...The Dream

M000033600

# RVing

# ADVENTURES

## with the

# SILVER

# GYPSY

# NON-FICTION TITLES

by
**Sharlene "Charlie" Minshall**

*RVing Adventures
with the Silver Gypsy*

*RVing Alaska! (and Canada)*

*Full-Time RVing
How to Make it Happen*

*RVing North America
Silver, Single, and Solo*

*In Pursuit of a Dream*

*Freedom Unlimited:
The Fun and Facts of Fulltime
RVing*

*...The Dream Continues*

# RVING
# ADVENTURES
## WITH THE
# SILVER GYPSY

**Sharlene "Charlie" Minshall**

**GYPSY
PRESS**

**Copyright © 2001 by Gypsy Press
150 Rainbow Drive, #5024
Livingston, TX 77399-1050**

First edition 2001

Printed in the United States of America

Library of Congress Control Number: 2001126231

ISBN: 0-9643970-6-4

Cover photographs by Gary Clark

Inside photographs by Sharlene "Charlie" Minshall

# Dedication

Thank you, Lord, for guiding
the Sprinter and me across North America many times
to experience your beautiful world and encounter delightful people.
Thank you for touch for I feel the breeze in my hair,
sunshine and saltwater on my face,
and the encircling hugs of family and friends.
Thank you for sight for I see
snow on the mountains, clouds in a blue sky,
and joy in a friend's face.
Thank you for sound for I hear birds singing, a cascading stream,
and my grandson's laughter.
Thank you for silence for then I hear you.
Thank you for hunger for it proves I still have an appetite,
even for my cooking,
or for chocolate chip cookies baked with my granddaughter.
Thank you for a sense of smell for it thrills me with the fragrance of flowers and
warns me of danger.
Thank you for aches and pains for they remind me I can still do the things I love
to do, walking, hiking, biking, kayaking….
Especially thank you for loving daughters, interested sons-in-law, fun
grandchildren, and the good health we all enjoy.
Thank you for RVing friends, new friends, old friendships, and family.
Thank you for your forgiveness
when I don't meet your expectations
or "boot" up the computer unnecessarily during frustrating moments.
Thank you for giving me this life.

# Acknowledgements

Thanks to Janet and Tracey for their constant encouragement, and for not reminding me that midway through each book, I always say, "I'll never write another one." A huge thanks to computer guru, Steve Schlake, who patiently struggled with me and taught me about a Pagemaker cover, PDF text files, and more than I ever wanted to know about graphics.

Thanks to Bill and Jan Moeller for their time, effort, and encouragement to try a new direction with Book-on-Demand. If Gary Clark didn't meet the cover photography criteria, "Make me look tall, thin, young, and gorgeous", it wasn't for lack of trying. Thanks Gary. Thanks to Jan Carmichael, Uteva Powers, Peggy Day, Frieda Clark, and Bill and Tom, for reading and/or giving me editing suggestions.

And last but not least, thanks to Charlotte White for her spelling of Beijing. She and Irv kindly kept me in salads through the winter. And thanks to friends who put up with my griping about lack of time when it was my own schedule I was working against. God Bless

# CONTENTS

# *Introduction*

In November of 1985, neighbors gave me a surprise birthday party and asked what my goals were for the next five years. Still awed with a six-week trip to the Orient and Hawaii, my first response was that I wanted to return to Japan. With a little more thought, I added that I wanted to be published and travel more. Little did I know! I never returned to the Orient, but on September 4, 1986, four years after the death of my gentle giant at age 47, and still with an aching heart, I left Niles, Michigan, in pursuit of a dream.

Jack and I and our two daughters had tented and RVed wherever and whenever time and money allowed. Traveling was already in my blood. It took four years to create new solo goals and dream new solo dreams to enhance a "second life" of traveling and writing.

I sold the house, moved to what I didn't know was an "interim" apartment, and six months later into a 25' used mini-motorhome. That "interim" RV took me to live on Baja, Mexico, beaches for six months; on my first venture to Alaska and Canada; and across the lower 48 at least four times. That mini lasted 1½ years until I bought the new and present 1987 27' class A Sprinter.

The Sprinter has changed drastically to fit my office and need for solitude without a landline. I added three solar panels, four in-house batteries, and a 2000-watt inverter, among other changes. I have always thought of the motorhome as "Six wheels to adventure." Given the rough back roads and questionable destinations you'll read about, he hasn't fared too badly. I have often said I plan to drive the Sprinter until the wheels fall off. That has begun, and you'll read about that later, too.

After doubling as my mobile garage for five years, the 1981 Mercury Lynx tow car retired to a vocational school in the Blue Ridge Mountains in 1998. I intend to replace it within the next year.

The Sprinter was not the only one to experience changes. My travels have included romance, intrigue, sorrow, general happiness, and a great many terrific "Moments in time." I've stayed healthy and made a lot of friends along the way. This "second life" as a full-time RVer has taken this average housewife and mother beyond her wildest imagination.

Out of the writing and publishing I desired, came my first book, "*In Pursuit of a Dream.*" I have since published four other books and over 300 columns and freelance articles. I still get a "Wow!" feeling when an article or column is published or a new book comes out or someone recognizes me. This is *my* life? I'm sure I'll never become blasé about my blessings.

Although I had sporadically given RV adventure talks when a new book came out, a few years ago I became an instructor for the annual Life on Wheels Conferences in Idaho, Kentucky, and Pennsylvania. The brainchild of Gaylord Maxwell, they are educational seminars for new or "Wannabe" RVers, and involve approximately 40 instructors.

It's not that I'm an expert on anything, but I am a female solo full-time RVer who has had multitudinous adventures with a correspondingly small amount of major crises. I give students the sub-basic straight scoop about life on the road, as I do in my books. My message is, "If I can do it, anybody can." Ahh, so true!

Do I worry about safety? No. And no, I don't have dogs or campground directories or a Global Positioning System (GPS); it's just me and my Co-pilot. I call these my "Wonder years." I have spent 9/10 of the last 15 years wondering where I am. If it wouldn't take all the mystery out of my meandering, I would be a prime candidate for a GPS.

Kind souls giving directions always end with, "You can't miss it." These are well-meaning words but it is only rarely that I *haven't* "missed it." When I hear, "You can't miss it," I am confident I am heading straight into a magnificent adventure.

My motorhome preference is due to the safety factor. I don't have to "get out to get in." The key is always in the ignition should I perceive danger in my surroundings. Beyond that, I say a prayer, add a smidgen of common sense to cut my vulnerability, and keep on truckin'.

The Sprinter is kept in the best possible condition with the help of the best mechanics I have found and keep "stashed" around the country, plus daily TLC and maintenance. I listen to the Sprinter's sounds. I give him a chance to get beyond the early morning grumbles and groans, then if he still sounds out of kilter, I find out why. Although I have had tire and wheel problems, I keep good rubber under me at all times. I try to follow my own advice as in *Full-Time RVing: How to Make it Happen*.

Memories are both thrilling and painful. I had never been without childhood, marriage, or land ownership roots. With the exception of a few middle-of-the-night qualms when I woke up wondering "Where am I?" and "What have I done?", there were few times I was frightened, and they were momentary.

I've had three things going for me - the encouragement of my two daughters, their families, and innumerable old and new friends; a tremendous sense of adventure; and more faith in the Lord than even I knew I had.

My personal "life on the edge" has included all that you will find in this book. Adventures in other books involved flying, driving, and wilderness canoeing beyond the Arctic Circle; horseback riding the beaches of old Mexico; ultralight flying over Quartzsite, Arizona; a Mississippi RV barge trip; and working as a cabin girl on the Bar-M Dude Ranch, among others.

All I had to do was open my arms to adventure and I did; but, all adventures are not big ones, as you'll read in the Daily Life Vignettes chapter.

If every day were filled to the brim with excitement, it would wear me out. The charm of full-timing is having "every day" kinds of days fitting between extraordinary moments of pure pleasure.

Meeting people was not a goal but it became a highlight. RVing is a great leveler. Around the campfire, the person driving a new $300,000 coach usually does not care that mine is 15 years old. In what other life could I sit around a desert campfire listening to stories from a Los Angeles cop, a retired U. S. ambassador, two Iowa farmers, and three sea captains from British Columbia? Sitting in Barrow, Alaska, eating muktuk with the Eskimos wasn't too shabby either.

Comments are priceless. A charming cowboy poet I interviewed in Arizona was as fascinated with my story as I was his. He said, "I may just have to come courtin' you." He was 81 at the time, but I sorta kinda hoped he wasn't kiddin'. I learned this winter that he married a fifty-something bride a couple of years ago. I should have hung in there!

The really neat thing about extensive traveling is the mention of a place, a road, or an activity, and I have either experienced it or can visualize it.

Relationships are more precious than ever. My daughters say they are comfortable with my travels after all this time, but sometimes I wonder. Janet, my older daughter, created maps for my *RVing Alaska!* book. I located Inuvik for her in the Northwest Territories. "Mom, I didn't know you drove that far north."

"I told you it was 205 miles beyond the Arctic Circle."

"But I didn't know it was *way up there!*"

She is the only one who voiced a forlorn wish to be in the canoe with me on the Yukon River trip.

I told my younger daughter, Tracey, I thought I had found a partner to hike the Chilkoot Trail with me at Skagway, Alaska. She asked what it was like. "It's a 33-mile, steep, rugged rock trail used by the 1898 gold rushers on their way to the Yukon Territory."

"Keep in mind, Mom, we have a bedroom upstairs where you can convalesce."

They are still concerned on occasion. Tracey said, "I don't worry about you except when I hear about blizzards, flooding, tornadoes or hurricanes and I don't know where you are. Then I hear from you and everything is o.k." They are both amazed when I find my way back to visit them. They know from personal experience that I can get lost grocery shopping.

Sons-in-law, Bill and Tom, love my lifestyle, especially when they can pack up the family and meet me in the mountains or on the seashore for a few days. At our last bi-annual family reunion, I had the privilege of having them both all to myself on my 6 a.m. daily walks.

Full-timing allows me to spend quality time with my two grandchildren, although they have 3,000 miles between their doorsteps.

At almost 13 years going on 34, MBG (My Beautiful Granddaughter) Rebecca, is not as interested in RV trips with me any more, but we manage a few "grandma" type activities like baking cookies. At 5'8", Rebecca and I no

Introduction

longer see eyeball to eyeball or exchange sweatshirts.

In Virginia I babysat grandson, Will, for over three months. He nestled into an oversized pillow on the motorhome dash and laughed delightedly as he watched his first autumn leaves belly flop to earth. He won't remember any of it, but I will. This winter, at 3½, he and his mother visited me in Arizona's Wild, Wild West. Dressed in cowboy hat and vest, his look of pure unadulterated joy sitting astride "Whiskey" while being led around the corral, was priceless.

This book is not necessarily in chronological order. These stories are not in other books but where appropriate I have used my published columns, usually with additional information. Readers have prompted me to be more specific about my routes. Photographs, plus the numbered map, will give you an idea where my travels have taken me.

I loved turning 62! I bought my once-in-a-lifetime $10 Golden Age Pass. Now I zip through National Park entrances for free and pay half price for camping (depending on concessionaire arrangements). Our 370+ national parks are magnificent in their own uniqueness, important examples of our nation's natural and cultural heritage, and protected for our "awe" ful and lawful enjoyment. It has been my privilege to visit most of them, as well as National Monuments, Preserves, and Scenic Rivers.

I'll take you for a glimpse of near-to-the-border Mexico and as far northeast as you can go in Canada and the United States. Although I have made major Alaska trips since writing *RVing North America, Silver, Single, and Solo*, they are told in *RVing Alaska!*.

After reading awhile, you may think I don't travel alone often but I seldom caravan with anyone. Occasionally I meet up with special guy friends whose company I enjoy and I'm off for great spur-of-the moment kayaking, hiking, motorcycling, or maybe just sharing a campfire. I also feel privileged to have women and couple friends who are either from my first life or new friendships I have formed since being on the road.

One time I woke up in the night and planned my whole spring route for heading north. I even had a good idea of my fall return route. It's a little like buying computers, my plans were obsolete before the plans got off the board. I covered very little of either route. I treasure these friendships and last minute plan changes.

I rarely carve my itinerary (when I am rash enough to make one) in rock. March, July, and September Life on Wheels seminars have put specific destinations and major curves in my already circuitous path. This year I will fly to all three of them, including a flight from Alaska for the July Conference as I did in 1996. There is really no mystery to my travel routes– whenever we aren't required to be somewhere in particular, the Sprinter and I are somewhere else.

RVers experience the United States in different ways. My friend, Rich, whom you will read about in the beginning chapters, decided he would visit all the lower 48 States within two years. Parking his RV in each place and exploring thoroughly with his motorcycle, he did an admirable job of it.

I didn't have specific plans or a time period in mind. I visited some states extensively and others hit and miss, choosing instead, to stop again later and see something else. I had the advantage of knowing I would probably make many cross-country trips with children on opposite ends of the country.

"Are you lonely traveling by yourself?" Not usually. If I am, I stop for coffee and talk with people or make phone calls to friends or family. A major problem with being alone is that there is no reinforcement. If you feel sick or down, there's no one within reach to care. If life has dealt you a blow, big or small, there is no one to say, "I'm sorry, this too shall pass." When there is a beach to walk or a path to hike, there is no one to give you a hand up, over, through, or just to hold your hand or just hold you period. That I still miss.

When I see RVing (or landbound) couples destroying their marriages a nit-pick at a time, or almost worse, having no dialogue at all, I want to shake them. Wake up! Don't be "Just married;" be friends. Invest some of your "quibbling and sparring" time into putting zip and spark back into your marriage. Compromise. Learn to have fun with each other. Absolutely nothing warms my heart more than seeing couples who are still in love after 30 or 55 or 60 years. Wow! The reason, in my opinion, is that they are friends as well as mates.

O.K., I'll get off my soapbox but I feel strongly about enjoying each other through whatever years you are given. It is what I once had, *lost in a heartbeat*, but would cherish again if the right opportunity presented itself.

Where will I settle when I hang up my wheels? The "Upsizing" chapter will partially answer that question. Michigan will always be the place of my heart. My first love, children, friends and family climbed its sand dunes, splashed in its freshwater lakes, hiked and camped in its forests, and canoed its streams. Ah…but west of the Mississippi and north, beyond the Rocky Mountains, following the westward trek of Lewis and Clark and Sacajawea…there I can breath. And the far northwest, Canada and Alaska…I'll never live there but I leave a piece of my heart each trip.

The more I travel and write, the more I realize how much I haven't seen or done. If you never travel beyond North America, you can be busy for a dozen lifetimes. If you never leave home and only see the miracles in your own kingdom, you will be busy for a lifetime.

People often ask me how long I stay in one place. With gasoline prices going off the charts as compared to what we considered high 15 years ago, it makes sense to stay longer and see more before moving.

Though I have been in all 50 United States, all Canadian Provinces and Territories and 17 Mexican States, I keep traveling because I still love finding myself in the "Middle of Nowhere."

The purpose of this book is to give you possibilities and spur you on to living whatever dreams you have. With that in mind, join me for a journey through *RVing Adventures with the Silver Gypsy* and see what *"life on the road"* is really like.

Our first stop is truly grand with a capital G…

# Map Relating to Silver Gypsy Travels

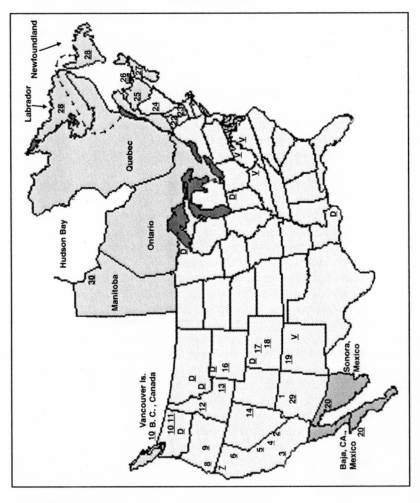

**Map numbers correspond to chapter numbers**
**"D" corresponds to "Daily Life" Chapter**
**"V" corresponds to "Various and Sundry" Chapter**

# Grand Canyon National Park

Rich Edwards was a Pennsylvania Life on Wheels student, a retired English teacher from Long Island, New York, who had never traveled west of the East Coast. In a chance meeting in Texas, he said he didn't believe any place existed until he had visited it. Arizona had just come into existence (Thank God since I was in it!) and he was coming to North Ranch. He asked if I would show him around.

In his circuitous route (is there another kind for an RVer?) between New York and Arizona, he had witnessed many wonders of our beautiful United States, but I knew he hadn't seen the equal to Grand Canyon National Park.

We left North Ranch on St. Patrick's Day, communicating via our CBs. Every few minutes he entertained me with a bit o' his Irish brogue and a brief blast of lilting Irish music.

A full-timer's world is seldom ruled by calendars and watches. Thinking that March would be an ideal time to avoid tourists, I had forgotten something called "Spring Vacation." We found two National Park Service campsites in Mather Campground as the sun went down. Because Rich's RV was having an electrical problem, we moved to hookup sites in Trailer Village for the next four nights.

Morning found us with typical free-soul skepticism, reluctantly boarding the free shuttle bus. It was wonderful. We didn't have to drive narrow crowded roads or maneuver into limited parking spaces. The shuttles ran on time, often, and dropped us off. We were then free to climb back on whenever we chose or hike along the rim and catch another shuttle at a different place and time.

With over five million visitors a year, the shuttle bus system is only the beginning. In a few years, a light rail transit system will eliminate visitor vehicles and parking problems altogether. This is a good thing. The alternative to enormous crowds is to visit off-season and frankly, I prefer the cooler seasons anyhow. Though I had misjudged spring break time, it was gratifying to see college students enjoying their national park and the outdoors.

The high desert terrain leaving I-40 and traveling north on SR #64 toward the Grand Canyon gives you no clue that an outstanding world wonder awaits you. Richard's first canyon view at Yavapai Point was comical. It was great fun to see this sophisticated New Yorker's reaction to a truly awesome sight. His jaw literally dropped. Within an hour, he had used two rolls of film.

The canyon deserves that complete awe. Its length is 277 miles, encompassing 1,218,375 acres. Standing on any one of its precipitous cliffs, you can look down well over a mile into its depths. In places it is a mile wide, in others, over 18 miles wide. No matter how many times I return, it is impossible to explain my feelings standing on the edge of this amazing sight.

Yavapai Point has an observation station where you can identify major temples and landmarks, as well as read about the geological history. You get a panoramic view of the canyon's orange and red splendored formations. With good eyes (or binoculars) and a clear day, Phantom Ranch can be seen roughly 10 miles away in a canyon bottom oasis. Plateau Point is visible a ways beyond the Indian Gardens halfway point. Although I haven't hiked quite that far, from Plateau Point you can see the Colorado River.

There are those who would disagree with this, but I don't take unnecessary chances. I'm not afraid of heights so I thought nothing of standing a foot from the rim. I heard, "Ah, ah, ah, aah -- get back from that edge!" from the resident protective male (who was standing in the same proximity). Well, you know what happened. My "I am woman" attitude took hold and I promptly ventured closer than I ordinarily would have just to yank his chain. In his Alan Alda voice, he warned me again.

I laughed, "You go near the edge, why can't I?"

"I'm a guy and you're a girl!"

"What's the difference?"

"I'll explain that to you later. In the meantime, I don't want to remember Grand Canyon by scrapping you off the rocks."

Actually I have to admit it was nice having someone care one way or the other if I dropped a 1,000' over the edge. Rich not only sounds like Alan Alda, fresh off the M*A*S*H set, but his humor is in the Alda category, too.

In support of his caution however, far too often people ignore guard rails, climb around on loose shale, and rock hop for that perfect photograph. The year previous to our visit, five people fell to their deaths, avoidable with a little common sense.

It was cool and sunny, perfect sweatshirt weather. For pure drama, however, you'll find nothing like storms, sunsets, and sunrises for viewing the Canyon.

Hiking the 1½-mile rim path to Bright Angel Lodge brought on near starvation. A stew-filled sourdough bread bowl really hit the spot. After fresh air, hiking, and unbelievable views, we ended a perfect day the perfect way, with Ben and Jerry's ice cream, hot tea, and a movie.

The next day we shuttled to Bright Angel Trail. Though we were armed with small water bottles and snacks, we weren't really prepared for hiking deep into the canyon. The more curves we rounded, the more magnificent the views -- the farther we went. Going down was easy.

Here we have to consider the facts. Rich is 6'2" with 6'1" legs so he hikes much faster than I do. On a good day, I am 5'2" with 1'1" legs. When I wanted to keep up with him, I grabbed his belt and he slowed up. My other deterrent, and probably more of an excuse than I wanted to admit, was my four-month post-bunionectomy foot. I knew from experience that he wouldn't consider carrying me back up. In favor of my right foot and Richard's hankering to reach Indian Gardens, the halfway point, I suggested he continue and I meet him later. I gave him my water and snacks and he disappeared in a cloud of dust.

At this 1½-mile point where we parted, are toilets. Never one to miss an opportunity, I partook. Given my expertise in technology, I couldn't get the door unlocked. After several minutes and with the encouragement of those needing to use the facilities, I finally jiggled the lock loose. With great dignity I passed the waiting "pee"tisipants, and started up the trail. I often stood aside giving right a way to the mule trains headed for the Phantom Ranch oasis, nine miles down.

Rich made good time and was happy to have done it, but he returned admittedly exhausted. He is a runner but I would have felt terrible if he had bounded in with great energy after I wimped out. With cold drinks in hand, we did happy hour recovery time rocking on a lodge porch.

On prior canyon trips I had taken a helicopter flight to see the Anasazi Indian Ruins 1500' below the North Rim, and the mule ride to the bottom. It was hard to remember where I had hiked previously and it really didn't matter. With my CRS (Can't Remember Sugar), it was all new again anyway.

West Rim Drive views were entirely different. Bright Angel Trail twisted and turned below us as we hiked the rim from Trailview Overlook to the Lost Orphan Mine. When it was opened in 1893, it was a copper mine but uranium ore was discovered in the 1950s. It was abandoned because of the difficulty transporting the uranium up the canyon sides. It is ugly, but part of the Canyon's history.

We caught the shuttle near the John Wesley Powell Memorial, the Civil War Major who lost his arm at the battle of Shiloh, for his 1869 Colorado River exploration. He and his crew made the first recorded trip through the Grand Canyon by water.

Although I couldn't claim his bravery, he expressed how I feel when I move ahead with an adventure rather than turn back. When they considered calling it quits, he said, "To leave the exploration unfinished, to say that there is a part of the canyon which I cannot explore, having already nearly accomplished it, is more than I am willing to acknowledge, and I determine to go on."

Hopi Point promontory, considered *the* place from which to watch sunsets or sunrises, gave us 45 miles of temples, thrones, and towers to view in either direction. I wish we had taken the time for a sunset visit but by evening we were usually exhausted from our activities.

We caught a first-hand look into The Abyss without ever getting off the bus. If we had leaped off at that point, we would have plunged 3,000' to the next plateau. Somehow that didn't appeal to me. The Pima Point Colorado River view is the best on the South Rim and you can see Granite and Boucher Rapids as well.

**Grand Canyon National Park**

At the end of West Rim Drive, is Hermits Rest. This log and stone edifice, built in 1914, has a very unusual walk-in fireplace. While I had no desire to walk in it, if I ever build that cabin in the woods, I want one just like it. The building was named for Louis Boucher who came to the Canyon in 1891 and was considered the local hermit. While we drank in the beauty, we sipped coffee and munched grandé muffins.

Another day took us on a short bit of the extremely steep, winding South Kaibab Trail. My mule-ride memories returned. The mules walked confidently on the very edge of Bright Angel Trail, all the way down and across the narrow swinging Colorado River Bridge to an overnight at Phantom Ranch, and back up the South Kaibab Trail. I also recalled the flatulent mule I followed coming up that arduous trail, a di"stink"tly smelly memory.

The Kaibab Trail is 21 miles long and connects the North and South Rims. We had excellent views of its switchbacks as we dawdled our way along the rim to Yaki Point.

The Canyon is far too grand (in enormous) and far too grand (in beauty) to even think of seeing or absorbing it all in one trip. It is a World Heritage Site, but don't go there if you don't give a schist. The geology is fascinating, the formations are wondrous, and the colors are magnificent.

The human history is captivating from prehistoric North American Indians to the Spanish to the explorers, miners, surveyors, trappers, and to the young couple who embarked on their honeymoon trip in 1928. They were last seen at Bright Angel Creek, 26 days into their trip. They continued and were never heard from again.

In 1956, two commercial airliners collided above the canyon. A memorial to the 128 people who died in that crash, is in the Grand Canyon Cemetery near the Shrine of the Ages west of the Visitor Center. Many of the canyon pioneers are also buried there.

Even if you can't hike, you can satisfy your curiosity of mesas, buttes, and major points by car or shuttle bus. Museums, ruins, restaurants, shops, Visitor Centers, and campfire programs fill in the gaps.

The more I read, the more hiking I want to do, and I definitely want to experience a weeklong raft trip through the canyon. The neat thing about water travel is that you don't see footprints of those who have traveled before you. It feels like you are the first human to see it. So I'm dreaming, what's your point?

We experienced a Yavapai Point sunrise our last morning, a nice goodbye to Grand Canyon National Park.

I can almost guarantee you will feel you are really flying or boating through the canyon, without getting wet or being quite so close to the canyon walls, if you visit the Imax Theatre Grand Canyon presentation at the south entrance. Prepare to hang on.

We caravanned out of the park along East Rim Drive, stopping at various points including the Watchtower. This 70' stone building is a re-creation of the prehistoric towers that were once scattered all over the Southwest. The Hopi Room houses Indian Art with an extensive explanation of the painted figures. The Watchtower also has curios, a snack bar and a view from the observatory. Richard teased me because I wasn't quite tall enough to see out of some of the observatory windows but I knew the view was there.

On other trips I have continued north at the SR #64 and US #89 but never when I could visit the North Rim. It averages 1,000' higher than the South Rim's roughly 7,000' and is closed due to snow from approximately mid October until mid May.

To take advantage of mule, river, or air trips, you need to make reservations many months in advance. Calling at the last minute may get you in on a cancellation but that's chancy. When I knew Rich was headed for North Ranch, I asked if he would be interested in a mule ride to the bottom. He said yes, but when I couldn't get reservations, he admitted he was glad. He has never been on a horse.

Grand Canyon was established as a National Park in 1919. My love of the canyon is expressed best by John L. Stoddard in 1898, "To stand upon the edge of this stupendous gorge, as it receives its earliest greeting from the god of day, is to enjoy in a moment compensation for long years of ordinary uneventful life."

At US #89, we turned south. The San Francisco Peaks north of Flagstaff had very little snow on them but they are always beautiful. We continued on #89A through Oak Creek Canyon into Sedona. This 27-mile, snake inspired, curlicue road through the Coconino National Forest is a Scenic Byway. If you are in a hurry, take paralleling I-17. Years ago this route could be driven with very little company. Now, especially with RVs, locals chewed on our bumpers, but the scenery was worth their impatience.

One good stopping place is Oak Creek Overlook. At an elevation of 6,400', we not only had a dramatic canyon view but Native Americans selling crafts. Pull-offs were not large enough for big rigs and definitely not for two caravanning RVs as we meandered through the ponderosa pines, campgrounds, picnic areas, and Slide Rock State Park following Oak Creek.

Driving into Sedona feels like driving along the Grand Canyon bottom. You spend a lot of time looking up at the awesome red and orange formations that dominate this tourist town. The remaining time is spent parking-space hunting so you can walk around. It is definitely not RV friendly as far as parking.

It is a delightful town with a wide variety of restaurants, galleries, shops, and jeep tours that will take you into the red rock boonies. As for us, we gave up and continued on to a Cottonwood campground recommended in Richard's campground directory. It was a resident park with few RV spaces. The main reason we chose it was for the Laundromat. It was closed. We had more fun going to the town Laundromat anyway, fitting in trips to Wal-Mart and the grocery store between washing and drying.

Connie Gillespie, a Michigan high school friend, was visiting her daughter. She picked us up in her rented car the next morning and gave us a marvelous Sedona tour. A really good place for panoramic Sedona pictures is along the airport road. We enjoyed a streamside lunch on The Hideaway Restaurant deck in downtown Sedona.

Connie drove us to Polatki, or Red Cliffs, opened recently to the public. It was much more fun visiting these ruins because the area was rugged and underdeveloped, a little like stumbling into it on your own. It was one of the largest Sinagua Indian Villages in the Sedona red rocks, a combination of several archaeological sites.

The small pueblo-style dwellings in this box canyon were built against red sandstone cliffs. Site interpreters explained the rooms, petroglyphs, pictographs, and the agricultural lifestyle.

We said our goodbyes to Connie and drove up to Jerome, a favorite ghost town I have written about many times. It was late so we walked around Jerome just long enough to buy fudge and post cards. It is a charming place for strolling and enjoying. SR #89 is steep and winding going into and beyond Jerome, with only a few places big enough to adequately park big rigs.

Jerome is a former copper-mining town that nearly died when the mine closed. During a family trip many years ago, Jerome had two inhabitants. Through the years it has accumulated more residents who opened shops, galleries, and restaurants. Although many buildings are still slowly creeping down the mountain, others are stabilized (hopefully).

We stayed overnight in Prescott's Point of Rocks Campground and had breakfast with my brother, Dean, from Prescott Valley, the next morning.

One of my favorite drives and I think it should be a Scenic Byway, is SR #89 from Prescott to Congress. The locals refer to the first section to Wilhoit, as "The Corkscrew." I couldn't agree more. Many people choose to drive Iron Springs Road from the back side of Prescott, through Skull Valley, and connect to SR #89 below Wilhoit.

We arrived at North Ranch. I had one day to prepare for a flight to Virginia and a two-week visit with my youngest daughter and her family.

Richard dropped me off at Phoenix Sky Harbor International Airport early the next morning. He left for California, continuing his RVing adventures.

But a change of plans brought us back together again in…

**Zabriskie Point, Death Valley National Park**

# Death Valley National Park

Death Valley became a National Monument in 1933 and changed to a National Park in 1994, the lower 48's largest. It is a magnificent panorama of fascinating history and deadly statistics.

Its names are deadly as well, the Funeral Mountains, Hell's Gate, The Devil's Golf Course, The Devil's Cornfield, Coffin Peak, Tombstone Flat, and Deadman Pass. Those devilish names are enough to give you the Ubehebes. Actually Ubehebe Crater is only a few miles from Scotty's Castle but somehow I've missed going there. Fortunately, other names offer more uplifting references like Wildrose Canyon, Confidence Hills, Teakettle Junction, and Jubilee Pass.

Over the years many modes of transportation have taken people into this valley. Pre-historic man came by foot, Indians by horseback, pioneers in covered wagons, and miners and prospectors by mule. Now we see bicycles and the modern version of the covered wagon, the RV. But I'll tell you about another type of transportation that was new to me.

You all know how I open my arms to adventure when it appears. Well, if this story seems a bit windblown, it's because my notes were written on the back of a biker.

My daughters complained, "You never let us do things like that. "My reply, "You can ride motorcycles anytime you like...as long as you're at least 85 years old and I'm dead!" I donned his extra helmet, leather jacket and gloves for safety, plus warmth against the wind, and immediately metamorphosed into "Motorcycle Mama."

The biker was my friend, Richard. After his brief foray into California (Just long enough to prove it existed), we met in Nevada and caravanned into Death Valley National Park, this time with Richard's beautiful emerald green GoldWing machine tagging along in a trailer behind his Class C Coachman motorhome.

We learned a lot from each other over the next few weeks. He had been full-time RVing less than a year and he had a lot of questions. I had rarely ridden on a motorcycle so I needed major instruction. First I had to learn how to climb on the bike behind Richard so I wouldn't dump us both in a heap. I never did learn that to his satisfaction.

Richard was properly awed as we drove into Death Valley on SR #178 from Shoshone. It is one of my favorite routes. At Badwater, it is 282' below sea level, the lowest point in the Western Hemisphere. A sign denotes sea level on the mountainside above. We hiked out on the salt flats. It was about noon and I can tell you it was too hot for me. For just looking and enjoying, the weather was perfect, but hiking heats the body considerably.

Continuing to Furnace Creek, we drove below sea level. We dry-camped two nights at Furnace Creek Campground. This was handy to the Visitor Center, the general Store, TCBY, the post office where we got our general delivery mail, a Sunday church service, and the indoor/outdoor Borax Museum, all part of Furnace Creek Ranch oasis.

The museum building itself is the oldest structure in Death Valley. It houses an extensive rock collection as well as the colorful valley history that intertwines with "The Borax Era." In the 1880s, the famous Twenty-mule teams trekked the 165-mile "*Death Valley Road to Mojave*," hauling 46,000-pound borax loads to the railroad.

The team carried its own water, 1,200 gallons, and hay for the 10-day trip. The teams dropped hay and barley at stationed wagons on their return, to serve the next team's trip to the railroad. A feed wagon is in the outdoor display.

For a small fee, a guidebook explains the equipment behind the museum. Displayed is everything from the gold arrastra (a means of crushing gold ore with materials at hand) to a rocker quartz mill. Conestoga wagons and a 60-ton oil-burning locomotive are on display too. At the entrance to Furnace Creek Ranch is a complete set of Twenty-Mule Team wagons, and Old Dinah, a steam traction engine and her ore wagon train.

Rich and I usually took turns providing the evening meal or they were a combined effort so neither of us cooked more than absolutely necessary. I was dealing with a "New Yorker" though. He assured me that one could find every kind of food (or anything else) within almost any New York City block. He talked of fantastic ethnic restaurants, fabulous bakeries with unbelievably good rye bread, and he had not found a rival for New York pizza anywhere in all the States he had traveled.

If you've read my columns or books, you know that cooking is not my forte. One night I fixed a dessert that I really like even if I did come up with it by accident. I served a waffle with ice cream and chocolate on it. Granted the waffle was a little mushy with thawing, but hey, I made the effort. He didn't let me forget that one.

Do you remember the haunting ballad, "*Ghost Riders in the Sky*?" This song recorded by Vaughn Monroe is still one of my favorites. Guitar-playing Ranger, Stan Jones, created that song around a Death Valley campfire in 1949. He progressed from the campfire to Hollywood and Disney fame with his music and acting.

Who did the work so we could access and enjoy this park? Does the "CCC" ring a bell? The Civilian Conservation Corps was established in 1933 by President Franklin D. Roosevelt to provide jobs during the Great Depression. They built 343 miles of new road and five campgrounds within the park.

The Furnace Creek Golf Course, outlined with swaying date palms, was adjacent to the campground. Richard is an avid golfer. I drove the cart since I figured driving *was* my forte, at least more so than cooking. At the ninth hole, he phoned in for hamburgers. We drove up a ramp to the counter, picked up our order and back down. Cool! Always be grateful for the little things in life.

The GoldWing was so big and comfortable, we overheard a "spitfire" motorcyclist refer to it as "One of those Winnebagos on two wheels." My seat curved around my back and his seat pushed back against me in front, making me feel very secure (after several 100 miles). I had my instructions, "Don't lean into a curve, just turn your head toward it." At first I was a little tense on corners but thanks to Richard's safe and capable driving, I relaxed and went with the bike instead of fighting it.

The seven-mile Artists Drive loop road is slow going in a car but was even more so on the bike. Although the switchbacks and curves slowed us down, it was the danger of sliding on the sand-covered paved road that was scary. The narrow, some-times steep, roughly 10-mile road led into canyons where we had a close view of the erosion process. Halfway through the loop is a sideroad to the Artist's Palette with subtle yellows, pinks, greens, and purples in the minerals, iron salts, and manganese. The road cut across great alluvial fans before returning to the main highway.

On another day, the GoldWing protested the last steep hairpin-curved mile to Dante's View, 5,475', but it was worth the spectacular panorama of the 130-mile-long Panamint Valley. The snow-filled crevasses of 11,049' Telescope Peak were in the distance. Near its peak, Bristlecone pines grow, Mother Earth's oldest living things reaching for the sky in their unique twisted way.

The day was clear enough we could see both the highest and lowest points in the lower 48 States. Beyond the Panamint Range was snow-capped 14,495' Mt. Whitney in the Sierra Nevada Mountains, the highest point in the lower 48 States. As the crow flies, it is less than 80 miles away. Looking down, we saw the lowest point at Badwater. If you were to jump off the sheer cliff at Dante's View, you would land in Badwater pool. You might bounce off a few rocks on the way down, and since the pool is not all that deep, it isn't highly recommended.

Thirty million years ago, we would have looked over a lush green tropical Paradise where "thunder beasts" 13' long and 8' high feasted. The Titanothere was one of the largest mammals in North America, a cousin to the rhinoceros. The species is called *Protitanops curryi* but they are locally known as Tom, Dick, and Harriet.

Archeologists believe primitive man lived 10,000 years ago on the shores of Lake Manly. They left behind petroglyph and pictograph stories of their lives. When the waters evaporated leaving the great salt flats, Indians referred to it as "Tomesha" or "Ground Fire," for the relentless summer heat.

Experts tell us this stark dramatic driest, hottest spot in North America is very young, still growing and changing with each sand grain blown in the wind or rock eroding onto an alluvial fan. At first glance, it looks barren but Death Valley lives in its many creatures and plants. Desert Bighorn sheep live in the park, but in five visits, I have yet to behold a ewe turn.

African burros domesticated by the Spanish in the 16th Century and eventually used by the prospectors, were abandoned to roam and proliferate, causing great destruction to water resources and valley habitat. This same thing has happened in the Grand Canyon. The burros are available for adoption, but somehow I couldn't picture one in my Sprinter. I wonder if they would be good for stamping out mice?

It is unlikely you would encounter the scorpions, rattlesnakes, black widow spiders or other creepy crawlies. They survive the harsh climate by hunting in the nighttime coolness. They live among the over 900 plants that spring to life with the miracle of rain, two inches annually. Even the remaining puddle of Ancient Lake Manly at Badwater is surrounded by ditch grass and pickleweed that teems with soldier flies and water beetles.

Hawks and ravens bent on dining, look for rabbits or anything small enough to eat. On moon-filled nights bats, coyotes and owls converse, telling tales of goldseekers and prospectors like Shorty Harris or Seldom Seen Slim. Old abandoned mines, ruins, and equipment corroborate their stories.

As merciless as the summer heat is, so the mountains that frame it have cold and unforgiving winters. Legend has it that as families on their way to the Gold Fields in 1849 suffered their way over the snow-covered mountains, one woman turned and said, "Good-bye, Death Valley," giving the area its name.

Richard had agreed the night before to ride the GoldWing to meet the sunrise at Zabriskie Point. The groggy voice that greeted my knock on his RV window at dawn was deep and slightly menacing. A short bike ride later, we paced to keep warm while the sun created highlights and shadows in this ancient eroded and tilted lakebed, the rugged Badlands of Death Valley. Manly Beacon is one of its most photographed landmarks. After an hour of taking photographs, we made a beeline for the Furnace Creek Café, breakfast, and hot coffee.

On our way to Stovepipe Wells and two nights with full hookups, we stopped at the Old Harmony Borax Mill to see a borax-processing site.

I hiked into the Death Valley dunes from behind our campground one early morning. Sand dunes are not new to this Michigander but I always love walking in them. I did sort of miss Lake Michigan. There are several valley dune areas, each unique, but the one near Stovepipe Wells is the most accessible.

We headed west on the bike to Wildrose Canyon but the road was closed. At Panamint Springs a fellow told us a landslide had covered it the year before and it was being fixed. "You could probably get through with the bike but they fine you $250 if they catch you on it." It didn't take long to decide not to try it. Panamint Springs didn't have gasoline as they usually do so we opted not to take the long way around to Wildrose Canyon and possibly get caught in the boonies with no shelter. Desert nights are extremely cold no matter how hot the days are.

I really wanted Richard to see Scotty's Castle and a rare desert rain brought cooler weather for our next day trip. When I visited the castle in 1994, I went for the Living History evening tour. With rangers characterizing Scotty and others who had lived and worked there, the 1930s came alive. It was downright spooky and y'all know how I loved that.

Death Valley Scotty was Walter Scott, described by some as a prospector-hustler. Others called him a humorist, a philosopher, and a teller of tall tales. This legend in his own time was talked about from New York to Los Angeles because of his escapades involving great amounts of money. He once hired a train to take him on a 2,265-mile trip to Chicago to the tune of $5,500. He wanted to break the record for the fastest trip. They did.

Chicago millionaires Albert and Bessie Johnson befriended him. During their strange friendship, the Johnsons funded the two million-dollar castle that eventually became known as Scotty's Castle. It is nestled in an oasis in Grapevine Canyon.

It has the original massive hand-carved furniture and original rugs, woven on the Island of Majorca. Hand-tooled leather draperies hang in the windows and fine European paintings on the walls. A modern humidifier maintains a certain temperature to preserve the furnishings.

The Johnsons especially tailored Scotty's bedroom for him. His clothes hung in the closet as though he were returning shortly. The room held mementos of Scotty's marksman days with Buffalo Bill's Wild West Show.

The ceiling of the music room, which had a $160,000 Welte Mignon organ in it, was made from 60 different hand-carved panels. Neither the Johnsons nor Scotty could play a note but famous musicians gave private concerts in the castle. All the rooms were lit with magnificent hand carved wooden chandeliers.

Mr. Johnson was an engineer and had many innovations well ahead of common usage, such as solar-heated running water and diesel-generated electricity throughout the castle.

Outside, the Westminster Chimes could be heard from the 56' clock and tower. Rich and I walked up the steep path to Windy Hill and visited Scotty's grave. Where did Scotty get his money? Speculation says a hidden gold mine. Many people tried to find that gold mine including the government, but it was never found. Scotty is buried overlooking the castle grounds and he isn't talking.

The highest recorded temperature in Death Valley is 134°F. It wasn't quite that hot the day we left but it was definitely getting hotter and we had other frogs to fry (so to speak). We packed up.

When Richard and I checked out of the campground, I asked the Stovepipe Wells storekeeper how she could stand the heat in mid-summer. She quoted a favorite saying of her mother's, "It's better to burn here than in the hereafter." Amen.

By the flip of a coin, I was back in Death Valley again that fall with my kayaking buddy, Art Hill. Although he lived in California for most of his life, he had never visited Death Valley. We dry-camped awaiting the Forty-niners Annual Death Valley Encampment. This is an early November fun way to spend two weeks. Pre-encampment campground evenings are blessed with "Y'all come," a standard invitation to play and/or sing, or just relax and listen. We enjoyed everything from New Orleans Jazz to German polkas to sad bluegrass songs.

My Sprinter and Art's Safari were backed in beside each other on the top row closest to the mountains. It was so neat to sit under his awning for great sunsets, balmy evenings, eating by candlelight, and listening to impromptu "jamming."

With his four-wheel-drive Suzuki, we explored Twenty-Mule Team Canyon on a steep gravel one-way loop road. Small abandoned mines are posted against exploring, but interesting to peer into.

While having breakfast at the Red Buggy Café in Shoshone, a neat little western town east of the park, they told us about local caves called "Castles in Clay." Single miners and prospectors have lived in them since the 1920s. They were hollowed out of the Tecopa Lake Bed deposits with chimneys for cook stoves, wooden floors, and even sidewalls were added to some of them. I had boondocked near some of them on a previous trip.

I was completely amazed to find the Tarahumara Indians living in caves 400 miles below the U. S. and Mexican border, but I never realized caves were used in California. The last cave dweller died there in the 1990s!

While waiting on breakfast, we read in the Red Buggy Dispatch about the escapades of famous Shoshone lawman, Charles Brown. He became sheriff when the powers that be sent a badge to the Citizens' Committee and told them to "Pin it on some husky youngster who is unmarried and unafraid and tell him to shoot first." He wasn't just a flash-in-the-pan local law enforcement dude; eventually he spent 20 years as a California State Senator.

Next door is a little indoor/outdoor museum with all the local history. They are reconstructing a woolly mammoth found in the area.

Art and I found Shoshone's China Ranch. The drive to it gives you no clue that you will soon be twisting down through a narrow canyon. At last you turn a corner into a green Amargosa Canyon oasis. It is referred to as "The Hidden Ranch" and they aren't kidding.

We walked through the sorting room and the workshop. It was definitely a mistake for either of us to peruse the gift shop. We both bought yummies but we didn't succumb to the date shakes.

The first date grove was planted in the 1920s, now full-grown trees.

Other groves were of various ages and stages. A worker told us about the brown paper and colorful cloth wrapped around the date bunches. "We first put brown paper up to keep the birds off but the ravens tore the paper off. Then we went to a used clothing shop and bought 30 bags of dresses for a dollar a bag. We tied the dresses around the hanging dates. The birds can't tear the cloth and the dresses can be reused." With a glint in his eye, he added, "The hardest part was finding the right dress sizes." It was colorful, comical, and the first time I was ever in a date grove with a dress code! Come to think of it, I don't think I've ever had a date that wore a dress.

Considering our early arrival and the extraordinary dust, we opted to leave Death Valley before the Encampment. Art left for the Pacific coast and I went on to North Ranch.

You and I are going from clay castles to real castles when we meet up with Richard again.

**Ye Olde Swimming Hole, Hearst Castle**

# *Hearst Castle*

Our caravanning adventure continued out of Death Valley to US #395 and south. Our ultimate destinations were Sequoia and Yosemite National Parks. Due to late April travels, high elevation weather, and individual plans, our travels would take us on a really strange path throughout California.

Back in Michigan, you can find shortcuts to almost anywhere, especially if you are willing to take the back roads. In the west, it's different. "You can't get there from here" is more the rule. Usually this means deep canyons or high mountain ranges bar your path with no connecting roads, in this case the Sierra Nevadas.

We turned west on SR#178 crossing Walker Pass to Lake Isabella. As our elevation rose, the wind died down but it became really cold. We intended to travel north around the lake but if it was snowing in Lake Isabella, it was definitely snowing at 6,102' on Greenhorn Summit. After grocery shopping and advice from locals, we continued to Kern River County Park east of Bakersfield.

The next morning I was being lazy, laying in bed daydreaming, when Rich called a hello on the CB. A few minutes later he knocked on the door with creamed and sugared coffee just the way I like it. Now *that* was a treat!

Where would any self-respecting full-time RVers go after being in the desert for a week? You guessed it, Wal*Mart.

Our next 100 miles took us from oil-well orchards near Bakersfield to orange and lemon groves. The fragrance was heavenly, but the bees were so thick they crashed against the windshield, making a real mess. I'm sure it caused them a headache or two as well.

I had stayed at Lemon Cove Core of Engineers Park previously. It is a good stop for exploring Sequoia National Park. Two other times I had made April trips to the park and couldn't get beyond the Lodgepole Visitor Center. Both trips, one in a friend's truck and another time with the motorhome, I was caught in a blizzard. With friendly park host advice and a phone call for high-country weather conditions, we took advantage of our full-time RVing status and changed our plans.

We headed northwest across lush green rolling country to the Pacific. We stayed two days at Betabel RV Resort in Gilroy, catching up on e-mail (we had our own phones!), laundry, and exploring.

On May Day, we took the GoldWing through Seaside, Pacific Grove, and Monterey, and along John Steinbeck's Historic Cannery Row. We photographed the purple ground cover, Monterey pines, and beautiful homes while the ocean crashed in the background. I never get tired of sea sounds or smells.

I had been on the 17-Mile Drive many years before in a rented car but my disappointment was for Rich. We pulled up to the gatehouse with the bike. The attendant explained it was a private community and motorcycles weren't allowed. We had no choice but to turn around.

If Rich was reluctant to spend $350 to play the Pebble Beach Golf Course, he at least wanted to see the famous course as opposed to watching the rich and famous playing it on TV. He did eventually get a picture of the 18th hole from the highway. His comment, "It would be a once-in-a-lifetime experience, but at that price I could fly to Scotland and play the Old Course at St. Andrews."

Nancy's Café at Seaside provided our pasta dinner. It was one of those very tiny, hole-in-the-wall places with atmosphere and good food. We perused the Sunday paper and read "stuff" to each other.

It was warm in mid-afternoon but very cold as the evening approached. I don't think I have ever been that cold. Jeans are not known for warmth and on the bike, they lent no warmth at all. A hot tub bath was the only solution.

Since there was seldom anyone on our CB frequency, I left mine on. The next morning at 6 a.m. Richard was singing taps. Uh huh!

Who could not be impressed with the Monterey Peninsula? The 123 miles from Monterey to Morro Bay is a Scenic Byway. We caravanned beside the ocean where every curve brought a prettier scene than the one before. A shoulder is mostly non-existent. The road is narrow, winding, as steep as a 1,000' above the ocean in places, but beautiful even in the rain showers. Richard bemoaned the fact that we were driving motorhomes rather than the bike. The openness was also one of the features I enjoyed most about motorcycle riding.

In our coastal driving, we experienced everything, the good and the bad, the wind and the rain, and the sunshine. We stopped often but sometimes enjoyed the view from inside. This chilling weather had Richard wondering about "warm, sunny" California.

At the California Sea Otter Refuge, enormous elephant seals were sleeping beach blobs. Very few were up and moving. They lounged on rocks all along the coast, protected as well, outside the refuge.

We talked with a ranger about parking at an ocean viewpoint. She said the authorities generally look the other way on the eight-hour parking rule unless you "set up camp" and stay for a week. The only other RV looked like an abandoned unit that had been there for months.

Richard had never boondocked until we caravanned together. He soon realized the advantages of free dry-camp nights in between expensive campgrounds. For what more could we have asked than to sleep with our bedroom windows open toward the ocean's song? Yesss!

Although this was a familiar route, I had never been to Hearst Castle. The weather was lovely one minute and raining and windy the next. It was a good day to be inside.

People often ask where I would plant roots again if I stopped traveling. It would have to be somewhere within sight of mountains, and preferably where the sun sets on the ocean, and green trees live. Big Sur fits the bill. The Santa Lucia Mountains run right down to play on the Pacific beaches. Of course to afford living along that coastline, I'd have to sell the Great American Novel big time. Maybe I could get a job at Hearst Castle cleaning the pool.

We bought bus tickets for the steep winding five-mile, fog-shrouded trip to the castle atop "La Cuesta Encantada" or "The Enchanted Hill." Two docents accompanied our tour, giving no chance to dawdle for an extra peek, picture, or pry into "The Golden Days of San Simeon."

William Randolph Hearst's love of the outdoors was reflected in the San Simeon zoo and game preserve, the largest private collection in the world. At one time the 2,000 fenced-in acres was home to 90 species of grazing and jungle animals. That didn't include the "unfenced." Your castle-bound drive might have been blocked by anything from a zebra to a musk ox to a giraffe.

In 1865 William Randolph Hearst's father bought the land for what is formally called "Hearst San Simeon State Historical Monument." This isolated and difficult-to-reach land was used for family camping, the end of comparison between the Hearst family and mine.

I try not to compare apples to oranges to prunes but as we walked up the West Terrace steps, I thought about my visit to Biltmore Mansion in Ashville, North Carolina. The Biltmore is a National Historic Landmark with 255 rooms and North America's largest private residence. It has an indoor swimming pool and a bowling alley.

The Hearst "Big House" or "Casa Grande" has 110 rooms in the middle of nowhere with fabulous mountain and ocean scenery. It has two major pools, one inside and one outside. They both have many major fireplaces. I was born in a tiny log cabin with five rooms and a pot-bellied stove on the Dowagiac Creek in Michigan. Guess who's the prune?

On the West Terrace we were given the castle history and "The rules" which included "Touch only the concrete and metal handrails." We could only envision the scenery. It must be magnificent on a fogless day.

Richard teased me about "Mythical Michigan" and "Mythical Michigan humor" because he had not yet visited my home state in his travels. The guide said something that prompted Rich to look across at me and mouth the words, "Like they do in Michigan?" She saw him do it and with a glint in her eye said, "Is this a joke? Is this funny?" I fully expected her to make him explain himself and stand him in the corner. I would lay odds she was a teacher. It was funny. As a teacher, I'll bet he has called many a student on the carpet for not paying attention. I only barely resisted, "Yanananana." We quickly switched circumstances.

I'm more into nature than man-made structures, but the 104' long Neptune swimming pool was really outstanding in white Vermont marble with an antique green marble mosaic floor shimmering below the water. According to the brochure, the "Temple Façade is a composite structure incorporating pieces from ancient Greek and Roman buildings. The Italian Renaissance figures depict Neptune, Roman god of the sea, with sea nymphs." It was far more beautiful than anything I saw in Rome!

Seventeen dressing rooms surrounded the pool. Back home in Michigan we had a 20' X 40' pool with flower-filled tree stumps and a 40' authentic Baja fishing net draped on the wood fence. We had big splashy gatherings, providing our 20-foot mini for a dressing room. Ah, back to prunes.

Then this always-follow-the-rules person took a picture, barely touching a marble column to balance the camera. The guide called me on that – eyes like a hawk. Richard smirked.

Alas the pool was too big to pull behind the motorhome. We went on to Renaissance Spanish and Italian gardens with enormous pansies, sculptures, and winding paths to see the guesthouses. One of many guesthouses, the La Casa del Sol, had eight bedrooms, eight bathrooms, and two living rooms.

We followed the Esplanade to the Main Terrace and went into the Casa Grande via a wrought-iron convent gate from 16th Century Spain. This building looks more like an elegant cathedral than a castle with its two Spanish Renaissance towers and 18 bronze carillon bells in each one.

Mr. Hearst loved interesting people and built the castle for entertaining. He made sure his guests enjoyed themselves and was noted for his unique parties. Guests were offered a wide variety of outdoor activities and in the evening, they gathered in the Assembly Room for cocktails and conversation.

The only dining room was The Refectory. Mr. Hearst liked casual. In contrast to 16th Century wall tapestries, a 17th Century Italian wood ceiling, and the antique silver, catchup bottles and pickle jars were stationed along the long polished dinner table.

His guest list read like the who's who of the world, Charles Lindbergh, President and Mrs. Calvin Coolidge, the Shah of Iran, David Niven, Maureen O'Sullivan, Claudette Colbert, Clark Gable, George Bernard Shaw. And of course Richard and I were there only slightly after that time period.

Beyond the Morning Room, the Billiard Room, and the 50-seat theatre where we watched home movies taken by guests over the years, we arrived at the 84' indoor Roman Pool below the tennis courts. It took three years for artisans to place thousands of gold-faced tiles in intricate patterns to finish this room.

Alas, I couldn't get this into the motorhome either. I appreciated going through this magnificent castle and really enjoyed the stories, but as I climbed back into my 8' X 27' motorhome, I had a hard time relating to the 60,645 square feet in La Casa Grande. I mean, what would I do with 38 bedrooms?

The story of the castle complex creation is fascinating. I would be remiss if I didn't mention that the architect/engineer who worked directly with Mr. Hearst on this major 28-year project was a woman, Julia Morgan. On returning to the Visitor Center, we watched an Imax Theatre movie about building the Hearst dream and the castle party life.

William Randolph Hearst owned 26 newspapers, 13 national magazines, 8 radio stations, produced newsreels and made nearly 100 feature films. He referred to his vast collection of art and beauty creatively arranged in a private residence and guesthouses, as simply "The Ranch." So much was he into conserving the giant oak trees in the construction path, he spent thousands of dollars moving them. The estimated weight of each was 600 tons. It proves that if you have enough money, you really can move mountains, or at least giant trees.

Another day we explored the artsy village of Cambria. We had breakfast in a tiny café, then Richard split for a barbershop and I walked around town. Richard is very much a family-oriented person. In discussing our children's growing-up years, he said he had read Dr. Seuss to his kids so often that he had the stories memorized. Yeah, right, I know the stories too, but could he really have memorized every page. A Dr. Seuss book was in a children's bookstore just waiting for him to prove it.

"You turn the pages and I will recite each page as you turn it." He recited page after page and never missed a word. I was impressed. I think I lost a quarter on that deal.

We vacated our ideal ocean boondocking location, crossed country east on SR#46. Little ranches were tucked into the rolling green mountains. It was wine country with big wine tasting buildings and grape vineyards, a great morning.

Sunset found us setting up campsites at Park Sierra Escapee Co-op near Coarsegold, California. Our intention was to branch out into new territory and visit some very tall trees.

# National Park Twins
# Kings Canyon and Sequoia

Richard wore a mike-outfitted helmet for communicating as we traveled to Fresno and southeast on Kings Canyon Highway (SR#180). It was a warm sunshiny foothills ride to the Kings Canyon Big Stump Entrance and Sequoia, our National Park twins.

We walked through the Grant Grove giant sequoias. It was my third time to see Richard completely awe-struck, and to his credit, he never recovered. I cannot imagine anyone not being impressed with these majestic ancient trees, not to mention the mountain scenery.

Millions of years ago the redwood species covered much of North America, now only 75 giant sequoia groves exist, growing naturally only on the western Sierra Nevada Mountain slopes. Coast redwoods grow in a narrow 500-mile strip along the Pacific Coast.

Although they can reach a height of 311', at least three tree species grow taller. The bristlecone pine lives longer than the sequoia's 3,200-year life span, and at least one tree has a greater diameter, but the Sequoias have them all beat in sheer size. Compared to the taller more slender coastal redwoods, these trees are tougher, huskier looking with sometimes eight-foot-in-diameter branches, the Arnold Schwartzeneger of trees.

Because of their chemical make up, sequoias are highly resistant to fire or insects. They have a shallow root system and no taproot. They are far more apt to die from falling over due to wet ground or high winds, than disease. Once they are down, tannin preserves them against decay. One wonders, if we drink enough tea (tannic acid), will we be thusly preserved against decay? Hmmm.

Some trees are severely fire damaged but they still live. Natural fires are needed to open the cones and allow seeds to reach the forest floor ash seedbed, critical to seedling growth and germination. Green cones could conceivably hang on a tree for 20 years before the right conditions release their seeds. Seed release gets a little help from squirrels and beetles between fires.

"Prescribed burning" is used within the parks to keep the undergrowth down. With no undergrowth (duff), fires pass quickly through the trees, burning them only at their bases where they are most fire resistant. Although protected by thick, resin-less bark, big fires reaching into the tree crowns can kill them.

Man's attempt to harvest these giant trees for their unbelievable amount of board feet, failed when it was discovered the brittle centers shattered when the trees were finally toppled. After all the difficulties cutting them down, the wood was only fit for making small products.

It is one of our fastest growing trees. Growing one to two feet per year until it reaches 200-300' in height, it then grows outward. Over a year, its overall growth is the equivalent of a 60' tree that is a 1 ½' thick!

Our walk took us to the only *living* memorial to our war dead, the 2,000 year old, 267' General Grant Tree, the world's third-largest living tree. It is designated by Congress to be "The Nation's Christmas tree." Services are held there every Christmas.

The Centennial Stump is the remains of a tree felled in 1875 as a Philadelphia World's Fair exhibit. Obviously they weren't as concerned about preservation then. Seeing is supposed to be believing, but Easterners couldn't believe the incredible Sequoia size, labeling them another "California hoax."

The King's Canyon Highway continues 30 miles through Sequoia National Forest, then back into the national park to a dead-end just beyond Cedar Grove Village. I understand the Kings River Canyon has some of the most rugged, dramatic scenery in North America.

At this point, you either hike east to US #395 (a big chunk of hiking let me tell you) or turn around and go back. Three paved roads west from US #395, the villages of Lone Pine, Independence and Big Pine, don't quite reach the park boundary, but do lead to hiking trails and/or campgrounds.

If you intend to hike, check with the rangers. The higher trails do not open until July. Elevations go from desert foothills to 14,494' Mt. Whitney. The closest you can get to Mt. Whitney except by foot power, is from the Whitney Portal Road at the Lone Pine entrance off US #395. Whether driving or hiking, weather should be a factor in your plans. The weather becomes cooler and wetter as you climb.

Unfortunately, riding the GoldWing from our campground and the total distance involved, we opted to turn back at Grant Grove. We headed south on the General's Highway into Sequoia National Park.

Sideroads often lead to viewpoints or hiking trailhead parking. Hiking will take you to see the best views away from the usual crowd. If you aren't into hiking, it is like Alaska, you can experience the beauty of Sequoia National Park without ever leaving your car.

A sun-warmed boulder was a perfect spot for us to relax and listen to the mountain stream rushing madly along below us. We didn't talk. We didn't need to; we were enjoying the moment's tranquility.

I always recommend viewing the park movie. You may not remember everything but it gives you a good overview. This will reinforce other information you pick up and help you remember it. We watched the park movie at Lodgepole Visitor Center, both of us nodding a bit in the warm room. Rich bought souvenir shirts for his kids, then we headed for the Giant Forest.

Anywhere else, we would be impressed with the white firs, sugar and yellow pines, and cedar trees that add to the park beauty. We tended to ignore them in awe of the giant "Sierra redwoods."

The statistics of the world's largest tree, the General Sherman Tree, are mind boggling. General Sherman is nearly 275' tall. If anyone were ever so incredibly insensitive, they could build a 13-story condo beneath its lowest large branch. Its age is only slightly more than the mirror reports I am after a sleepless night, approximately 2,500 years. In perspective, this tree grew from a seedling to a tree more than twice the age of our country by the time Christ was born.

The Moro Rock-Crescent Meadow Road twists through the big trees like a snake. We drove on top of the Auto Log, a giant fallen sequoia, just to say we had done it. As I write about the next place we stopped, I am once again reminded that one really needs to have at least two weeks in any national park to experience even the barest of high points.

We did not have time to climb the 400 stone steps up Sequoia's great monolith, 6,725' Moro Rock with a 4,000' drop into the canyon. It was hazy enough that day we wouldn't have been able to see much of the Great Western Divide anyway.

Unless you have looked up at these giants, you can hardly imagine being able to drive through them, build a house in one, or house a store, but that has all been done somewhere. We took pictures after driving through Tunnel Log, a live tree. It is the turn-around point and well worth the six-mile round trip.

So many activities await anyone with a few days (or few weeks or several trips). What it boils down to is there never is enough time to see everything. Definitely one day is not enough. I'd love to go back for hiking, horseback riding, see areas we didn't visit, and just have time to soak it all in. Also, snow still closed areas we would like to have visited.

The drive to Ash Mountain Entrance is so curvy and twisty and full of hairpin turns that we took our time. Layer after layer of curved road wound down the mountain before us. We went from the magnificent Giant Forest wonders to high desert country decorated with blooming century plants.

Stopping often to feed on the view, we also let feisty little motorcycle wheel-chewing cars go flying by. We followed SR #198 to SR #99N, passing the Lemon Grove campground we had visited two weeks before, continuing in the dark to Park Sierra.

Park Sierra is the prettiest of the Escapee parks I have visited. It is nestled into the nooks and crannies and mountain rocks with lots of trees and interesting places to walk. On my rented lot, the Sprinter's open door faced a green area and a view of the Sierra Nevada Mountains that I could see as I worked on the computer. Richard's site was about a block away on another hill. We usually combined talents for the evening meal. Unless we were eating outside on my picnic table, we usually ate in his

RV because I have changed my booth area into a couch.

In between visits to the national parks, Richard played golf, I wrote columns and we did other exploring with the GoldWing. We often went into Oakhurst, the nearest town large enough to get major supplies, gasoline, or see a movie.

I couldn't believe the cost of the protective leather jackets. Richard's new black one cost over $600. The one I wore was 12-years-old and cost $125 new. He said its well-worn look made it a "jacket of distinction." I wasn't going to argue with that and still expect to wear it!

As much as I enjoyed seeing the special places we visited, we found scenery every bit as beautiful just out knocking around. We drove around Bass Lake (Crane Valley Reservoir). This area boasts movie locations for such as *The Deer Slayer*, *Spencer's Mountain*, *Last of the Mohicans*, and *Small Soldiers*. Richard bought a book on Father's Day and read portions to me while we sat outside a bakery eating non-fat (?) treats with tea and milk and local atmosphere.

Eventually we turned on Sierra Vista Scenic Byway Forest Road #81 going into the mountains. We went up and up through the Sierra National Forest with views of Mammoth Pool Reservoir and Dam, and the San Joaquin River, as well as distant snow-covered Sierra Nevada Mountains.

The paved road was almost completely ours. It was a peaceful scenic ride until all of a sudden, Rich put on the brakes, laid the bike to one side, jumped off, and frantically removed his helmet. In the meantime, I was sitting at a very odd angle with my foot touching the ground, had visions of falling off, and had no idea what was going on. Mother had warned me about going into the wilderness with leather-jacketed bikers.

I had never seen anyone with a bee in his bonnet before but it definitely wasn't funny. Rich jiggled the helmet around and out fell a big bumblebee. Neither of them were happy campers. He said he felt only a pinprick and that it didn't hurt badly. I decided that was not the time to be humorous with a comment about hard heads. He never wore that helmet again; consequently, we lost the fun of communicating while we traveled. The bike was so heavy, I pushed from my side and he pulled from his until it was upright.

Considering the perfect warm spring weekend, we were surprised to find several neat primitive streamside campgrounds that were almost empty. We walked over the water-smoothed rock and sat listening to the cascading stream. Potholes were worn into the rocks over who knows how much time.

At Mile-High Vista, an enormous dead tree stuck out over the vista. The ground was covered with tiny white, blue and yellow flowers. We rested and snacked on orange slices. Continuing up through the ponderosa pine and other forest growth, the road became narrower and narrower until it was a two-lane only on the curves. Pine needles and cones carpeted the road.

We ran into snow about 7,000'. We bypassed one drift but a quarter mile farther along, we ran into another snow patch with no way around it. Our intention had been to connect with Forest Road #7 back toward Bass Lake, making it a loop trip. With more elevation ahead of us and that early in the spring, we had no choice but to turn around, making it a really long return trip.

We let Taco Bell do the cooking when we got back to Oakhurst. We ate and read the newspaper just like an old married couple (Don't tell him I said that!).

Many moons ago, my third oldest brother, Leo, and I were discussing California. I will never live down calling Yosemite, "Yose-mite." I finally had a chance to visit my downfall.

**Sequoia National Park Tunnel Tree**

**Richard and the Mean Green GoldWing Machine**

# *Yosemite National Park*

It rather annoyed Richard that I had already visited many of the places we went together. More than once he said, "I hate it when you tell me you've been there!" With many years of full-time travel, it was difficult not to have been there and done that. The marvelous thing is that at this age if you have already visited, you can't remember it anyway! He was pleased that I hadn't been to Yosemite National Park. Actually, a few years between visiting places and it is a delight to return and discover something new anyway.

I loved seeing the awe on Richard's face. We followed SR #41 through Coarsegold on our way to "Yose-mite" National Park's southern entrance. If we had blinked we would have missed it, but back in the days when it was known as "Gold Gulch," Oakhurst was filled with miners.

Yosemite National Park has everything and its charms drew us back three times via three entrances and they were equally beautiful. With the great distances, our biggest problem was not having our houses on our backs. Next visit, I definitely want to stay within the park borders.

Mariposa Grove, the largest of Yosemite's three groves, has nearly 250 giants, some standing 200' tall. The Grizzly Giant is Yosemite's oldest known living giant sequoia at 2,700 years old. While we were at it, we walked through the Wawona Tunnel Tree.

We "Wow"ed and walked a lot. This was still early May and Glacier Point Drive remained winter closed. It leads to the 7,214' overlook, 3,214' above the valley floor, and I can only imagine the view. Surely Glacier Point couldn't be any more spectacular than our stop at Wawona Tunnel View. This was our first inkling of what Yosemite is all about. Bridalveil Fall plummeted in the distance. Beyond that, El Capitan rose ahead of us to 7,569', said to be the largest single hunk of granite rock on earth. Toward the end of the day, we would become aware of climbers inching their way up its sheer face.

At the eastern end of the valley, the distinctive 8,842' Half Dome impressed the heck out of us. This massive granite plutonic block is a young 87 million years old. Its other half is thought to have been carried away when the glaciers receded. Legend says that a husband and wife quarreled and were turned into stone. She became Half Dome and he became North Dome. I think that's called a "dom-e-stic" fight, probably by taking each other for "granite." Not only that, but what can they expect of a "plutonic" marriage. Sorry. I wonder how many fights would be avoided if couples knew they would both be turned into stone. Hmmmm.

While Rich climbed around the rocks for the perfect picture, I talked with a couple from New Jersey. This was their first trip west and they were major impressed.

None other than Abraham Lincoln provided this valley's first protection in 1864, the Yosemite Grant, creating the world's first state park (and California's), and the basis on which future national and state parks were established. Forestlands surrounding this portion made up our nation's second National Park in 1890, Yellowstone National Park being our first in 1872.

The California State Park, made up of the Mariposa Grove and Yosemite Valley, was not included in Yosemite National Park until 1906. This happened thanks to the efforts of President Teddy Roosevelt and conservationist, John Muir, two names we recognize as being very instrumental in preserving other magnificent trees, valleys, lands, and lakes.

John Muir, a Scotsman whose sight was regained after being blinded in an industrial accident, dedicated the rest of his life to natural environmental exploration and preservation. He first visited the Yosemite Valley in 1868. He is noted for helping to establish and preserve Yellowstone and Yosemite National Parks. In 1892, this authority on forestry and forest management became the first president and charter member of the Sierra Club. The John Muir Trail runs through the park, as does the Pacific Crest Trail.

Standing there in the sunshine of that May morning, the panoramic scene before me seemed unreal. It was even more unreal to believe that all I could see and what I was standing on, was under water 500 million years ago.

Sliding plates, heat and pressure, rising magma, tilting blocks, carving rivers, and receding glaciers have changed the park into what it is today but it hasn't stopped changing. In July of 1996, an 80,000-ton rock slab loosened, broke into two pieces, slid down a 300' slope, and went into an 1,800' free-fall to the valley floor below Glacier Point. It generated windblasts up to 100 mph, destroying hundreds of trees. On landing, its disintegration created a 50-acre dust coating.

A river runs through it, the Merced River. SR #140 into the park is still hampered with re-construction due to its major flood in January 1997.

Waterfalls were at maximum springtime flow and completely mesmerizing. Native Americans who lived here from 7 to 10,000 years ago, called Bridal Veil Fall, "Spirit of the Puffing Wind." At 620', the fall is small compared to Yosemite Falls, but in perspective, it is still the equivalent to a height of 56 RVs.

Other sights awaited us, each more awe-inspiring than the last. The valley itself is seven miles long, approximately a mile wide, and hosts more visitors than any other part of the park. As we drove through the lovely green meadow, we stopped by the Merced River several times to admire Cathedral Rocks, a closer view of El Capitan, the Swinging Bridge, and Yosemite Valley Chapel. The chapel was built in 1879, the park's oldest building. It holds weekly worship services.

The four RV campgrounds within the valley didn't look full but the summer season hadn't begun. Although of no interest to RVing visitors, I found the concession-run cabins in Curry Village interesting.

The first campers in "Camp Curry" numbered 290 in 1899. Although there are variations of their cabins now, they still offer a "canvas tent cabin." This is a wood-framed canvas on a raised wooden platform with electric lights, but no heat, plumbing, outlets, phones, or TVs. Great fun for kids and adults alike. Tents have probably changed little but the number of tent cabin guests has increased from 290 to 333,000 a 100 years later!

Someone asked us if we had ever seen the "firefall." This involved pushing glowing embers off Glacier Point (above Camp Curry) each night in a fiery red-cinder cascade, to die safely on a ledge below. This nightly show was discontinued in 1969.

We walked, rode, and admired greatly. Hunger drove us to the Terrace Meadow Deck at Curry Village Pizza. I had the impression Richard would have preferred New York pizza but I was content with anything hot and the initials P. I. Z. Z. A. I also just loved being there for that moment in time. Yesss!

With four offspring, two grandsons, various aunts, uncles, and friends, Rich kept concessionaire eyes bright everywhere he traveled. He was thoughtful with postcards, T-shirts, books, and whatever he thought might bring joy to someone back home.

It was fun going through the Yosemite Museum, the Valley Visitor Center, and the Ansel Adams Gallery. Ansel Adams' son, Michael (and daughter-in-law, Jeanne), operate the gallery.

Each of our three trips, we visited Degnan's ice cream parlor, enjoying cones at shaded tables within view of Yosemite Falls. There were lots of places to people watch or stretch out and let the falls mesmerize you into dreamland.

Our second trip into the park took us north along SR #49 and #140 into Yosemite. Mariposa's claim to fame is having the oldest courthouse west of the Rockies still in continuous operation. We picked up bluegrass festival information and discovered #140 was closed. Decisions, decisions.

The road was normally closed nights to work on 1997's flood damage. However, now it was closed due to a major landslide that had happened within the last two days. We had called ahead for road conditions but the newest information had not been recorded. The change to driving CR #132 to #120 made our day trip a very long one.

Now if your driving desires include a serpent-inspired highway, SR #49 north of Mariposa is it. Fortunately, although it is steep and narrow with extreme hairpin curves, it is also a beautiful route. The GoldWing is such a big, heavy motorcycle that you can't go around a hairpin curve sliding your knees like the little spitfire bikes do. However, Rich nearly did it on this highway.

**Yosemite Falls, Yosemite National Park**

Even though the scenery was as western, as dramatic, and as different from Long Island as it was possible to get, I had a hard time convincing Richard this wasn't New York. An IHOP, or even signs for a pancake breakfast, did not live on every corner. It was even many miles between corners and with most men without breakfast, he was becoming a bear.

How appropriate that we stopped in historic Bear Valley where buildings were built around the turn of the century (the Twentieth), for a pleasant breakfast with service that was hard to beat. They served only waffles and Richard's palate was set for pancakes. He charmed them into making a special plate of pancakes for him. The chef came out to see who preferred pancakes to his wonderful waffles.

We turned right at historic Coulterville, passing the Hotel Jeffery, built in 1854. It had provided beds for John Muir and President Roosevelt once upon a time. This short cut took us 17 miles to Buck Meadows. We turned right again and took SR #120 to the northern Big Oak Flat Entrance into Yosemite National Park.

From this point you can drive north to Hetch Hetchy Valley, Hetch Hetchy Reservoir, and Hetch Hetchy Dome. Catchy, Hetchy. The O'Shaughnessy Dam was built to restrain the Tuolumne River, a source of San Francisco's drinking water.

You can imagine the major controversy that building project sparked, destroying a natural area said to be much like Yosemite Valley. John Muir fought the good fight against it, but President Woodrow Wilson authorized the building of O'Shaughnessy Dam. It was completed in 1923, the only dam built within a national park. Time constraints kept us from taking this drive where you can still enjoy the remaining waterfalls, towering cliffs, and generally fewer people on its many trails.

At Merced Grove Trailhead, Richard discovered snow. I turned around just in time to see him mold a snowball. I know the devil made him do it but as soon as I said, "You're not that brave," he nailed me with it. The battle was on. I can't hit the broad side of a barn, let alone a string bean from New York. However, I don't get mad, I get even.

Eventually his mind wandered to other pursuits. Never turn your back on a vindictive female. My snow was soon down his neck along with, he claimed, an unreasonable amount of gravel and dirt. I was raised with too many brothers and do not comprehend the danger in such retaliatory actions when one is the passenger. He was kind.

Snow kept us from driving scenic, 39-mile Tioga Road over the mountains to US #395. It was still closed for the winter, as it had been the several times I have wanted to cross from either side of the Sierra Nevadas.

*However, I left Arizona's 110° heat on June 1, 2000. Three days later I started across SR #120 from Lee Vining and got caught in a blizzard that closed the road temporarily. Eventually I crossed over beautiful Tioga Pass and appreciated another overlook view of Half Dome.*

Tioga Pass is California's highest vehicle pass at 9,945', and encompasses lakes, domes, forested countryside and has the Sierra Nevada's largest subalpine meadow at Tuolumne Meadows.

We were in awe of Yosemite all over again, seeing different views of El Capitan, Half Dome and other sights from the opposite canyon wall. Kodak stock rose again.

After our daily dose of ice cream and hot coffee in Yosemite Valley, we spent some gaping time at Yosemite Falls. At 2,425', the combined upper, middle, and lower falls are the tallest in North America, and fifth highest in the world, exceeded only by two in Norway, one each in South Africa and Venezuela. Venezuela's Angel Falls wins the prize at a towering 3,212'. Are you going to remember that?

The unbelievable wind force and mist next to the falls make photography better a short distance away. The "Spirit of Puffing Wind" being forced down through that canyon is so strong, it is difficult keeping your balance against it. We walked backward to the GoldWing. It was too beautiful not too look.

Our return trip along SR #41 south, again took us past the National Historic Landmark, Hotel Wawona. Built on the 1857 site of Galen Clark's "wayside hotel," this tree-nestled Victorian-style structure was built in 1879 and is the oldest hotel in the park. You can take a bath in your room for $103 a night, in some cases in a clawfoot tub, or you can go without a bath for $74 a night. If I didn't have a motorhome, I'd stay there just for the beautiful veranda that wraps around it.

Galen Clark is considered Yosemite's "First Guardian." A lung disease brought this New England miner to Yosemite to await his demise. He lived another 54 years fighting for the creation and preservation of the park. He died at age 96.

The Pioneer Yosemite History Center at Wawona gives his story as well as others who have contributed to the park's history and preservation. Historic buildings, horse-drawn carriages, a covered bridge, and other memorabilia are on display. Although it is a 30-minute self-guiding tour through the early Yosemite years, costumed docents are available to answer questions.

Remember that festival information we picked up last trip? On a bright, cheery Saturday, we rode the GoldWing to Mariposa County's 8th annual Bluegrass Festival. The fairgrounds had a hilly site, shade trees, picnic tables, and choices of BBQ chicken, Mesquite BBQ, and garlic polish sausage, with boysenberry pie to complete the picture.

We settled into the afternoon program. The GoldWing was a bit small for carrying lawn chairs so we lounged against a tree or sat at a picnic table. My introduction to Bluegrass was thanks to a guitarist named Walter at the Coast to Coast Spirit of the Suwannee Campground "Pickin' Shed" in Live Oak, Florida, a lot of years before. This was my first actual Bluegrass Festival.

*"Peach pickin' time in Georgia, Apple pickin' time in Tennessee"*

California's Brushy Peak Bluegrass Band and Colorado's The Bluegrass Patriots were the first two groups who played. Our favorites and the feature group were California's Laurie Lewis and Her Bluegrass Pals. She has appeared on TNN TV and The Grand Ol' Opry.

I closed my eyes, felt a slight breeze pull at my hair, and listened to the sad bluegrass sagas. While they "fiddled" with banjos, mandolins, guitars, violins, and a Dobro, we tapped our toes and smiled.

Two county sheriffs stood in the gathering, quietly relaxed. One leaned against a garbage can. It didn't appear to be a troublesome group. Hands in their pockets, they chatted about fishing and community matters. Birds collected bounty from careless eaters.

Babies barely walking were followed by mamas not walking so many years themselves. Little girls pranced in long dresses. Boys chased boys. Adults in all manner of jeans, tie-died tee-shirts, denim, fancy cowboy hats, suspenders and big belt buckles, listened in their own fashion. They were completely engrossed, thoughtful, asleep, day dreaming, or eating.

*"Arkansas I can hear you calling."*

As we browsed the booths, an uninhibited grey-haired woman with long hair, barefoot in an ankle-length billowy dress and flowery straw hat, danced in wild abandon. We clapped for her. To watch her was to feel her joy. A paunchy fellow's hat proclaimed, "Been there, done that, now back to plowing."

Some of them wrote their own music. One song was written just for the town of Mariposa.

*"Born in a cabin built with his own hands, Mariposa man..."*

To get the full benefit of a festival, it is better to stay in the campground for however long the festival lasts. Lots of pickin' and jammin' is done evenings and everybody joins in. Maybe next time. On leaving, we discovered our tickets covered three days. We decided to go back on Sunday morning for the Gospel Sing.

Along with gifts for his family, Rich bought several bluegrass tapes that we listened to on the way back. Riding along with music playing, it was almost like riding through a movie set. The countryside fragrances and the scenery were much more up close and personal than within a RV.

We purposely went early enough the next day for Sunday breakfast. Richard had never had biscuits and gravy before and quite possibly, never will again.

Early Sunday they had the Mountain Bluegrass Boogie two-mile and five-mile runs to benefit domestic violence victims. The Muir Trail Girl

Scout Troop sponsored the festival but they weren't selling cookies. Only in high desert country could they get by with selling icewater.

California's Witcher Brothers started the Sunday morning Gospel sing. Virginia's Lynn Morris Band was next. Richard said, "Bluegrass Gospel Music under the trees on a cool, sunny California morning is a more religious experience than being in church." I had to agree but perhaps he felt that way because as a little boy the nuns cracked his knuckles for saying, "Hail Mary, full of grapes."

*"Please mamma don't you cry, things'll be better in the bye and bye."*

Sunbeams filtered through tree leaves but it was cool enough for light jackets.

*"I'm on the road to my father's house and he is lighting the way..."*

Blankets provided roll-around space for tiny babies. Guys sported bushy beards, baseball caps, and overalls; Gals wore braided hair, straw hats, and shapeless dresses. We were among the very young and the very old; everyone entranced with the music.

A 60-something couple sat on lawnchairs, tapping their feet. His gold-banded finger glinted in the sun as he rested his hand on her shoulder. They had a cooler on one side of them and a newspaper on the other. Every so often, they leaned together and kissed each other. A day spent together in loving comfort, a testimony to wedded bliss.

The last group before lunch break was California's "The Lost Highway" and we figured to get on down it, returning for the last time to Yosemite National Park.

SR #140 (El Portal Road) was open from Mariposa to the Arch Rock Entrance. It is considered the easiest and least mountainous way into the park. The construction zone was rough but livable.

We watched kayakers running the Merced River. It was wild with spring run off and probably so were they. They were quick, skillful, and fun to watch. I wasn't quite envious. I like the longer kayak and quieter water. Color me chicken.

All entrances ultimately lead to Yosemite Valley so we drove through again, always awestruck, always hitting a couple of places we hadn't seen before. This time it took us down the short side road to the Ahwahnee Hotel. It has a spectacular setting in the trees at Yosemite Valley's east end. Rooms are $250 a night.

If one brought one's coat, tie, or Sunday dress, one could dine elegantly while feasting on Yosemite's beauty through the Ahwahnee Dining Room full-length windows. The dining room of the 70+ year-old hotel, a National Historic Landmark, boasts "a 34' tall trestle-beamed ceiling and twinkling chandeliers." I was quite sure they wouldn't even let us peak inside wearing our leather jackets and jeans. Their Indian Room and Late Night Grill are for casual diners.

More casual dining and convenient fast-food places are available throughout the park. We kept our date with Degnan's ice cream. Richard went to sleep on a park bench, using me for a pillow, while I people watched and daydreamed to the tune of Yosemite Falls.

We said our goodbyes to Yosemite Falls, the Valley, the Wawona Tunnel Overlook, and the fabulous scenery going south on SR #41.

The park's top speed limit is 45 mph and that is sometimes too fast for a road that is narrow, steep, winding, and filled with vehicles heading home. Three *extremely slow-moving* RVs led the pack. As a RVer, that really annoyed me. With many safe, easily used pull-offs, there is no excuse for not stopping momentarily and allowing long strings of smaller vehicles to pass. This is called by several names, courtesy, safety, and in some States, the law.

We saw Yosemite National Park blooming in full springtime magnificence. I have never, ever seen such large dogwood blooms anywhere.

Though the higher elevations will be closed, I definitely recommend mid to late May for beauty and fewer people. Four million people visit Yosemite National Park yearly. Going in spring, fall, winter, or into its wilderness area, will give you a tad more room to enjoy its unparalleled splendors. With three limited day trips, we barely touched the surface. From the young to the young-in-spirit, if you leave Yosemite National Park bored, you'd better have someone pinch you because you are probably dead.

Time goes fast when you're having fun. Richard was headed northwest to San Francisco. I hadn't tossed a coin yet so I really didn't know where I was going except it included going north.

Richard was ahead of me checking out of Park Sierra. As he came out, I started down the hill. I said, "Aren't you from New York?" He in his best Brooklyn accent replied, "Whatsitoya?" We said our goodbyes.

As I paid, the woman asked, "What route are you taking?"

"North along SR#49."

"No, don't take that route! That's a terrible route for motorhomes or trailers. I always advise people against it."

"I drove it several years ago in the motorhome and just last week we were on it with the motorcycle."

She got the map out, showed me the curlicue road, and did her level best to dissuade me. I didn't try to make her understand that the route is exceptionally beautiful, a challenge, and my kind of road.

Having said that, let's go!

# Criss-Crossing Toward Lassen Volcanic National Park

I rarely feel lonely. When I do, it is usually immediately after I have shared time and exploring with a friend. Richard was fun and I knew I would miss our exploring together.

In my 13th traveling year, I bought a TV dish. However, with moving around a lot, I decided it was too much trouble to set up and largely ignored it. It is also seldom that I pick up a newspaper. My world information comes in bits and pieces and generally I don't miss knowing. I know that murder and mayhem continues without my specific knowledge. On this day, national news met me face to face.

For lunch and a rest, I stopped at a vista overlooking the upper reaches of Don Pedro Reservoir. I sat outside on a log enjoying the view. In the corner next to me were bouquets surrounding a small wooden cross. I thought it was a strange place for a traffic fatality memorial but thought no more about it.

Two ladies pulled in and asked about the flowers. I had no answers. One lady probed a bit and said a band was attached to a bouquet that said, "Julie, we love you." Suddenly we realized this was the place where one of the three young women who were killed at Yosemite National Park, was found a short time before. It was very sad but reminded me once again that life is so precious, and often, much too short. I called my daughters. It was suddenly very important to touch bases.

A sign declared Sonora Pass open along SR#108 east. I thought about it for a few minutes and decided to cross it and come back on SR#4. Why? Well, one, both passes were open. Two, I had never been on either one. Three, it would take me into high snow-scenery country that I enjoy so much (as long as it isn't on the road). Four, the roads were there and I wasn't expected in Washington for another month. I turned right.

At Stanislaus National Forest Ranger Station, the Ranger saw me drive in with the Sprinter and informed me, "We don't advise motorhomes, trailers, or trucks to go over Sonora Pass. It is too narrow and extremely steep."

He proceeded to give me horror stories of a RV that had gone over the edge and several that had to be towed. The lady working with him said, "If you're not faint of heart and take it easy, you probably won't have any problems. SR#4 coming back across is only 1½-miles wide with pull outs for passing."

"I don't want to make it dangerous for anyone else but I have 454 strong horses. Are the steep stretches really long?

"No, short spurts of 20%." I continued east and met several rental motorhomes. I figured if renters who had no idea what they were getting into could cross that mountain pass, I could too.

The road narrowed and snow filled the rocky nooks and crannies. Through the years I have heard people refer to "Hells Half Acre." According to the map, it was out there north of me. A scenic vista overlooking Donnell Lake and Dam was hard to get into with no good parking for RVs. I climbed through boulders to see a distant falls and look off into the Carson Iceberg Wilderness.

I stopped to photograph a stream pounding down through a narrow rock canyon and just sit and listen. When I hiked a half-mile back into a valley to see the Columns of the Giants, I had them all to myself.

Very little traffic came my way and even less was going my way. A signed warned of "26% grades" going over Sonora Pass! The ranger had said 20%! The steepest grades I had ever driven with the motorhome were 18%. Aaagh! I backed into a Eureka Valley National Forest Campsite next to a stream.

Ah, this morning is already fantastic. The sun is coming over the mountains as I leave for my morning walk, dressed in long-sleeved turtleneck and a heavy sweatshirt against the somewhere-in-the-40s, over-5,000'-elevation coolness. With long strides (well, as long as possible with short legs) I am soon toasty warm.

Around a curve and over the hill walking along the Mark Twain Highway that has just opened from a long winter's nap, I continue through sequoia and ponderosa pine shadows to see the sun glinting off Relief Peak's snow at 10,808'. I know farther south are the even greater elevations of Whorl Mountain, 12,019', and Excelsior Mountain, 12,448', in Yosemite National Park.

The mountain stream hurtling through the canyon calls to me. I scramble into the forest. Though it is nearly the end of May, snow still clings to the crevasses. The wildflowers and grass are showing tiny green shoots. Early flowers are small but already in bloom. Tree leaves are unwinding. The mountain air is so fresh I breath deeply, filling myself with springtime. It is great to be alive.

Following the river brings its own challenge. I leap across a small stream that will dry up once the snow is gone, mindful of landing properly and not injuring a hamstring as I did the year before in the Blue Ridge Mountains.

A fat ponderosa pine log fallen over a ravine is an invitation. It is a bigger struggle to pull my 60-something body up without falling than I want it to be, but the exhilaration of gracefully (?) balancing across it, gets my heart going. It isn't really necessary to walk across the log to get where I'm going you understand. The ravine is dry but the log literally begs to be walked across. Mark Twain made me do it. Huck Finn or Tom Sawyer would have walked it.

Boulders are strewn about. Trees grow around and through the rock, breaking it up. Huck and Tom wouldn't hesitate to find little paths up and over the jumble of enormous boulders, so I do too. This is fine for a while but then I come across a solid wall I can't negotiate. I can see the Sprinter below me but I can't reach it from here.

I get as close to Deadman Creek as I can and lean against a boulder, watching the wild stream a few feet below me, wondering at its name. This was a place that friend Richard would have tsked, tsked me away from the edge, but I am part Michigan mountain goat. I wonder what the stream and the trees would tell me if they could talk, tales of mountain men looking for gold, and pioneers finding their way west?

My friend Steve, the mountain climber, would have found a way around it but Huck, Tom, and I back-tracked to the top and another fantastic scene of Deadman Creek and the distant mountains.

I am now back to the Sprinter's comfort zone turning on my computer thanks to modern technology, solar panels and an inverter. The day has hardly begun but my adventures are already many, and not everybody starts their day with Mark, Huck, and Tom.

The mouse (or mice) had eaten the peanutbutter. Oh for a better mousetrap. The campground host suggested I use Bounce sheets to discourage them. It apparently worked for him but I stuffed Bounce into all possible mouse entrances until I nearly suffocated, to no avail. They loved it.

I walked down the road to where Deadman Creek passes between solid rock walls, carving fascinating whorls where it roiled and boiled through in its breakneck descent. Water puddled in huge boiling pots. Sheer canyon walls forced the water quickly on its way.

A car stopped and a fellow searched the area, finally asking me if I had seen his companion. They were fishing and now he couldn't find him. If he fell into that fast water, he was probably already sitting on an ocean beach.

I thought I was alone in the campground until a man came around the RV. As he got closer, I realized he was drunk. He kept repeating that he was a medical engineer, someone was looking for him, and he was on his way over to Bishop (on US#395). I asked if he realized how steep and winding the road was over the pass, especially that late in the day. He said it didn't make any difference, he was a medical engineer and he was needed at the hospital. He gave me his card. He was from

Connecticut which didn't make too much sense. I gave it to the host when he returned.

My neighbors affirmed that the road did indeed have 26% grades in a few places with lots of curves and hairpin turns, but they didn't think it would be a problem if I drove carefully.

Again the peanutbutter was eaten off the cheapo mousetraps. The live trap had a big fat mouse in it. I cleaned the camper again and left about 8:30.

They weren't kidding about the 26% grade. It started shortly after I left camp. By the time I reached the Vista Point overlooking the Emigrant Wilderness, I had lugged down to five-mph and prayer. I hadn't any more than parked, when an extremely long flatbed truck went flying by. I'm glad he didn't catch up with me, I wouldn't have a bumper or the back half of the motorhome! So much for trucks being warned against that road.

It was a winter wonderland. The road was clear to 9,624' Sonora Pass but the snow became deeper and deeper and the road narrower and narrower until I was driving through a snow canyon. Sections of it were extremely steep but for only short distances. Fantastic! The Pacific Crest Trail was deep with snow. A few other people gawked and took pictures as I was doing. It was very cold but with few places wide enough to stop, I appreciated the scenery from inside my cozy motorhome.

On the down side of the mountain, I stopped at Leavitt Falls Vista and talked with a fellow who had just come the short distance from Death Valley the day before. It was 109°!

I reached US#395 as two 40' motorhomes with tows turned toward Sonora Pass. They waved me down and asked about the road. Given the narrow roads, hairpin curves, 26% grades, and lack of places wide enough to park, I discouraged them. I don't know if they turned back.

The propane lady couldn't believe I had driven Sonora Pass or that I was now returning across Monitor Pass. I had driven from US#395 up SR#89 to 8,314' Monitor Pass and Markleeville on a previous trip, only that time I was still new at pulling a car. Simultaneously praying that I wouldn't need a tow truck and talking the Sprinter through each grade, I made it to the top. The top looks east over miles and miles of Nevada.

On SR#89 and #4, I passed through Toiyabe National Forest and between Mokelumne and Carson Iceberg Wilderness areas, then back through Stanislaus National Forest.

It was great to be without a schedule. I moseyed on to SR#4, enjoying spectacular views. I stopped for lunch near a stream and took a nap to its music. I continued along the 1½-lane road through snow country again. A few lakes were melting, coloring the snow green. I watched streams make their way through the snow, so cold, so beautiful. I let the occasional car pass.

I really wanted to stay the night but the campgrounds were snowed in and the snow narrowed the possibilities of boondocking to zero.

Back on SR #49, I bought gas and groceries and finally honored my promise to call Richard. He had conquered San Francisco with a 20-mile walk through all the tourist areas and was heading up the coast.

I love driving SR#49 but even with using gears and brakes judiciously, my brakes got hot. The Sprinter and I crawled in and out of mountain ravines and drove through trees and pastureland before stopping at Coloma and the Marshall Gold Discovery State Historic Park.

James Wilson Marshall built Sutter's Mill for Captain Johann Sutter on the American River's South Fork. Perhaps with knowledge from his goldpanning one afternoon, he had the water shut off in the tailrace. The next morning, January 24, 1848, he found gold in the cracks of the tailrace's exposed granite bedrock.

After discovering that it was almost pure gold, James and John swore their workers to secrecy. Human beings being human beings, the word leaked out. This discovery that turned into a major goldrush and helped launch California into statehood two years later, brought little compensation and no recognition to Marshall during his lifetime.

I stood in the very spot that the first bits of gold were found, now high and dry due to major flooding and the river's changing its course several times in the last 150 years. I thought about where I had visited gold rush areas or gold panned during my full-timing years, Dalonega, Georgia (First gold rush in the US, 1828); Dawson City, Canada's Yukon Territory (1898); and Nome, Alaska. I nearly froze my feet off panning in Resurrection Creek at Hope, Alaska. Ah memories. Recreational gold panning is allowed on the north side of the American River.

I didn't see any "spreading chestnut tree" under which "The Village smithy" stood, but as always, I was fascinated with the working Coloma Blacksmith Shop. It was being utilized as it would have been a hundred years before. The fire smell, the clanging of hammer against metal, and the sizzling of hot iron put to cold water could easily make you believe the time period.

Two restored 1856 stone buildings are all that are left from a large Chinatown, first destroyed by rampaging Irish miners, then by fire. They are open with displays.

Where once grand balls, lavish benefits, and major gold rush life took place, now we walk Coloma, trying to picture it's colorful history as "Queen of the Mines." Many nations were represented from Australians to Chileans, from Germans to Spaniards, Native Americans, and a parade of other nationalities who flooded the area looking for gold.

Only a few of the Gold Rush buildings are standing. Buildings were vandalized, cannibalized for their materials, or torn down for the gold that might be lurking underneath them. Coloma later became a major wine-producing area using the mining ditches for irrigation and the denuded hillsides for terraced vineyards.

Although there is nothing to discourage anyone from driving a RV to the mountaintop where Marshall's statue sits atop his grave and points to where he struck gold on the American River, I would discourage you. It was not wide enough for two vehicles to pass, trees limbs were not cut back, and parking would be nil during the tourist season. A 1½-mile Monument Trail exists and I would definitely take that next time.

As I continued north, all of nearby Sacramento's population must have been out for a warm spring outing. Fishermen lined the rivers and the young, the old, and the in-between were tubing. Now that looked like fun. My only inner tube, unfortunately, was "waisted" and not available for floating the river.

Can you tell I was wandering? I turned east again onto I-80 toward Reno. That very l-o-o-o--ong steep mountain grade over Donner Pass, 7,239', seems like it will never end. The engine had heated to just past the half–way mark several times in the mountains on this warm spring day. I checked the oil at the Donner Lake Vista. It guzzled a quart. Ah, the Lord was still watching over me.

The Emigrant Trail Museum is at Donner Memorial State Park, west of Truckee. Being late on a Sunday, this was not an option for me, but I did stop at the Donner Party picnic area after turning north on SR #89.

I walked the 1/3-mile loop trail. The emigrants left Springfield, Illinois, in April 1846, headed for California. Captain George Donner and his brother, Jacob Donner, and families, were forced by George Donner's broken wagon axle, to stop at Alder Creek. The others went on but were unable to cross the summit due to early winter storms. They built cabins near the (Donner) Lake only eight miles beyond Alder Creek. Due to a lack of trees large enough to build cabins, the Donner families lived in crude brush sheds covered by wagon canvas.

Even as I read their story on trail signs, I couldn't imagine the struggle of two families with 12 children living in such severe conditions with so little to protect them. Three adults and two children died at Alder Creek. After the March death of her husband, George, Tamsen Donner got as far as the Lake cabins and died. Two children died during rescue attempts. Jacob died in mid-December. His wife, Elizabeth, lived until early April. Eight Donner children were eventually rescued and lived to marry and have families.

In all, 42 of the 90 people died, most of them from starvation and exposure. The last survivor of the Donner Party died in 1935. She was one-year-old when her family was trapped at the Lake. It has long been questioned whether some lived by cannibalism. I hope we will never face such dire circumstances or have to live or die by such decisions.

Distances and time – it took me an hour to drive to the Sierra Nevada Mountain summit on I-80. Two days before I had driven two other snow-filled mountain passes across the Sierras just for fun. I pondered all this 135-year-old wagon-train history as I boarded my cozy Sprinter motorhome. People tell me I am brave to travel alone. No way. Bravery was living for months in unbelievable winter weather in a brush shed! The pioneers continue to amaze me.

It never fails. I intended to stay in the national forest overnight but I passed several campgrounds, than didn't see any more. In a lovely valley near Clio, I stopped at Rivers Edge RV Park. They advertised both Good Sam's discount and Woodall's rating. For $18, they even had an e-mail hookup. Civilization is great in small doses.

After one last e-mail fix, a long RV question and answer session with a friendly elderly gentleman while I pumped gas, I looked for a church. I concluded that Church Street should have a church on it. I parked by a tiny Methodist church. As I was getting out, I ran into a delightful lady coming out of the first service. I asked if she thought they would object to my wearing jeans. She said, "Of course not. The Lord just wants you to be there." (I can remember arguing that point with my oldest daughter when she was a hippie teenager. Now I'm a hippie keenager!) We talked a couple of minutes then I hugged her goodbye.

The lady next to me on the back seat was very friendly and shared her bulletin with me. The minister asked if there were any visitors and I didn't raise my hand. My new acquaintance stood up and revealed that her pewmate was from Michigan. So much for remaining anonymous in my jeans. It was a nice service and good choir. My friendly pewmate introduced me to several other friendly people, a good beginning to my traveling week.

Lassen Volcanic National Park was in my path. I had never been there. Having my Golden Age Pass at the ready, I sailed right through the Southwest Entrance Station fee after gleaning the information that my sailing would end in a snow-clogged highway approximately 11 miles into the park.

When I'd seen references to this park in the past, apparently the "Volcanic" part didn't register. I just thought it was a high mountain park. Think again Minshall. Until superseded by Washington's Mt. St. Helen's eruption in 1980, Lassen Peak's eruption in 1914 was the most recent volcanic outburst in the lower 48 States. Lassen Peak is one of the active volcano zones extending around the Pacific Ocean in a great Ring of Fire. Included in this are California's Lava Beds National Monument and Oregon's Crater Lake National Park. Hey, I was on a learning kick!

Considering I was surrounded by deep snow, it was quite warm, sunny, and pretty neat walking the boardwalk at Bumpass Hell and looking down into the water boiling up through the snow. A 50-something couple with their young son was traveling at about my speed. As we shared the stops, it was fun listening to Dad explain everything to his little boy.

It was my kind of road but clear of snow although I drove between high banks of it. At the barrier was a large area to pull off. One fellow who was sitting in a lawn chair reading a book, said he went up there often for peace and quiet. Actually, he wasn't getting it there. A number of people looked like they had spent the day in noisy fun.

I found a nice pull-off with a big rock on the way down. Someday I'll go back and see the rest of Lassen Volcano National Park, but for that moment in time, I had peace, quiet, a panoramic view, and a picnic on the rocks.

O.K., it was time to get out of snow country and find the beaches. First I spent the evening with Fred and Erma Cushman in Orland. Their house was right across the road from the fair grounds and the fair was in full bloom. While we scarfed baked potatoes with all the fixin's, a Mexican band played *Phantom of the Opera* Mexican style. Vely intelesting!

I went to Alaska for the first time in 1987 with Dick and Mary Carr and Fred and his first wife, Madeleine. Madeleine died a few years later and Fred and Erma had just celebrated their fourth wedding anniversary. We spent several hours at their kitchen table eating Fred's homemade ice cream and reminiscing about old times and newer times. They were all the best of times.

Over breakfast both Erma and Fred said I shouldn't take SR #36 from Red Bluff to the coast. But I had taken SR #299 across several years ago and this would be a new adventure. They said it was winding, narrow, and curvy. They didn't understand that it was my kind of road. Once I started into the mountains, the road also became steep, with views of distant snow-covered Mt. Shasta's 14,162'.

A side road pointed to a Vista Point but after following it for seven or eight miles and driving through minor landslides and snow patches, I wondered where it would end. A big drift, even though it had tracks through it, made me do something I really hate to do, turn back.

When I connected with SR #3, the signs said, "Road Narrows," they weren't kidding. Sometimes it had minus no shoulders. The edge of the road was the edge of the road minus crumbles, with nowhere to go but down. Fortunately, traffic was almost nil because I'm sure I would have given anyone coming toward me a heart attack in those steep, narrow places. However, it was great scenery driving through the Shasta-Trinity National Forest. By that time I had a goal in mind so I didn't dawdle and stay in several of the interesting campgrounds I passed. Another time now that I know they are there.

Nearer the coast, I drove through Grizzly Creek Redwood State Park where the huge redwood trees were at the road's edge with reflective signs. If you have never experienced these trees, I urge you to go and see them. Twisting through them is an awesome drive. It was about 140 miles to coastal US #101 but it seemed three times that distance. I enjoyed it all day but I was getting tired of twisting and turning.

From our phone calls, I knew that Richard was somewhere along #101. With five strong bars on the cell phone, I decided to find him. He had just pulled into a campground and was on his way to the office to register. When I discovered he was only 30 miles from me, I asked, "Want somebody to cook dinner for you?" Suspiciously perhaps, he said, "Who?" Since you already know my reputation as a cook (and so did he), you might wonder at his sanity in accepting.

I was soon on my way north with a quick stop for groceries. In the meantime I discovered I hadn't locked the medicine cabinet when I opened it for an aspirin. I had an interesting array of contents all over the bathroom and throughout the RV. Well, it wasn't the first time.

The chicken (Stores with already roasted chicken are great!), fresh asparagus, potatoes with herbs, the Knicks game (You know how I love sports) and making plans for exploring Redwood National Park, made for a fun evening at Sounds of the Sea RV Park at Trinidad. The three Musketeers were together again (Me, Richard, and the beautiful mean green GoldWing Machine).

P. S. The ice cream and strawberries weren't bad either. Of course Richard being Richard, spied the fact that it wasn't "real" ice cream, but "non-fat." But on to visiting another branch of the redwood family tree.

**Lassen National Park Hall of Snow**

# Redwood National Park

A morning walk took us on a wooded path to Palmer Point where we explored among the boulders. Richard took snail and lichen pictures while I conversed with the slugs. A baby sea lion rested high and dry on a rock formation. At first we didn't see that it was surrounded by seven adult sealions bobbing in the froth. While we snapped pictures and explored, they watched every move we made. The steep climb back up the cliff was a great excuse to stop and breathe, listen to gulls screeching, and just look. It was nice to be near the ocean again.

It was also fun to be on the Mean Green GoldWing Machine again. Steps and walls were built into Wedding Rock at Patrick's Point State Park. It is an enormous monolith connected to land by a bridge. A great view for a wedding but I wouldn't want to serve drinks.

A short curvy, narrow dirt road took us up the mountain and through the redwoods. It was familiar. Janet, Bill, Rebecca, and my kayaking buddy, Art, had gone this way in Bill's Forerunner a few years before. That was in April's wet weather. This was May and much nicer. A huge fallen redwood created a tunnel, perfect for pictures of Rich and his motorcycle.

Though we had seen their cousins, the giant Sequoias, the coast redwoods are even more awe-inspiring. They grow only along this Pacific Coast strip in California and southwestern Oregon. Discovered almost 40 years ago, the world's tallest redwood, 367.8', is here on the bank of Redwood Creek.

Coast redwoods have been known to survive for about 2,000 years. Like the Sequoias, they do not suffer diseases or insect damage but have extremely shallow root systems. While the base of a Sequoia might reach 40' in diameter, a coast redwood might be 22'. Sequoia bark might be up to 31" thick as opposed to a redwood's 12" thickness.

We turned off US #101 on to Newton B. Drury Scenic Parkway. All roads through the redwoods accommodate the trees, weaving around them rather than making a straight path. Richard tilted his head back until his helmet touched me. I'm not sure how he drove in that position. I continued to be impressed with how "Wowed" he was by everything.

The very first time I saw a redwood was in the late 60s when our family dropped into California as far as Crescent City and headed north again along US #199 to Crater Lake. I have a picture of them all standing in a redwood cavity. No, matter how often I have driven this area, it continues to thrill me.

Both California State and National Park cooperative management protect the Coast redwoods. They are considered a World Heritage Site and an International Biosphere Reserve. Some side roads we explored are marked as not advised for motorhomes or trailers.

Case in point, the Coastal Drive where we took the GoldWing. It alternated between a reasonably good paved road and very bad bumpy gravel and/or dirt. We followed the grassy bluff above the beaches, passing the WWII radar station. It was built in the 1940s, disguised as a farmhouse and barn. They housed a power supply, an oscilloscope, and radar technicians.

Our panoramic views took us to the Klamath River mouth and the old Douglas Memorial Bridge with the original golden bears on it that was wiped out by the 1964 flood. After reaching US #101 again, we went north over the new bridge with its shiny new golden bears to the town of Klamath and food. After trying several places, our eating choices were limited to a bar that served food. We were both hungry enough to eat the golden bears, shiny or otherwise.

The hamburger and fries served by friendly personnel were excellent, even the New Yorker admitted. He bet me a quarter I couldn't answer questions about the area but I came out even, I won two and lost two. We returned tired but happy to Sounds of the Sea RV Park.

The owner of the park was helpful with area maps and information. We headed south through Trinidad. Although we were early for seasonal activities, blooming flowers absolutely took our breath away. Trinidad State Park is in town and there are numerous other state and county parks along with Redwood National Park. The combination of spring and coastal waters was magnificent.

This bay was discovered in 1595. Trinidad, the town, was rediscovered several times, as a supplier for the gold rush, a local lumber shipping seaport, and even later as a whaling station. Now tourists revel in the considerable natural beauty, fishing, and history.

We criss-crossed through the 19th Century Eureka seaport "oldtown" and restored waterfront. We passed my favorite house and apparently the entire country's favorite place. It is supposedly the most photographed house in the world. Built between 1884 and 1886, William Carson lived there with his wife and four children. I have a feeling this lumber baron did not have to paint all that gingerbread! This is not open to the public but it is a fascinating place. Horsedrawn carriages have tours through town.

We drank coffees and ate no-nos outside the Eureka Baking Company in Ferndale. It was a delightful step back in time. We sauntered through a couple of antique stores, art galleries, and an old-fashioned mercantile. Richard had to forcibly pull me away from the candy shop. There should be a law against making candy in windows in view of vulnerable people. Speaking of vulnerable, I don't think I'll recount the conversation about the red cowboy boots we found in the handmade saddles and leather goods shop!

On Main Street and beyond, we admired the restored Victorian houses, gardens, and the Catholic Church. In the 1800s, this was an agricultural and transportation center with predominantly Scandinavian, Swiss, Italian, and Portuguese inhabitants. This is a place I may have to return to at Christmas. Although there are many festivals throughout the year, the lighting of "America's tallest living Christmas tree" and decorated Main Street Christmas trees plus a merchant-hosted Hospitality Night, sounds like great fun to me.

Leaving Ferndale, we went up through more redwoods into the King Range National Conservation Area via a (what else) narrow, winding, steep paved road. Rich said he had never taken the bike on that steep a road before.

Cows grazed unimpressed with their dramatic vistas. We rode along the ridge above the remote "Lost Coast," or "Forbidden Coast," so named for the lonely, treacherous coastline, final resting place for more than one hapless ship. Ranches were scattered in this rugged area. Weathered fences partnered with yellow buttercups, other wild spring flowers, tall green grass and together strained against the wind. We rode on the very top of the world.

Tight curves and a fierce wind accompanied our descent to the ocean. We climbed down the rocky shoreline to find a cave but tide and wind kept us from that side of the rock. We walked a bit on Cape Mendocino's rare black sand beaches before the wind pushed us back into the mountains again.

We rested at Honeydew. The business district was an old country store with its share of lollygaggers. The talkative owner grew up in Honeydew.

Rich asked, "What is the chief source of income?"

"Pot," he replied, without batting an eye. "We had an exciting day yesterday. The Feds brought in the helicopters. Everybody swarmed into town so they wouldn't be home. That's always a good day for business."

We sat on an old church pew watching kids play in the shade beside a county bookmobile.

I commented, "Your motorcycle is less intrusive than if I had come here with my motorhome. William Least Heat Moon and Steinbeck traveled in vans. As men, they could walk into local taverns, strike up conversations, and feel right at home, something I wouldn't be comfortable with."

"I wouldn't either."

"Why?"

"Saloons aren't my kind of place."

"You're unique."

"Why?"

"Some guys would think they weren't macho if they said saloons weren't their kind of place."

"I don't think saloons are macho." He was already tall but somehow he was even taller after that.

It was another 26 miles to the Avenue of Giants where we turned north paralleling US #101. This was old territory to me and since we were both tired from a long day, we drove slowly through the redwoods.

The Avenue of the Giants is a 31-mile stretch of old US #101, surrounded by Humboldt Redwoods State Park. While it takes only about 30 minutes to drive straight (like a snake!) through it, it could take weeks if you took advantage of hiking every trail, staying in all the campgrounds, and visiting all the attractions.

Redwood trees have been used for many novelties, Chimney Tree, an Eternal Tree House, a Shrine Drive Thru Tree and a Log House. We were careful in the land of "hobbits" near Phillipsville. You can hear their story while you're visiting the 1,500-year-old hollow living redwood tree. The "Immortal" redwood still lives next to the Burl 'n' Drift Novelty Shop. It is 950 years old and has survived fire, flood, and the logger's axe.

At Eureka we had dinner at Marie Callendars and then finished the day with Law and Order. During commercials I was grilled, "I can't believe you never heard of that (whatever the subject)!" Richard has a hard time with my not knowing what is going on in the world or who is who in sports.

I moved to the Redwood National Park beach south of Orick to boondock. Richard postponed his return south until Memorial Day and came with me. This stretch of beach is a favorite camping spot of mine. The ranger said it was the last fee-free year.

You just can't beat a picnic lunch oceanside with sealions performing in the surf, except maybe an evening fire. It was cool but the wind had died down. A la-a-a-zy time to watch the sunset, a time to talk and reminisce.

Richard said, "I don't like roasted hotdogs or sausage because of the ashes."

"There is no hope for you at all." As usual, we ended the evening with hot tea and Law and Order.

The GoldWing swam through foggy soup through Orick and on to Bald Hills Road. It was new territory to me but we could hardly see it. Our mile-loop trail through foggy Lady Bird Johnson Grove was eerie. We walked within a process called transpiration. Each hour the redwood trees exchange many gallons of water with the surrounding air. Without the fog protection, and the 85' annual rainfall, the giant redwoods could not replace their moisture losses.

As with the Sequoias, the redwoods often suffered injuries due to fungi and fires. These injuries created hollows that the pioneers, who made use of everything at their disposal, used for confining livestock and fowl. These are called "Goose-pen trees." Nature also uses the protecting redwood hollows for growing other types of trees and ferns. Trees were standing despite whole rooms opened beneath them from fires or rot. Fallen giants are effective nurseries to abundant life forms.

The trail was well marked with numbered signs following the brochure. It is really amazing that a tree that could weigh over 500 tons was grown from something as tiny as a tomato seed-sized seed (That's a tongue twister!).

Standing in a clearing surrounded by old growth forest, I imagined the day in 1968 when Lady Bird Johnson dedicated Redwood National Park. What a thrill it must have been to know all this was protected at last. It was the 50$^{th}$ anniversary of the Save-the-Redwoods League.

Since the mountain man, Jedediah Smith, first stumbled on to these magnificent trees in 1828, gold, copper, and silver mining plus logging had changed the region's face forever. One company alone harvested 8.5 million board feet per year. By 1929, 500 million board feet of lumber was being cut. Several presidents and many other people were involved with saving the redwoods, grove by grove. The 1978 Redwood National Park Expansion Act added 48,000 acres, and established a 30,000 acre watershed protection zone, plus establishing funds toward rehabilitating cutover forest lands and erosion control.

Richard took photographs while I sat on a bench and listened to the trees. On the overpass bridge to the parking lot, I asked Richard for a quarter. He said he could beat me around the loop and I reached the bridge first. You be the judge. We completed the loop and were at the end of the trail, right? He said he meant to the bike and started running. He beat me out of more quarters that way. You can see our time was spent in serious contemplation of life's greater meaning.

Continuing up the mountain, we finally went beyond the fog but we still couldn't see a thing below us. The ridge road turned to gravel with a ranch tucked in here and there. Distant snow-covered mountains poked through the valley fog with Mt. Baker significantly higher and more snow-covered than the others. In the foreground were open meadows thick with bluebells and birds singing. No doubt from all that fog, the trees were covered with moss or lichen.

What goes up must come down and it did, in spades. The road became washboardy in a very steep curving descent. With the heavy GoldWing, it was downright dangerous with loose gravel on the curves.

A couple local yocals blasted by leaving us in a cloud of dust. The road was doing a good enough job of that. When we finally reached pavement at SR #169 and 96, we were totally brown with dust. Rich zapped the dust from the not-so-beautiful GoldWing. Although he knew when we started that the road eventually turned to gravel, he was not prepared for just how much we would encounter.

Rich must have been praying! We drove into tiny Weitchpec on the Hoopa Valley Indian Reservation. Would you believe there was a car wash? After the GoldWing was once again a shiny green machine, Richard smiled again.

A pleasant local restaurant provided great hamburgers. The potato salad was whipped. I looked at Richard expecting a discourse on the Epicurean delights of New York potato salad. He loved it! He also raved about the apple pie and ice cream. He was either extremely hungry or the dust had dulled his Epicurean New York appetite! They not only had good food but this tribal town was a very happy place to stop, with a good bit of the population right there, including the tribal cops.

The Yurok and Tolowa Nations still exist. The Chilula were absorbed into the Hupa culture. They used the giant redwoods for dugout canoes and continue to keep traditional arts and crafts alive. They speak their native languages and take part in traditional ceremonies.

We were soon on SR #299 heading west toward the coast. I had driven this highway from Redding several years before and discovered it to be another very curvy but beautiful drive through Six Rivers National Forest. The seashore was still under a fog cloud. We were both cold and tired.

Turning on my heat full blast, I crawled into a woolly blanket and slept soundly. I wasn't sure if Rich was sleeping or watching the game when I woke up, so I drove the Sprinter to the store. I wanted to celebrate Rich's birthday early, before he headed to parts unknown. Orick's tiny grocery had few items with which to make a birthday party.

I built a fire and requested Rich's presence. He was surprised all right and the goodies were up to my usual gourmet standards. The strawberry frosting, ice cream, and Cool Whip helped cover the infirmities of the thawed and shapeless carrot cake. The candles wouldn't stand straight in all that goo. They wouldn't stay lit either.

My cooking disasters don't usually bother me because I'm the only one to see them but this one really embarrassed me. We forked our way through about two bites before I dumped it in the trash. I'm not sure when I have ended the day feeling so incredibly stupid.

What started out as a gray day was spectacular by the time we left on the GoldWing. Shafts of sunlight forced their way through the redwood darkness. At the Trees of Mystery north of Klamath, we walked around the gift shop. The museum has extensive Indian craftsmanship and artifact displays from throughout the United States and Canada.

I grew up with the legend that the big feet of Paul Bunyan and Babe the Blue Ox had made the Great Lakes. I'm not sure he made it as far west as northern California so I think they were stretching things a bit to make claims on *MY* Paul Bunyan and *MY* Babe the Blue Ox. Statues of both are outside the Trees of Mystery.

Rich had no interest in walking the Nature Trail or the Trail of Tall Tales to listen to Paul and Babe stories or see their fabled friends carved in redwood. Since I had already been through it a couple of times, I just had fond memories of the Candelabra Tree, and the Cathedral Tree where weddings are often performed. We walked across the street for coffee and a roll at Babe's Iron Tender Restaurant, passing the End of the Trail sculpture carved from one redwood tree.

I told Rich a story but he was looking off in space so I just continued with, "of course I'm talking to myself." Then he quoted exactly what I had said and added, "I can ignore you and hear every word you say." That struck me funny. I laughed so hard I almost cried. Actually, I was crying but he won't know that until he reads this at some far distant time.

We pulled off the main highway and took a route to the Requia overlook. Foamy waves rolled incessantly onto the rocks and beaches. I wondered if the gulls soaring above it recognized its beauty.

Crescent City's Battery Point Lighthouse was built in 1856 and can be reached only at low tide by crossing a 100', rock-strewn beach. It was fast becoming the high side of low tide. We balanced on rocks against a strong wind and progressively higher waves. Long Legs had better balance so he went on up to the lighthouse.

I stayed behind and took pictures of the beautiful spring gardens and remembered an eerie moonlight night I had boondocked there in the parking lot with the fog enveloping the motorhome. Rich said the lighthouse and the flowers were worth slightly wet feet.

We took SR #199 east to Hiouchi Information Center and southwest to Stout Grove. When I had driven very narrow Howland Hill Road previously to see Stout Grove, the ranger had said, "No problem." Now the map is marked, "Motorhomes and trailers not advised."

On the hike around the grove, we wondered how loud it would be when a mammoth redwood crashes to the ground. A path led downhill and through the mid parts of one that had fallen and smashed onto the ground. After admiring the trees, all of which seemed to have specific personalities, we continued. Even though Rich had to thread his way through the potholes along this narrow, one-way road, it was a direct route to US #101 and "home."

The park beaches are a great place for seeing unique driftwood, colorful stones, and tidepools filled with sea creatures. The ocean was in a big froth, making channels behind the sandbank as the tide came in.

Rich grew up surrounded by the Atlantic Ocean and was as fascinated with it as I am. An enormous tree trunk tossed about in the powerful tide. He challenged me to run and touch it for a quarter but then said I shouldn't. Of course he did it. "After being around the ocean all the time, I can gauge it." I'm amazed that I didn't take on that challenge. I was getting soft or maybe I had already lost too many quarters.

The ocean's movement was mesmerizing. We watched the sunset around the campfire and talked until late, late being relative, 10 p.m.

Sunday morning Rich took his chair to the beach to sit and read. I walked two miles into town to church. The tiny room was full. The minister acknowledged visitors.

"I'm originally from Michigan."

"You've been here before haven't you?" What a memory! That was at least four years before. I hoped I hadn't done anything outrageous to cause him to remember. I especially remembered his sense of humor. We all gathered for coffee and cookies and I talked with a full-time RVing couple from the Coast to Coast park (A few miles south of Orick) about Alaska. I asked for a ride back to the beach.

It was a wonderfully, sunny, lazy afternoon. Rich was occupied with a game on TV. I saw a movie at the Information Center.

At sunset we explored the beach. Rich again dodged the waves. He said he used to do that with his kids when they were little. We watched a sea lion ride the surf to where the river and ocean collided. The river pushed him back as the surf subsided. Then he rode the surf back into the river again. A fire was the perfect end to a perfect day.

That afternoon I had made an appointment to take a jetboat ride on Tuesday. That meant I would only be going about a hundred miles on Monday.

Rich asked, "Do you know where you'll be camped on Monday night?"

"No."

"Doesn't it bother you not to have a specific place to stay ahead of time?"

"No. There will be a place." (If they build it, I will come, right?)

Rich had already made reservations for his next few stops and lives by a camping directory. Almost every time I have done that, I have either called and cancelled because of changed plans or changed arrival dates. I have also found that the campground descriptions often do not coincide with the real thing. My exception to making reservations is when I must be in a populated area during the busiest season.

After the evening campfire, we shared our usual tea and cookies. I asked, "Who will make tea for me after this?" I was definitely spoiled.

Memorial Day arrived, calm and warm, but not any clearer than usual. We had breakfast at the Palm Tree Restaurant in Orick, another small town favorite from past trips. (They have the most delicious homemade pies but you didn't want to know that did you?).

We went back to the beach and he cleaned his windshield and mine. I patted the beautiful green GoldWing machine goodbye. Rich soon had the bike tied safely in his trailer and hugged me goodbye.

Rich turned south. I headed north. My glasses fogged with tears. I really hate goodbyes, but then again, a new adventure awaited me. We have kept in touch by occasional phone calls but mostly e-mail. Our paths haven't crossed again.

Let's head into Oregon and meet a real rogue!

# The Hydro-Jet Set

In the wee hours of June first, I awakened to a foghorn's deep mournful voice warning those who navigated the Pacific waters. Although I have long since given up "jumping" out of bed within the Sprinter's small confines, I was intrigued with spending the day with a rogue, in this case, the Rogue River.

With the gas gauge in its usual state of teetering emptydom, I pulled into a Gold Beach, Oregon, gas station. The high school sophomore who pumped it (I _love_ Oregon because they pump gas for you!) asked me a very strange question, "Are you with the circus?"

My long locks generally resemble something combed in a wind tunnel, and nobody ever accused me of wearing anything other than casual clothes, but they weren't especially colorful nor did they sport splashy circles. I don't drink and I wasn't cold so my nose wasn't bigger or redder than usual.

"Why do you ask?"

"There's a circus in town. From the filled map on your RV, it looks like you've been everywhere, so I figured you were with the circus."

Good sound reasoning I suppose.

Full-time RVers rely on the mail to keep them current on business matters, friendships or if they're very fortunate, affairs of the heart. I experience hassles getting mail because I don't know which road I'll be traveling or where it will lead me. The folks living along the Rogue River had it even harder. They had no roads, only the river. In 1895, enterprising Elijah Price established a Rogue River Mail Boat Run from Gold Beach to Agness.

That wasn't an easy feat considering the 130' rise in 32 upstream river miles. That trip took four days going up and two coming back. Of course they didn't have jet boats in those days. While the original mail carriers struggled to push themselves upstream with poles, our 1,000+ horsepower Hydro-jet was taking us on a 104-mile round trip in 7 ½ hours and that included a two-hour lunch break!

By 8 a.m. we gathered by the river, the beautiful, the beautiful river, dressed in layers covered with wind and splash protection. We carried sunglasses, cameras, binoculars, and whatever else, in plastic, and made a final stop at the necessary. If you didn't need that stop, I guess it wasn't necessary.

I sat in a front corner, almost protected by the windshield. After giving us safety instructions, Stan, our guide, added, "98% of what I tell you will be the truth – better than the average politician." I would have given him higher marks than that.

The Rogue River consists of three areas, Recreation, Scenic, and Wild. These names don't describe the river's character, but its accessibility. The Recreational part has a developed shoreline and is easily accessible by roads. We saw lovely homes with electricity and telephones and views that wouldn't quit.

RV resorts and USFS campgrounds were also on the river. Later on, we saw homes reached only by boat. They were without amenities except possibly for solar, wind, or waterpower, but then the view and the isolation made up for it. No cell phone service in that area.

A few roads access the Scenic River area, but it is mainly reached by trail. The Wild River is accessible only by trail, undeveloped, and generally unpolluted. Our "Handle with Care" Mail Boat trip took in all three.

It wasn't long before we knew why our belongings were plastic wrapped. Stan warned everyone to hang tight. He swirled the boat warp speed in what he called "a spin around." Come on, from paragliding, I remember those twisty things are called "360s." At any rate, he got our hearts started big time. Now we were ready for anything. He put the nose of the unbelievably maneuverable Hydro-jet into a waterfall. The boat sinks only six inches and draws only three inches of water. Mileage is worse than the motorhome. I get six mpg and the Hydro-jet gets less than one. It is only feasible to make the trip with a full boat.

He stopped momentarily and talked with a fisherman who proudly displayed his huge catch for us to admire. Stan yelled, "What'd you catch it with?" Grinning, the fisherman held up an enormous oversized lure. I smelled a conspiracy. One fisherman caught a fish just as we jetted by (surely they couldn't have staged that!). He handed the line to his wife and Stan said, "Now we have things under control; she has the pole."

We stuck around to watch. They pulled anchor to play out the fish but before they moved, he filled the gas tank. I'm sure the audience flustered them. Playing the fish took forever but amid good-natured remarks and laughter from the jet-boat bunch, it was finally landed.

A harbour seal lurked close by awaiting the right moment to grab the fish before it was netted. He lost. Their dog was excited. He jumped and carried on, "Come on Boss, lemme help! lemme help! I know I can get it! I know I can get it!" Drama on the high seas.

Glen told about the famous people who had fished the Rogue River like Clark Gable and Zane Grey. Zane Grey had a river cabin and used local background for one of his novels. It was almost as rugged an area as his *Call of the Wild* setting.

Early on we had riffles. The riffles had ridges. We flew through Bacon Flat, Rachel's Delight, and Nail Keg Riffles and later between the

400' walls of Copper Canyon. A cement truck skeleton was wedged on shore. "That was carried down here from Agness by a flood. For a long time it had a sign on it, 'We deliver anywhere.'"

Remember my seat behind the windshield? Occasionally I ran the wipers to keep it clear. When we experienced a big spray, Glen laughed, "Refreshing isn't it?"

He showed us quartz, which usually means gold is in the area. He pointed to the way rock was twisted up to make a natural sleuce.

We stopped for a 15-minute break at Agness. A truck transported those who couldn't or wouldn't walk the arduous climb to the ridge and Singing Springs Resort for snacks, souvenirs, and by that time, the necessary necessaries. Although this resort was high above the river, the 12/22/64 flood proved it was not above flood level. The Rogue, which normally flows at 2,500 cubic feet per minute, accelerated to a raging 750,000 cubic feet per minute, and enveloped the restaurant.

Before we continued the Hydro-jet ride into the Wild Rogue Wilderness above Wilson Creek, we were required to don life jackets.

Streams poured into the Rogue, using its corridor to find their way to the sea. The water was about three feet higher than usual for that time of year so we didn't experience as much of the whitewater excitement as normally we would have. We went through Old Diggins, Little Wildcat, and Solitude Bar Rapids, no doubt each with a story behind its name.

The Rogue River travels 215 miles from its headwaters on the Cascade Mountain's western slope. It is innocuous enough as it passes through orchards and farmlands but eventually it hurls its way through the Hellgate Recreation Area and the Wild Rogue Wilderness before it riffles and cascades to the ocean.

It doesn't surprise me that it was one of the original eight rivers included in the Wild and Scenic Rivers Act of 1968. Mountains, high cliffs, thick forest, and rugged shoreline surrounded us. The outfitters refer to it as going "up the down staircase." At Devil's Staircase Rapids, we knew the end was near. We could go no further than Blossom Bar Rapids. If you were on a raft trip coming west and down the Blossom Bar Rapids, they claim it is the most exciting whitewater on the river.

We reluctantly turned around and made tracks (or maybe waves) for Singing Springs Resort. We were starved. Again we climbed the steep trail, this time for a delicious dinner. It was my kind of meal, substantial enough I wouldn't have to cook later. Glen commented, "If you leave hungry, it is your own fault." During July and August they serve a "Traditional Indian Salmon Bake" on Thursday and Friday evenings. Oooh, why am I always too early or too late?

Good food, a morning of excitement, constant engine rhythm, and my eyes desperately wanted to sleep. It didn't work. Just like on the way up, around every corner somebody saw something. In Bear Canyon, Glen said, "Keep your eyes peeled. We see a bear in here about once a week." "Yeah, right," I muttered. "We're going to see a bear on cue in

Bear Canyon." When will I ever learn? No sooner was the mumble out of my mouth when we spotted a furry little black bear, about two years old and freshly kicked out by his mother, foraging for food on the steep mountainside. Two or three people saw another but most of us didn't see it. Glen said, "We see a lot of 'five-second bears.'"

Black-tailed deer, the only kind on the river, grazed, barely acknowledging our presence. A frisky fawn tumbled along behind her. Elk and cougar are occasionally seen as well. Considering the number of animals we encountered, the boat obviously didn't disturb them.

Suddenly he beached the Hydro-jet on a sand bar and asked if anyone had questions.

"Do you ever hit rocks?"

"I think I've hit every rock at least once. If you ever have a driver tell you he has never hit a rock, look for another company.

"What were the oldest and youngest passengers you've ever had?"

"96 years and five weeks. I also had 92 year old twin sisters."

"Where are you from?"

"I've spent my whole life near the river and the last 23 years doing this."

He pointed out the western common pond turtles sunning on logs, just like they used to do during my Michigan childhood years. They were probably Midwest common pond turtles. River otters, a bit smaller than their sea otter cousins, gamboled in the water. A huge sea lion begged for food where we dropped guests off at their hotel near the U. S. #101 bridge.

Daylong river trips sometimes leave something to be desired. The Hydro-jet maneuverability certainly made the trip more amusing since he could stop on a dime, and often did. We stopped to see whatever piqued anyone's interest. Stan shared a bit of history or humor, identified animals or birds (on cue), or answered questions. There was never a dull moment from the first river otter to the roughest rapids.

I highly recommend this fun trip, but button up your overcoat, those "spin arounds" can get you wet! And maybe next time I'll spend a week at Singing Springs Resort, if they promise not to have a flood.

Now lets go visit a national treasure.

# A National Treasure

Some say it is indescribable. Others call it magnificent. To many it is awesome. Still others describe it as Mother Nature's theater-in-the-round. It is Crater Lake National Park, Oregon's only National Park.

Nearly 8,000 years ago, Mount Mazama, one of many Cascade Range volcanic mountains, was a majestic mountain rising to 12,000'. In a violent eruption, the mountain caved into a caldera six miles wide with lava cliffs rising 4,000' in a nearly perfect circle. Over the next 7 to 15 centuries, rainfall and snowmelt created Crater Lake. With no inlet or outlet, the lake's level is maintained by evaporation and seepage, fluctuating no more than three feet per year. A volcanic cone forming Wizard Island is 800' above the lake and has a 90' crater in its top.

Picture standing on Hillman Peak, the highest peak along the caldera rim, viewing a panoramic winter scene. Whimsical waves of deep snow blanket the earth and sparkle in the full moon. Crater Lake is a deep Prussian blue. It is peaceful. Trees, shaped by harsh winds, are coated with the day's frozen cloud vapor. The hoot of a snowy owl echoes in the clear night. Snowshoes crunch with each step.

Yes, you would definitely need snowshoes. The annual snowfall is approximately 50'. Crater Lake, 1,932' deep, is the deepest lake in the United States and maintains an average temperature of 38°F. The lake last froze in 1949.

The three remaining seasons explode into July and August with lush greens and flower-carpeted meadows where black-tailed deer browse in the early morning. Subalpine and Shasta red firs; Ponderosa, whitebark, and lodgepole pine; and Mountain hemlock are awakening along with conversing ravens and singing robins. Stellars jays scold and chickadees chatter. Yellow glacier lilies, pink monkey flowers, lavender shooting stars, purple lupine, and red paintbrush, along with others, create riotous color.

Yellow-bellied marmots in high places pose in furry charm for photographers. While their peers romp in the meadow, these sentinels guard against attack by martens, hawks, fox, or golden eagles.

A two-lane highway circles the caldera for 33 miles with a seven-mile spur road leading to Pinnacles Overlook. Thirty awe-inspiring vistas offer a look at this self-contained bowl of unbelievable color called Crater

Lake. Due to its great depth, the water is purer and clearer than any other. It is this deepest blue that astounds the park's half a million annual visitors.

Ninety miles of maintained and well-marked hiking trails vary in difficulty. Sun Notch Viewpoint is a half mile one way with views of Crater Lake and the Phantom Ship. Mount Scott, 8,926', the highest peak in the park and five miles round trip, offers 360° views including Pumice Desert, Crater Lake, and even California's Mount Shasta. The only safe and legal access to Crater Lake's shore is the Cleetwood Cove Trail. The trail is two miles round trip and drops 700' in elevation. Returning is an exhausting climb comparable to ascending 65 flights of stairs.

Activities include Crater Lake Volcano Caldera Cruises, geology talks, history programs, ranger-led nature hikes, and campfire programs. Winter activities are snowshoeing and skiing.

Pikas and ground squirrels prepare for the cold season. Cottonwood trees turn gold and aspens quake with the thought of winter winds and blowing snow. Facilities close; roads drift. The cycle is complete once more. Crater Lake National Park is truly one of our national treasures.

In June of 2000, I visited Crater Lake again. I had turned off I-5 to SR #62, and north through the park to SR #138, heading for US #97 and my daughters.

I had problems with the Sprinter's engine overheating on I-5's steep mountain passes. I surmised with its similarity to the clutch fan going out on a previous occasion, that I could get to Leavenworth and a "stashed" mechanic before having it fixed. I drove with the hood up. It didn't interfere with my windshield vision and it helped keep the engine cool.

At the Visitor Center, a young lady with the park police asked if it was my RV with the hood up. I explained I was babying it along. She was concerned because of the steep climb ahead of me. It was only nine miles through the park so I figured I could wing it. It was windy and cold. Signs warned of possible icy conditions. The deep snow made a canyon. The other 3/4s of rim road was still closed. At the few plowed overlooks I peered into an incredible amount of nothingness, remembering instead, the blue water, blue skies, and little girls playing...

It was raining and I knew without too much encouragement it would turn to snow. By the time I reached #97, the rain stopped and the wind started. I white-knuckled it all the way to Leavenworth and the warm arms of family.

Let's continue north and cross the Canadian border to visit a very special limestone quarry and something for the soul.

# Something for the Soul

## Butchart Gardens

Dan, a friend I'd met at a Florida FMCA Convention many years before, and I, ran into each other in Washington. Didn't I tell you it was a small world? He went with me on the Victoria Express from Port Angeles to Vancouver Island, British Columbia, Canada. It was a perfect September day, but cold on the water. The ferryboat captain warned us, "Don't take any weapons, Mace, machetes, knives, or guns through customs." I told Dan I really hated giving up my machete.

The scene going into Victoria's stone-walled Inner Harbor was busy with helicopters and pontoon planes taking off and landing, and water taxis scooting back and forth. US and Canadian Coast Guard were there along with ferryboats and yachts.

We docked in view of the blocklong, ivy-covered Empress Hotel and Parliament buildings. Victoria is British Columbia's capital. A much older culture is present in Victoria, too. Totem poles are everywhere, representing the Pacific Coast Indian civilizations that were there well before Victoria was settled.

After going through customs, we boarded a double-decker bus. A sign said, "No Sex Please, We're British," advertising a long-running comedy. Douglas Street and the Douglas Hotel were named for Sir James Douglas who established Fort Victoria in 1843.

Our guide, Chuck, gave a running commentary, "Notice there are no overhead wires. In the 60s, they were buried for aesthetic value. There are 700 hanging flower baskets that are watered each night. Victoria's population is roughly 325,000, with 500,000 on Victoria Island. Any buildings over a hundred years old must have a permit to be altered or torn down.

"The island is 300 miles long and 50 miles wide with about 7,000 coastline miles including all the inlets. We have approximately 27" of rainfall here with roughly 200" at the island's north end. This is one of the world's largest ferry systems with more tonnage than the Canadian Navy."

Their main industries are logging, mining, and tourism. The summer temperature is usually 70°-85°F, with 32°F-55°F in the winter. "Sometimes we have no snow at all. Due to the mild temperatures, the island draws the 'Newly wed and the nearly dead.'

It was about 18 miles to Butchart Gardens. The Robert Butcharts were pioneers in the manufacture of Portland cement. They bought 125 limestone waterfront acres in 1904 and expanded their cement business. After 24 years (1928) the limestone ran out.

They had a lovely home and decided to turn the quarry into a sunken garden. The family entertained a great deal with garden parties. Up to 200 people a day came to see the gardens. They opened it to the public. Unfortunately with the public involved, things were stolen. It was closed until the Butcharts died. In the early 1950s, a grandson inherited the property and opened Butchart Gardens; the rest is history. Chuck said sometimes the grandson, who is now in his 70s, directs traffic.

A million visitors come through each year. It takes 400 summer staff members to run it, mostly gardeners, and about 45 in the winter. On our way in, the driver slowed so we could see the lovely entrance sign and the beginning gardens, which you do not walk through.

Chuck said, "This is bus #251. Let's synchronize our watches to leave at precisely 12:15. For those who believe in the hereafter, if you get *here after*, it is for sure you will be *here, after*. And don't forget, the gardens in this area are fertilized with humans – the ones who picked flowers."

With all the flower sniffing and garden admiring, it isn't hard to get turned around, but it isn't a problem because you are always in a beautiful spot. They have the Italian Garden, Rose Garden, Japanese Garden, Concert Lawn, Greenhouse, and Ross Fountains. They encompass flagstone walks, sunny open spots and shaded pools with little bridges and fountains. The Fountain of the Three Sturgeons is a bronze fountain cast in Florence, Italy.

My personal favorite is the Sunken Garden. The Lookout gave us a sweeping view of what was once the limestone quarry. Steps took us down through garden islands, another rock lookout, then between small lakes to view the Ross Fountain, created to mark The Butchart Gardens 60th anniversary.

Dan and I watched the dancing waters while we ate ice cream from the nearby Quarry Coffeehouse. It is a perfect spot to rest up before the trek back to the bus.

A Flower Guide can be purchased in the gift shop if you must know the name of each flower. As for me, I just colored them all magnificent. If you are fortunate enough to be there during summer evenings, the gardens are illuminated, musical entertainment is transmitted, and fireworks burst forth on Saturday nights.

Back at the wharf, the Royal London Wax Museum had a presentation of John Franklin and his expedition in search of the Northwest Passage. I had no idea that within a couple of years during a November trip to the Canadian Arctic, I would buy the book, "Frozen in Time," which chronicles the fate of the Franklin Expedition.

Dan and I walked through the Empress Hotel with its arboretum, fountains, and flowers. People sat in the lobby and on the porch eating fancy tidbits and drinking high tea.

Carriage rides were available but we opted for a bicycle-pulled cab. The driver wasn't all that proficient and his patter was practically nil. At least he didn't charge us when we stopped to go inside Market Square. I think he wanted a cigarette. We went through the old buildings that held quaint shops and cafes, and later toured Trounce Alley as well. Our bike cab ride continued to Bastion Square where we paid him off. We decided it was more fun on the wharf.

It was really getting warm. We were fortunate to find a shaded lunch table at Milestone's Restaurant overlooking the bay. Something was happening everywhere we looked. A magician performed, an artist drew caricatures, and the gendarmes handcuffed a bike rider.

Besides the colorful people of all ages, crazy balloons, hanging flower baskets, and the unfolding wharf landscape before us, musicians played while laughter and happy sounds filled the air. It was wonderful. On top of that, the food was delicious.

On our wharf walk, we met Captain James Cook, as it turned out, a self-employed statue. A great crowd gathered but it was a few minutes before we realized what was happening. This statue wore an authentic captain's period costume with 3/4 frock coat, three-cornered hat and knee-length trousers with big shoes and stocks, all completely grey. His head, face, and hair were painted grey.

People passed by. He stood perfectly still on a pedestal until they were beyond him. He followed them with his eyes and slowly stuck out his very red tongue as he turned his head. When the audience laughed, passersby would turn around, sometimes catching him, sometimes not. If they did, they really did a double take.

He didn't do anything except move his eyes, send occasional smoochy kisses, and smirk once in a while. For someone who was doing absolutely nothing, he drew a big crowd. He eventually moved very slowly off the pedestal, withdrew a real rose from beneath his coat, and gave it to a little girl about seven years old. She wasn't sure whether to take it or not. He presented his cheek for a kiss and she walked away. She was urged to go back. She gave him a hug. It was really cute.

He had been doing that daily for four months. The guy next to me said people never got tired of the joke. The statue ended his performance by saying we should all be willing to laugh and have fun. Amen.

We listened while Wharf Street Willy played piano on a rolling platform. We were enchanted there in the warm early evening and didn't want to give up the magic, but the ferry called.

Next to magical days, I love magical evenings...

**Butchart Gardens, Vancouver Island, British Columbia**

# The Sound of Music

A few years ago it was my privilege to travel Europe for six weeks. Germany's Bavaria was every bit as beautiful as I imagined, with snow-covered mountains, picturesque chalets, and shopkeepers dressed in lederhosen and dirndl skirts.

But I don't have to go that far for such things. My Janet and her family live in Leavenworth, Washington, a small village tucked in the eastern Cascade Range Mountainside. My friend, Jane Parker, had flown from Florida for two weeks. One of our stops on the Cascade Loop was Leavenworth. As a special treat we took her to see *The Sound of Music*.

Mountains and the Wenatchee National Forest surround the Ski Hill Amphitheater. In the early evening we gathered while the sunset painted the clouds. A ¾ moon came up as though on cue. The alpenhorns sounded on the mountainside above and behind the audience. From the Nonnberg Abbey on stage, the nuns sang "Alleluia," their clear beautiful voices ringing through the valley.

The hills really were alive with *The Sound of Music* as Maria made her way down the mountain path to the theatre. I have seen this play many times but to see it in that setting. Wow! Throughout the play, the summer bug chorus accompanied the singers and a soft warm breeze stirred the air. We were mesmerized. The players drew the audience in to sing "*Edelweiss.*"

We sang and cried with the von Trapps as they escaped Austria by the skin of their teeth. We shared their laughter, joy, tears, and heartache all the way. We climbed every mountain and finally reluctantly said, "*So Long, Farewell,*" and wound our way down the mountain path to go home ourselves.

Only the year before I had visited the von Trapp Family compound in Stowe, Vermont, and read the true escape story. Again, wow!

There are many reasons to visit Leavenworth, Washington. If you do, don't miss Leavenworth Summer Theatre.

And next to magical days and evenings, I like special times with my MBG.

# *Lake Chelan's Stehekin*

When I'm visiting in Leavenworth, Washington, MBG (My Beautiful Granddaughter) and I take short "RV/camping" trips together. We drove the Cascade Loop and on the last day we went to Stehekin. Since it can only be reached by plane, water, or leg power, getting there is half the fun. We settled aboard The Lady Express at Chelan, Washington, with strawberry milk, chocolate milk, and cookies for treats, or was that breakfast? You can do that with grandchildren.

We cruised through Lake Chelan National Recreation Area, which extends northwest into the heart of North Cascades National Park. Stehekin, a village at Lake Chelan's upper end, has a year-around population of about 70. We were fortunate it would take us only 2½ hours. When The Belle of Chelan was launched in 1889, it took the firewood-powered vessel two days and 10 to 12 cords of wood to reach Stehekin.

MBG, eleven at that time, was not particularly interested that this 50-mile long lake was nestled in North America's deepest gorge or that it was the third deepest lake in the United States at 1,486'. Only Lake Tahoe at 1,645' and Crater Lake are deeper. Chelan is an Indian word meaning "deep water." I guess I take after my second oldest brother, Dick; I like some statistics along with my chocolate milk (You didn't think I was the one drinking strawberry milk did you?).

The scenery begins in rounded high desert mountains and progresses to the rugged snow-capped peaks of North Cascades National Park. This natural lake was raised 21' by the Chelan Dam. Although the lake averages about 1½ miles wide, at "The Narrows" it is about ¼ mile wide. We picked up passengers at Fields Point. The road on the lake's west side ends a few miles beyond at 25-Mile Creek State Park. On the east side, the road stops at Manson. The terrain was too rugged for road building beyond those points. Now we were really wilderness bound.

The narrator called our attention to interesting points, Slide Ridge, Coyote Creek Incline, Refrigerator Harbor, and Railroad Creek, all with stories of their own. Holden Village, an abandoned coppermine, is now a non-profit wilderness retreat for all denominations, run by the Lutheran Church. We saw Domke and Bridal Veil Falls.

With no roads, residents and businesses depend on supplies, mail, equipment, and tourists coming by boat or barge. They send grocery lists and blank checks to a Chelan store. Orders are picked up and delivered to the Stehekin dock. Lake Chelan Boat Company also makes "flag" stops to pick up hikers and others. In Stehekin you are more apt to find a floatplane or a canoe tethered to the front porch than a car in the garage. A few cars, all barged in, are classics wearing early 60s expired tags.

The story goes that a dealer learned a big lesson about promotion. His company advertised the best mobile home deal by offering free delivery anywhere in Washington. A Stehekin resident bought two mobile homes. The dealer almost went bankrupt barging them to Stehekin, plus the use of a flat bed truck and subsequent blasting to reach the site.

After docking, Rebecca and I went to Stehekin Lodge and picked up our rented bikes, along with a daypack of information and maps, a bag lunch, and bottled water. We were on our way. Rebecca napped through all the scenery. Now she was wide awake. She loves biking.

The first four miles of the 23-mile Stehekin Valley Road is paved. We knew we didn't have time to go all the way to the end. We checked out the old schoolhouse, the last one-room schoolhouse in Washington State, closed in 1988, and on the National Registry of Historic Places. One teacher taught from 5 to 18 students, ranging from kindergarten through eighth grade. It was hard for Rebecca whose school has many rooms and many teachers, to picture it. I didn't have that problem. I went to a one-room school with all grades and one teacher until I was in the eighth grade. I'm positive Rebecca thought I was historic too!

After eighth grade, students receive home schooling or go "outside" for school. No wimps attend school in Stehekin. The snow has to be 15' deep before school closes or so a bus guide on a previous trip had told me. The new school is considered a one-room school for teaching but it also has a library and gymnasium. The new school has indoor plumbing, pretty important with 15' of snow!

Stehekin means, "The way through." This valley was used as a trade route by inland Indian tribes to the Pacific Coast tribes. Pictographs throughout the Upper Lake Chelan Valley evidence Native American habitation for hundreds of years before white men discovered the valley in the 1800s. They are credited with establishing the lake's first apple orchard at Wapato Point.

A later orchard planted in 1911 by the Buckner Family is one of the oldest and largest stands of Common Delicious Apples in the United States. A self-guided tour can be taken through the Buckner Homestead Historic District, now maintained by the National Park Service.

Rebecca was used to biking so she zipped up the few slight hills but I hadn't biked for 10 years. I gave up biking when I creamed the last one against a palm tree while I was backing the Sprinter out of a Mexico campsite.

We followed the Stehekin River to Rainbow Falls. Church…well, we weren't there for Sunday worship, but it claims to have the highest ceiling in the world, the sky. Come to think of it, they didn't have any walls either. Nothing was on the riverbanks but seats and inspirational scenery.

According to a previous bus guide, "The gas station is on the honor system. You dig through the money to make change and put your name on the log. You'll be billed every 30 days…or so. No one even takes his keys out of the car. The only place to run is to a boat." Good point.

The loneliest stop sign in America lives in Steheken and as the guide said, "Probably the only one that has no bullet holes in it."

A pipeline brings water from the creek. Pure water isn't a problem. Eleven glaciers feed the creek. Lake Chelan has the reputation of being one of the cleanest water bodies in the United States. Where possible, homes use the City of Chelan's sewage line. All others are required to have a septic tank.

Just about the time my panting tongue was dragging along the road, we met a ranger.

"How far is it to the falls?

"Hang in there. They're right up the road."

"Can we take a shower under the falls?"

"Definitely, no clothes required. It has been done before."

Rainbow Falls was 312' of sparkling water, not only beautiful, but the spray was blessedly cool. We had this great scenery all to ourselves except for the bees. Rebecca isn't too fond of bees and they were thick. We finally left a few crumbs for them to feed on and took our sandwiches to eat next to the water. They didn't like the spray.

Mule deer, cougar, and moose live here but the guide warned, "Mosquitoes are the only animals you are legally allowed to feed." Technically, I don't think of mosquitoes as animals but his point was well taken. We fed as few as possible.

The sack lunch was more than adequate but with all that talking and biking, the hunger pangs returned. It might have had something to do with the fragrance floating our direction. As if by magic, the Stehekin Pastry Company appeared. We watched them make all goodies right there behind the counter. Coffee and a yummy nut and cinnamon roll didn't taste all bad.

We returned with a little time to spare. Rebecca went through the gift shops while I picked up information at the Golden West Visitor and Information Center. The young lady asked, "How bad were the bees?" I explained our lunchtime solution.

"Did you see the 'really big monster?' It's a tenacious fly with bulging green eyes, an orange body and a voracious appetite for 'great chunks of human flesh.'" I was not only glad we hadn't seen it but glad I hadn't talked with her first.

We returned to Chelan and the waiting Sprinter on the Lady II. Making several delivery and pick up stops, it took about four hours.

Adventurous, yes; overly bright, questionable – Let's take a July tour of Hell's Canyon.

# Hell's Canyon
## National Recreation Area

It had really been fun being an instructor for the Moscow, Idaho, Life on Wheels Conference, but when that week was over, I was ready to find solitude and/or adventure. I found both. I headed south down the old Lewiston Grade. I suppose nobody in their right mind would go to Hell's Canyon in July but who ever accused me of being in my right mind.

After a hamburger fix at Hoot's Café, I found the turnoff, "Hammer Creek Recreation Area/Pittsburg Landing." Heading west, I crossed the Salmon River and made an immediate left to Deer Creek Road (FR #493). The road was written up as a one-lane gravel road with turnouts and steep grades. Yup, my kind of road. I smoothed the ruffled tires of the Sprinter first. I had promised no more rough roads. However, this road was an excellent gravel road with very few washboard areas.

Ten miles later, I reached Pittsburg Saddle. A pull-off with a picnic table had a Hell's Canyon panoramic view with the steep road's tight switchbacks leading to Pittsburg Landing. Pittsburg Saddle was supposed to be a good place to evaluate whether you wanted to continue. Did they really think I would go back?

Even in first gear, it was necessary to brake almost to a stop several times to maneuver those hairpin curves. Gorgeous country with a few trees here and there to break it up. I first checked out the famous fast-moving Snake River, then found a campsite. The sun soon disappeared over Oregon's Wallowa Mountains. Grasshoppers abounded with my every step while getting settled, and serenaded me along with other night creatures.

Upper Pittsburg Landing is the Wild and Scenic River Boundary dividing the scenic river where I am at Lower Pittsburg Landing, and the wild part south of me.

This campground has 28 units with level parking, graveled spots with campfire grills, very long picnic tables with wheelchair access and under a roof with shade toward the afternoon sun. The campground is quite high above the river. I can hear it but can only see it in the distance as it curves, like its name, north through HCNRA. It rushes beside an outcropping on the Oregon side of the river that was deposited by Mt. Mazama's volcanic eruption 6,800 years ago, forming Crater Lake 200 miles southwest of here.

It stayed very warm well into the half-moon night. The rushing water finally lulled me to sleep. I awakened about 5 a.m. to a cool morning and two deer grazing within 10' of my window.

Signs warned of "Natural hazards" like snakes and poison ivy, and the powerful currents if anyone was to go swimming. They also warned that it gets very hot in the summer months but I already knew that. It was a fee area but I never saw anywhere to register nor did anyone come calling.

I love mornings but I hesitated to stay, knowing how hot it was going to get. I had to make the decision to leave early if I was going. The Sprinter would have a very hot and steep drive out to I-95. With deer grazing peacefully and my shades drawn against the inevitable heat and only three other occupied campsites, I couldn't resist sipping a cup of coffee, feasting my eyes on the scenery, and staying hidden for a while.

Rarely worn shorts and a matching blouse with cut off sleeves were the dress of the day. The deer and snakes would care less about my hairy legs and cellulite-dimpled thighs.

There is no cell phone service in this canyon, no public phone, no e-mail connection, and no library. My dish is turned off until I get desperate for inane TV. There is no recreation hall for potlucks or gatherings, no swimming pool except the treacherous river, and 17 miles separates me from I-95.

It is a peaceful place to work. I find at the end of the day that I have done only two productive things. I created a new business card and started this story. I spent the rest of the time making a new friend. If that isn't productive, it is at least soul satisfying.

Her name was Gwen. She's probably a little younger than I am although her grandchildren are a bit older. She is volunteering here at Pittsburg Landing so the Forest Service personnel will give her occasional boat rides across the river to an abandoned farm where she does research.

She is a geologist working on her Master's Degree doing a paper on floods. These are not ordinary floods mind you, but the Bonneville Flood that raced through the Snake River Canyon 15,000 years ago, and the catastrophic flood that crossed northern Idaho creating a waterfall in Washington that was 3.5 miles wide with over a 400' drop during the last Ice Age. She nonchalantly speaks of alluvial fans and carbondating. She sees the same scene I do but she knows its secrets; I only know its beauty.

She was born and raised in Washington, D. C. wondering when the sticks she put into the small neighborhood creek would finally reach the Atlantic Ocean. She had an innate curiosity about the nature of the world around her. Spending summers with her grandmother in South Carolina, she picked cotton, knowing in her heart she really wanted to delve into natural world mysteries. She lived 40 years of a first life raising children and other jobs before she finally went to college and pursued her dreams.

A Seattle couple visited with us under the shaded office porch roof where Gwen greets visitors and offers information. These two people were SOWERs, Servants on Wheels Ever Ready. They build houses and churches and do repair work to help others. They also belong to the same national RV group I am active in, Escapees, and spend part of their winter in Arizona. A small world.

We chatted about our various activities and what we did. After they left, Gwen said that until she had become acquainted with the three of us, she thought RVers were people driving big boxes bent on destroying the environment. So I guess the afternoon was worthwhile if I changed someone's negative view of RVers.

Because I travel alone I suppose, I think about who might be reading this. I want to tell you what I'm doing right now. The grasshoppers report a coming storm but the dark clouds and rumbling thunder already announced its impending arrival.

The river rushes on, oblivious to it all until it temporarily rises with the extra water coming from mountain streams. It has been hot today but the cloud cover and eminent storm have cooled the air. That air has excitement in it, maybe its because we never know what drastic change the weather will bring. The buck and doe who munched outside the Sprinter's windows this morning, are probably bedded down under a tree. Daisies blow in the rising breeze. Other tall weeds sway in rhythm with them. Swallows dive and dine.

The storm is getting serious now. Three-pronged jagged lightning strikes something up on the mountain. It isn't too close yet although its display is magnificent, close enough I'm not tempted to go walking. I'm glad I'm not parked broadside to the wind that is getting stronger.

I am amazed that here in mid-July, this campground has only two RVers in it and the other people are gone in their tow car. I don't feel lonely but as I watch the lightning and the roiling clouds, I wish I could zap my two grandchildren here to watch the storm with me. While lightning is dangerous, surely we should teach them about the beauty of storms as well. Eventually the storm moves on down the canyon or over the mountains, wherever storms go after they finish their heavenly performances and give everything a drink of water and a wash job.

When I finally turn out my light and lay me down to sleep, I look out into a beautiful night sky. There are no artificial lights to mess up my clear view of the half moon dancing on the Wallowas. Night has brought again the bug concert. The Big Dipper is outside my window where it has been an almost constant companion throughout my full-time RVing years.

Before I go to sleep in this peaceful place, I say a thank-you prayer for being able to *see* and *hear* that storm, *feel* that breeze, and *smell* the freshness of the air, and just be where I am for this moment in time. And for my offspring and families that are healthy and happy, and hopefully, snug in their Washington and Virginia beds, I am also grateful. I give thanks that I am healthy and happy and snug in my bed here in the Hells Canyon National Recreation Area.

It was a struggle to get up in the cool morning when I felt so cozy in bed. It was also a toss up as to whether I started working on the computer right away with ideas that had been racing around in my head last night or go for a walk, both of which I needed to do.

The walk won out. I went up the hill and around the bend to see what I could see. Leftover storm clouds hung on the mountaintops and the weather didn't look too promising. I didn't mind getting wet if it came to that.

I stopped to view a tiny waterfall that may not have been there yesterday. A flock of quail startled me. One quail stayed when the others flew. She hunkered down on rock top, thinking she was invisible. I walked on by and then realized a nice plump doe was standing a short distance away, probably also thinking she was invisible. We had a one-sided conversation before she pranced off in the opposite direction.

The turnoff to Upper Pittsburg Landing beckoned to me with its dip through a hollow and onto a plateau above the river. Birds continued to accompany me. Another deer must have been close by because suddenly I heard heavy thudding behind me. I caught sight of a doe going over the edge toward the river. In the other direction a buck loped toward the mountains. Had I interrupted an early morning tryst?

I knew it was two miles to the upper landing but the canyon narrowed and I wanted a good look at it. Blue cornflowers grew profusely beside the paved road, along with delicate yellow blossoms and sunflowers. The road curved down to the landing and the empty tent campground. Across the river a small boat swayed in gentle waves. A tent and all the equipment was set up on a sand bar. No activity at this early hour. A narrow gravel path took me to the petroglyphs hidden in the rocks.

On the way back, I found a path with a gate. I thought it was a cow path. There is nothing so intriguing as a cow path and a gate. It went up a hill and followed a deep tree-filled ravine. It looked to be a great place for deer to settle in. I was right. Several burst from their hiding places. Their ears gave them away as they bounded through the deep growth.

After reaching the road, I looked down toward the river. A doe and twin fawns watched my progress. Toward the mountains, other deer watched me from a distance. I was the subject of much morning gossip.

Nearly two hours had gone by in my exploring. I swished a tumbleweed ahead of me to rid the shortcut of a million grasshoppers and any slithering creatures with rattles. Rattlesnakes could no doubt feel my big-footed presence but then again, some creatures can get awfully hissed if they are awakened before their alarm goes off. It would be my luck to run into Snarly Snake.

When I returned, I inadvertently chased away a hummingbird menacing the red colors in the U. S. map below my motorhome window. Two airplanes circled and landed near the farmhouse across the river. They had phoned for permission to collect land samples. People came in and out with private boats or just stopped by. Jet boats from Lewiston turned around shortly beyond our landing. It was really quite busy.

The weather got hotter and hotter. No one was in the campground by that time so I ran the generator and air conditioner while I worked. The evenings were cool, fooling me into one more day. Deer fed nearby in the mornings, then they went home, turned on their generators and air conditioners and returned in the evening cool. When I drove out at 6 a.m., the whole herd came to say goodbye.

I celebrated Pittsburg Saddle with a Dannon Yogurt while I looked back over the canyon, feeling the breeze coming through Ponderosa pine, enjoying the wild flowers and the wildness.

Following the Salmon River, I stopped to wiggle my toes in one of its beautiful sandy bars. It was incredibly soft. Great numbers of butterflies flew around me. Another RVer and I stopped at a fruit stand. He was a very friendly older African-American man who appeared to be all by himself. When I came out he stopped to talk.

"Are you driving that big rig all by yourself?"

"Yes, where are you from?"

"Sacramento. I've just come from Montana." We chatted about our travels for a few minutes before continuing. We passed each other a couple of times.

There is no direct way to Hells Canyon, or connecting loop roads. It's one of those, "You can't get there from here" places. Eventually I turned north at SR #71 to Hells Canyon Scenic Byway. This 22-mile paved road took me up steep grades and along the Snake River to the Dam.

Above the dam is a sign where John Eckels and Arthur Ritchie are buried. They settled Big Bar in 1890, using it for farming and fruit growing. The fruits and vegetables were then toted by packhorses to the Seven Devils mining area. The produce was of exceptional quality and prized by the miners. The dam water now covers Big Bar. I boondocked about a mile behind the dam, a very hot night.

Riverside at the Visitor Center, I talked with the amiable girl who ran a portable picnic-table Hells Canyon Tours office, and a jet-boat driver. They normally have an overnight to Lewiston and they did, but it was completely booked for a company outing. As they checked in and got their tags, one fellow said his wife couldn't come. I gave serious thought to volunteering to be a wife for a couple of days. After watching the boats filling and leaving, I finally said, "Gee I'd love to do that but I know reservations have to be made months in advance."

"We had six cancellations this morning."

"Aaaght."

"Sign here." It never takes me long to get into trouble. I was signed up for an all-day combination raft and jet boat trip for the next day!

At the Visitor Center, I bought the book, "Home below Hell's Canyon" by Grace Jordan. The story was so fascinating that I couldn't put it down.

In the late afternoon, two RVs parked and let their two dogs outside. The lady sat in the doorway. One dog became alarmed. She looked up into the old apricot tree next to their RV and a small black bear peered back at her. I went over to greet them later and they asked if I had seen the bear running toward the Sprinter about 20 minutes earlier. It went on up the mountain until they lost track of it. Talk about a day late and a dollar short.

As always, I had my window open toward the water which was only about 12' away. I awakened and heard splashing sounds. The moon was bright so I opened the screen to see better. Right then a small deer tiptoed

**Hell's Canyon Rafting**

under my window. She seemed aware I was there but was very unconcerned. I hoped the bear wasn't hanging around.

In the morning I still heard the flip-flopping sound and I saw constant surface bubbling. Huge fish were swimming right next to the top, sometimes jumping but always bubbling. There were hundreds of them. Then I realized it was probably salmon running.

Meanwhile, back at the landing, which was actually across the dam on the Oregon side, Art and Brian, guides for the whitewater-rafting trip, outfitted me with a life jacket and a waterproof bag for personal items.

Six German visitors were escorted into one raft. Two couples, one from Illinois and one from South Dakota, one other person and I, went into the other rubber raft. It occurred to me I was trusting my life to a guide who had his oars in the water only half the time! I pondered that point even more when he stood up and dove overboard. He crawled back in and explained that he was hot. I was glad he stayed cool in the Class III and IV rapids. Over the 20 miles we collectively dropped a 100'.

I was given a Recreation Use Study Map that described every stream, rapids, landing place, and historical point. Stud Creek was named for somebody's stud horse that wandered off "someairs 'bout 1910" and fathered colts for several years up on Summit Ridge.

After we all survived Wild Sheep Rapids, our first Class IV, the Illinois lady said, "Can we do it again?" She was more thrilled and more relaxed as we passed over each succeeding rapids without flipping.

At the 1911 Hibbs homestead, the story goes that he was found by his daughter, murdered. In the cabin ashes an unidentified body was found. The 1934 murder mystery was never solved. Jessica Fletcher where are you when you're needed?

Both rafts pulled to the river's edge. We walked to a mountain overlook to see Granite Rapids, another Class IV, and what we could expect. Hmmm. It added to the thrill factor, gave us a stretch, and we made it through just fine.

Avoiding the poison ivy, we landed and hiked up the mountain to a major delicious lunch under a shade tree. They really put on a spread with three kinds of bread with turkey, beef, and cheese. We had salads, brownies, cookies, lemonade and raspberry something. Being on strict diets, three people (I won't mention who but two of them weren't me) spread peanutbutter on the chocolate brownies. Yumm. We had strange conversations with our German visitors but communicated with signs and smiles.

The guides conveniently arranged for Rocky Mountain Bighorn Sheep to parade on the ledges above us. I led the way back to the river, picking my way gingerly through the rocks. I stopped mid-step with my mouth open and my hand up to stop the rafters behind me. With no argument from this pilgrim, a snake with an impressive set of rattles crossed the trail.

The guide yelled, "Stand still." Did they think I would move? The snake didn't come out the other side so I knew he had taken shelter under the rock. We let him be and re-routed.

We hiked a steep trail to the McGaffee Cabin, a National Historic Site homesteaded in 1901. It was a tiny cabin with a loft, a front and back porch, and a falling root cellar out back. The cabin was completely built with four-foot length boards. The guide explained that all the building materials were hauled over the mountain by mule. He was packed with lengths that wouldn't get knocked off when he turned along the switchbacks.

Neither the river nor the stream running beside it could be seen from the house. That seemed a shame but with the hard work they did just to survive, they probably wouldn't have had time to look at scenery anyway. It was amazing that pioneers wanted to live in this harsh environment but they considered it good "cow country."

The guide gave us the history behind the Pictographs under the cliff rock. Back at the river some people went swimming, others waded. That water was refreshingly cold. Behind us was the Nez Perce National Forest and across into Oregon was the Wallowa-Whitman National Forest.

They say that Hells Canyon is the deepest gorge in North America, but then again I was told that at Lake Chelan too. I guess it just depends from where they measure it. This canyon depth is measured from He Devil Mountain at 9,393' to Granite Creek. Under the Wild and Scenic Rivers Act, what we rafted was the wildest part of it. Originating in Yellowstone National Park at 9,500', the Snake River winds through Idaho and north again to join the Columbia River near Pasco, Washington, 1,036' miles from its source.

We didn't hike to it but the Winniford Place is one of the oldest canyon ranches. Cattle were raised there in the 1880s. A dogtrot-style log cabin was eventually built and the Winniford family lived there from 1913-1923.

At Rush Creek Rapids, we could look over our left shoulders and up to Hat Point Lookout Tower, 6,982' above where we were, and the highest point on the Oregon rim of Hells Canyon. Little did I know that two days later I would be standing on top of Hat Point looking down on this very spot.

At the age of 81, Ace Duncan was hired to dig a tunnel through the ridge separating Myers Creek and Big Bar. It took him two years. The irrigation pipe that was put through it made it possible to raise 13 acres of alfalfa on Big Bar. This was in the 1930s. If they were talking about the same Big Bar, the fellows I mentioned who were buried above the dam had a fruit farm there in the 1890s.

In some lengthy calm water, our guide dove into the water again. When he returned, the fellow from Illinois gave him a hand and was pulled into the water himself. He laughed and managed to keep his cap and glasses intact. He was getting severely sunburned shoulders that had seldom seen the light of day. I expect he had some uncommon evening misery.

We reached the point where Brian said we would normally land but a message from another jet boat driver said our return jet boat would be late. We traveled another half hour and pulled in. The rafts were unplugged and rolled up. We waited for the jet boat. In the meantime, it was play time!

As with all kids with time on their hands, we played follow the leader. Brian, wearing his life jacket as he said we had to, climbed 25' (or more!) onto a boulder and jumped into the Snake River. A couple others reluctantly followed him but then declared it fun and did it again. The Illinois husband went up but after several peeks over the edge, he came back down the rock. That took more guts than jumping.

**Fearless Leader jumping into Snake River**

I asked the other guide, Art, "Are you going?"

"I'm old enough to know better."

"I'm trying to decide whether I am or not." Then I made the mistake of saying, "If you'll take my picture, I'll go."

"I will."

Strangely enough, Art went up the rock with me. I don't know if he thought I might faint, or couldn't climb the rock, or what.

"Are you going too?"

"I didn't wear my life jacket."

"Are you going to push me?"

"No, I wouldn't do that."

I looked down; 25' is 3' plus twice the Sprinter's height. My stomach churned. I knew if I looked one more time, I wouldn't do it. I took a deep breath and jumped. Wow! I'm can't explain the feeling I had launching myself off that rock. My life didn't have time to pass before my eyes before I hit the water. Down, down, down. Then I popped back up. We did this in a spot where the Snake swirled us back around to the landing. My biggest problem was uprighting myself on the slippery rocks. The South Dakota lady gave me a hand. Brian had taken my picture. Yess!!! One strike for senior citizens!!!

They were all concerned because my face was bleeding. Nothing hurt and I could see so I wasn't concerned. They patted the blood off my face. I suspect a jacket buckle hit me between the eyes. I still carry a small scar –

my badge of courage. I know very well that as a kid I jumped off diving boards higher than that but it was a thrill.

After that Art had to prove himself so he jumped off twice. What fun.

The jet boat ride back through the rapids was an eye opener. It gave us a good view of what we had rafted through. The jet driver really had to do some maneuvering to get through the bigger rapids.

There are three licensed commercial rafters and two private rafters who use the river each day between May and September. Before that, lots are drawn to be allowed on the river. It would be too heavily impacted without regulations.

This trip was so much fun but it helps when you also have guides that are enjoying what they are doing…and are a little crazy to boot. My only disappointment was that my tour didn't go as far as the Kirkwood Ranch, the setting for *Home Below Hells Canyon*. Maybe another time. I've read the book twice, one in the Hells Canyon setting and recently at North Ranch. I don't know why I feel so akin to Grace Jordan because I know I wouldn't be that brave. They took three youngsters, ages six, three, and seven months and started a sheep ranch during the 1930s. They were broke but determined. Cut off from the rest of the world for eight years, they became self-sufficient, home-schooled the children, and made a beautiful, if rugged life for themselves.

Whenever they left the ranch, they had to go by riverboat or horseback over the mountains to what we term civilization. The story includes neighbors, friends, workers, history, courage, and fun. Their lives changed drastically in later years when her husband, Len Jordan, became an Idaho governor and a U. S. senator.

Just to prove I don't go out of my way to get into trouble, I checked with the Visitor Center ranger about other places to view the HCNRA. He said Oregon's Hat Point was a beautiful place. I asked about the road. The ranger called someone and they said the first two miles were rough. That much was true.

After a good nights boondocking sleep, I drove into Oregon on SR #86 and PFR (Primary Forest Route) #39. It was a beautiful route but baby, I was in the middle of nowheresville. Not that that bothered me particularly,

I turned north again on Little Sheep Creek Highway to Imnaha. It was late afternoon and I really wasn't sure I was on the right road but it fit the description. I passed the Imnaha Store and headed into the mountains. I can only say I did it with a lot of faith and excitement. It couldn't be too bad; it had two names, right? It was called Hat Creek Road, which was reassuring, and NF #4240, which wasn't.

Once I was beyond the first two miles of two-track that was reminiscent of cow pasture, the road improved as predicted. The last 22 miles of this 24-mile one-lane gravel road with pull-outs, was excellent, if you don't mind seven miles of hairpin switchback curves.

The Sprinter followed the mountain crest through the flowered meadows to Hat Point Fire Lookout. Boondocking and hiking the ridges afforded me magnificent Snake River views winding through Rush Creek Rapids where I had been rafting two days before. A spectacular sunset ended the day.

I awakened to sunrise over Hells Canyon and the Seven Devils Mountains, Where did I sleep, in "Granny View," where else? My truck-camper neighbors were still asleep. I had full sewers, a nearly empty gas tank, and a horrendous headache, probably caused from sunburned eyes. I had forgotten to wear sunglasses on the river, a no no.

Did I forget to mention the switchbacks were on 16% grades? Signs warned, "Avoid brake burnout. Stop here and cool your brakes." I did that, plus several stops to enjoy the mountain beauty, soak in the fragrant air and watch the deer. Amazingly enough, for that out-of-the-way place, two gas trucks twisted their way around me.

I stopped for breakfast to let my brakes cool and a really long equipment truck went by. Other than trucks, rocks, deer, and cattle in the road, it was a cinch. I followed other back roads to visit the Bar-M Dude Ranch where I used to work. I spent a little time reminiscing with the Baker family before taking off for the Northwest.

Turning off Interstate I-82 in Washington, I heard a terrible racket. Had something come loose? A second wrenching sound and I saw a dual wheel rolling down the ramp ahead of me, impatient to be on its way.

People are kind. I was already on the cell phone to my insurance company when Marla Pearson stopped. She noticed me peering into the wheel well with a puzzled expression. Actually, it was pure awe that the second wheel hadn't skipped town with the first one. We went tire hunting and found it innocently napping on the other side of a farmer's fence, after it had climbed a steep embankment and leaped over that fence. We drove to the farmer's house. Nobody was home (they say that about me sometimes, too). I wheeled the tire back through the field. Marla helped me put it in the car trunk and drove me back to the Sprinter. She left me with her phone number in case the tow truck didn't show.

Several, "oops" comments did nothing for my confidence as the Sprinter was towed backwards up the down ramp and across two lanes of traffic. Twenty-four hours, two new wheels, $205 and a new friend later, I was on my way.

For what was I grateful you ask? That I wasn't on the narrow gravel 16%-grade road from Hat Point in a cell-phone-dead area. See, you have to look at the bright side!

Does it sound like fun to go "Moonin?'" Let's go.

# Craters of the Moon

In my first life, I often wandered around our moonlit Michigan yard. I didn't howl or do anything outrageous; I just enjoyed the beauty. I wondered what astronauts thought about full moonlight nights, knowing they had actually walked on its surface. I experienced the closest I will ever get to moon walking when I visited Craters of the Moon National Monument. It was late and I wanted a taste of the day ahead. A trail loop was just beyond the 52-site first-come, first-serve, no hook-up campground.

After magma, or molten rock, overflows on to the earth's surface and solidifies, it is called lava rock. North Crater Flow Trail had all three types of basaltic lava found in the park. I hadn't seen any major mountains close by and wondered where the lava had come from. My vision brought to mind a massive eruption like Washington's Mt. St. Helens.

Not to worry, the "Around the Loop" guidebook answered my question. The lava comes from cinder cones. Cinder cones formed by fissures opening in the earth's surface, are anywhere from several yards to several miles long. As frothy, gas-charged rock erupts, it cools and falls back around the vent as cinders. It continues to build until voila, a cinder cone. The inside of the cone may continue to push lava out, eventually breaking through the cinder cone wall, causing the lava flow such as I was walking through. Having hiked a bit in Hawaii Volcanoes National Park, the landscape wasn't a total surprise. In fact, some of the descriptive words are Hawaiian.

While the surface lava rapidly cooled, the hot lava beneath continued to move, wrinkling and folding into pahoehoe (pa-hoy-hoy) that resembles giant worms laid side by side, pointing the flow's direction. Aa (ah-ah) is caused by a slow-moving flow that cools and hardens and tumbles, leaving it a jumbled mass of jagged spiny rock and a very good reason to stay on designated trails. It has been known to do the Chattanooga chew boots.

The monoliths were large rock blocks broken from crater walls and rafted to their eternal resting places on thick aa flows. Actually, "eternal" may not be apt. Although the North Crater Lava Flow is the youngest in the park, formed about 2,200 years ago, sporadic activity has kept the place erupting nigh on to 15,000 years. Who's to say that the rafted blocks weren't going to be re-arranged that very night! I think about these things.

I stepped lively to see the "block lava" (Hmmm, I always thought that was a Hungarian pastry). The thick block flows creep slowly, creating large, irregular, dense, lava rocks with smoother surfaces. On my return to the Sprinter, I looked up at North Crater Cinder Cone, progenitor of the flows I had just walked through. It was on my early-morning visiting list.

I looked forward not only to treading in astronaut footsteps, those who orientated in this desolate environment to get a feel for walking on the moon, but others who had gone before them. The Northern Shoshone once hunted bear, bison, elk, cougar and Bighorn sheep, animals rarely found here today. They made arrowheads and other hunting tools from the harder volcanic materials.

While the Civil War raged in the east, Tim Goodale led a wagon train eventually numbering nearly 350 wagons, along the lava fields' northern edge to avoid Indian hostilities on the Oregon Trail. This route became known as Goodale's Cutoff.

The area was explored in the 1800s by the military, and extensively by geologists in the 1900s. It was the exploration and publicity brought by writer, Robert Limbert, via National Geographic Magazine, that brought this unique conglomeration of lava flows, caves, and craters to national attention.

I drove the paved scenic seven-mile Loop Drive to walk the half mile around Devil's Orchard Nature Trail, neat in the late afternoon sun. This trail began where volcanic eruption had destroyed all living organisms. It proceeded through "pioneer plants" growing within the bare minimum of Mother Nature's nurturing, into a "secondary" plant community that creates, stabilizes, and nourishes soils. In the "climax community" was a prime example of the "survival of the fittest."

Again the threat. With at least eight known times that this area has literally burst through the earth's crust, geologists say forces are "building to a point where an eruption is imminent..." Unfortunately, they aren't sure whether imminent means tonight or a thousand years from now. I wasn't sure whether to worry or not. Should I take chances expiring from my own cooking or just wait for the inevitable?

The scattered occupied campsites gave me the illusion of being alone. I knew for sure I wasn't on the moon because its fullness lit up the eerie formations outside my bedroom window.

The next morning I watched a short movie at the Visitor Center, and other excellent presentations explaining the volcanic process and the Snake River Plain geology.

A short but steep path to Inferno Cone summit, 6,181', affords a view of the Great Rift, the "plumbing" system where the magma rises to the earth's surface. On a clear day, if you could see over the entire 635 square miles, you would see 60+ lava flows and 25 volcanic cones.

I parked the Sprinter at the Spatter Cones and Big Craters lot and prepared for hiking with water and a couple of Power Bars. The hike is listed as 1½ miles but it isn't a loop so you either have to retrace the path or take the road back. They suggested having someone pick you up but since I was alone, that suggestion didn't prove helpful.

The molten lava that formed the spatter cones was heavier and stickier and thrown out of the center in globs. When it fell back to earth, it stuck to other sticky lava and formed the steep-sided spatter cone walls. I looked directly into these miniature volcanoes.

It was a steep walk to the top of Big Craters with a Spatter Cone Chain view. I continued the up and down path between the west rim of North Crater (6,244') and the east rim of Silent Cone (6,357'). It was perfect hiking until the hot sun snuck up behind me, making me appreciate the icy cold shadows. I had the trail to myself and the silence fascinated me. The only sound was my hiking boots crunching on the trail. Everything looked barren and dead until little spring-loaded ground squirrels or chipmunks popped up between rocks.

Switchbacks took me to the crater bottom with no indication where the path led or so I thought. Then I remembered the ranger mentioning rock cairn trail markers. I really had to look for them. I picked my way across and up to the rim top on the other side, and down to the road. It was a two-mile return to the Sprinter. A mule deer sprinted across Paisley Cone and I passed on another chance to climb Inferno Cone.

But on to the most interesting of all, the Cave Area. Again, the fast-moving top lava flow cooled and hardened, forming tubes channeling the molten rock many miles from its source, leaving sinks, tubes, and caves in its wake.

I descended the stairway into Indian Tunnel. My flashlight wasn't needed in this large cave. Several collapsed ceilings allowed sunlight in. This 800' long tube is 30' high and 50' wide. It took me through "nondescript breakdowns," over rocks, and under the ceiling collapses. Birds were making use of the nooks and crannies for nesting. I was momentarily confused but eventually found the path again. At the far end I pulled myself up over a ledge and out a four-foot-in-diameter hole on to the lava flow.

Rock cairns directed me to the main path. It was rough, but interesting to see the big collapsed cave holes where I had been. I definitely had to watch where I was walking.

A Wisconsin couple had gone part way through and turned around. But then again he had his arm in a sling, two black eyes, and walked with a limp. Maybe in that condition I wouldn't have tried to pull myself up through that hole either. I didn't ask. They wanted to go through the other tunnels but didn't have a flashlight. We went together.

At 300' long Beauty Cave, we met another couple whose flashlight was going fast. We scrambled down the first rock slope and peered apprehensively into the blackest black I had ever seen. The map showed this cave to have tight passages necessitating belly crawls. Then I read the small print. It said three sources of light per person, kneepads, and hard hat *required*, and suggested three people per party. The only requirement we had were the number of people. I wondered why that wasn't explained at the Visitor Center. Imagine! They thought we could read! My flashlight wasn't doing much for five people. Each person really needed a light for his or her individual space. Reluctantly (I think), we made our way out.

I left early the next morning with the sun coming up one side and a ghostly moon hanging on the other. For miles after I left the park, lava flow fingers reached into farmland and cattle grazing country.

For my first lunar landing, it was a great experience.

Speaking of great, let's make a little splash in a Great Basin.

# Great Basin National Park

I love autumn; it's exciting. I also love connecting with RVing friends. My kayaking buddy, Art, was in Sacramento, California. I was headed south through Missoula, Montana, after spending the summer in the Northwest.

Neither of us had ever been to Big Basin National Park. We decided via cell phones that touring one of our newest national parks was the thing to do. Why not do it together? I continued on down the Bitterroot Mountains, crossing Lewis and Clark's trail, through Idaho and into Nevada along US #93, circuitously on my way to Arizona. Our ETA was about a week later in Ely, Nevada. No point in rushing.

At a Well's campground, I was doing a Sprinter "Walk-a-bout." A travel trailer pulled into the next site. "Charlie!" I was puzzled. "Remember San Carlos?" It was Sunny and Jim Reed from Washington. We had exchanged Christmas cards since 1988 when we all lived in Teta Kawi Campground, San Carlos, Mexico. I hadn't seen them since and if she hadn't recognized me, we would have passed like ships in the night. It's a small, small world.

A few miles north of Ely, I stopped at a Pony Express Exhibit. Its history causes me to wonder as I wander.

In February 2001, my Priority mail forwarding took nine days traveling from Livingston, Texas, to Congress, Arizona, approximately 1,300 miles. This packet was no doubt transported from Livingston to Houston and from Phoenix to Congress via a 60-70 mph air-conditioned truck. Presumably the package was flown by jet directly between Houston and Phoenix.

In 1860 and 1861, almost a 150 years ago, 1,900 Pony Express miles from St. Joseph, Missouri, to Sacramento, California, were ridden horseback through extreme weather conditions, road-agent attacks, and the Paiute Indian War. The riders also made the trip in nine days. Have we come such a long way, Baby?

I should admit that although I have RVed western Nevada, I really never thought of it as a mountainous state. The fact that "Nevada" is Spanish for "snow-capped" should have been my first clue. Numerous Nevada peaks are over 11,000' with Boundary Peak the highest at 13,140'. Will I never stop assuming.

Art left California and crossed Nevada on America's loneliest highway, US #50. I thought it would be rather an innocuous journey. I was wrong. He crossed at least nine mountain summits getting to Ely!

The Holiday Inn in Ely allows RVers two nights free hook-up parking. Art arrived in time to claim the last available site. When you buy a $2 nickel roll, you receive a $1 nickel roll free, a ploy to rid your pockets of much more. It didn't work.

We hadn't seen each other for a while so in the process of driving to Great Basin National Park and talking non-stop, we turned on the wrong road. No problema except we were nearly out of gas. I'm used to traveling that way (Lost and out of gas) so we gulped and continued, hoping to return to Ely before the gas fumes gave out.

Six miles west of Baker, Nevada, we made a short stop at the Great Basin National Park Visitor Center, Nevada's only national park, and signed on for the Lehman Caves tour. Winding our way along paved Wheeler Peak Scenic Drive toward Wheeler Peak, it seemed impossible that millions of years ago, this was all under water.

According to Geologists, the Great Basin was once the continent edge where landmasses "slammed and scrammed," the other part becoming what is now Siberia. Talk about a rift!

Once, the Great Basin was a tropical Paradise with palm and magnolia trees and attendant dinosaurs. Twenty million years after the dinosaurs became extinct, give or take a million or two, the land shifted again. The mountains rose and the valleys dropped, leaving Nevada with more than 200 parallel north-to-south mountain ranges and valley basins. And I thought Nevada was flat, the preconceived notions of a Midwesterner.

We had the drive to ourselves. Art's little four-cylinder Suzuki went up the 8% grades like a charm. It was sunny but October winds blew cold, a harbinger of winter.

At Mather Overlook, we viewed 13, 063' Wheeler Peak and the only remaining Great Basin glacier, a leftover from the most recent Ice Age. Glacier meltwater that sculpted these mountains formed western Lake Lahontan and eastern Lake Bonneville. Utah's Great Salt Lake is what remains of Lake Bonneville.

Above the sage and brittle brush, beyond the Douglas fir and Englemann spruce and 10,000' elevation, is the bristlecone pine, one of Nevada's state trees. One gnarled park tree is considered the earth's oldest living tree at 4,950 years of age.

Bristlecone pines are considered windows to the past and peeks into the future. Scientists have determined that the average bristlecone pine growth rate has increased, possibly due to increasing carbon dioxide. Is this another sign of global warming? I would hear more about global warming on Hudson Bay shores. You'll read about that later.

The second official state tree is the single leaf pinyon pine, also in the park, prized by mammals and birds as well as settlers for its pine nut food source and by miners who used the nuts for fuel.

Prehistoric habitation goes back to 12,000 BC. From about 1,300 on, the Shoshone and Paiute Indians farmed the valleys and hunted the mountains. In 1826, a name we recognize, Jedediah Smith, was the first Caucasian in the Great Basin. By 1869, the U. S. Army Corps of Engineers sent an expedition led by Lt. George Wheeler to survey the Snake Range. Guess for whom the peak is named?

The road ended at Wheeler Peak Campground, which was already closed. On our 12-mile trip, we had gained 3,400' elevation. Trails led to alpine lakes, through the bristlecone pine forest, and Wheeler Peak, another five miles. Though the view would have been spectacular, the air was frigid at 9,886', definitely not a hiking day for two silver-haired wimps. We didn't hang around long; the elevation was giving Art a headache.

On the way down we checked out the campgrounds and a number of mule deer watched us as we watched them.

Lehman Caves, reached through the Visitor Center, was declared a national monument in 1922 and in 1986 was further protected as part of Great Basin National Park. The tours are limited to 25 people but we lucked out given the season. We had the 90-minute tour and the guide all to ourselves.

The 1885 cave discovery and later exploration was credited to former Ohioan Absalom Lehman, a miner and rancher. During archaeological digs in 1938 and 1964, Native American skeletons were found. We were asked to be quiet and respectful near the natural entrance and Indian burial site.

Our first room was the Gothic Palace. It was magnificent. I have been in many caves, but I don't remember any as pretty as this one. This room alone would have been worth the tour. Stalagmites ("mity") growing from the ground up, correspond to stalactites ("tite" to the cave roof), dripping from a water source, possibly growing together into a column. At a growth rate of approximately one inch every 100 years, it takes a while. The little pools that should have had water were mostly dry because they didn't have much snow the year before.

In the Grand Palace, we found "The Parachute", a beautiful drapery. The Lehman Caves is considered to be "well-decorated" with cave formations, called "speleothems." Speleothems are stalactites, helictites, flowstone, draperies, and shields.

As with most living caves, it has its creatures, none of which we saw, of course. Some venture outside occasionally in order to survive; some could survive outside but spend their whole lives in the cave. Others never see daylight and depend entirely on food found underground. These may be blind or colorless but with acute hearing, smell, and touch. Lehman Caves is especially known for the pseudoscorpion, a critter about an inch long.

We saw fantastically long soda straws and delicate gypsum flowers. The guide backlit a drapery with his flashlight. It looked like a giant slice of bacon. Among the argonites, flowstone, and fascinating cave popcorn, it is best known for its shields. This limestone and marble cave also had a lot of its fascinating features combined with each other, as stalagmites rising from flowstone or shields with draperies.

The guide asked if it was all right to turn out the lights so we could experience complete darkness. He lit a candle inside a tin can with both ends out, and said that was what they would have used in early years for tours. We could see very little. He turned all the lights off. It was eerie. Art reached for my hand. I'm not sure whether he was comforting himself or me. He surprised me by admitting he had never been in a cave before. He loved it. He was impressed but then so was I.

As a measure of how much he enjoyed the cave, Art gave an inordinate amount of "Gollees," "Wows" and "Good Griefs." I had to agree, but our venture into the depths was all too soon over. How exciting it must have been to see all this for the first time.

Our big adventure ended with prime rib and steak dinners in an Ely casino.Do you remember what I said about having "Every day kinds of days…fitting between extraordinary moments of pure pleasure?" Follow me.

# Daily Life Vignettes

Often I have been asked, "How many miles do you drive a day?" That's hard to answer because it depends on where I am and if I am headed toward a specific destination. I move anywhere from 100 to 350 miles a day and sometimes I don't move for three or four or ten days. With gas prices soaring, I will probably stay even longer in each place.

People are curious about what full-time RVers do. My favorite activity is a campfire just about anywhere, but hey, you want to know what everyday life is like, I'll give you a few examples.

## Sechler's Fine Pickles

Do you want to get pickled? No, would you settle for eating something pickled? It never would have occurred to me to tour a pickle factory but my friend, Linda Bassett, who lives in Auburn, Indiana, was going with a group. I tagged along.

The Sechler family has been processing pickles for three generations. Working "dill"igently, and undaunted by depression or fire, the business has grown mightily since 1921. From a basement and barn business, they now have a capacity for 90,000 bushels of brined pickles, a new building just for sweetening pickles, and in excess of 30,000 square feet under roof for production and warehousing. That's a lot of pickles and vinegar.

Their showroom was almost my undoing. I love pickles but I couldn't stop with buying one jar for myself. Our family doesn't exchange gifts, but I had to have an excuse to buy more, so I bought a variety of pickle thank-you gifts for various and sundry friends.

They have Candied Sweet Orange Strip Pickles and Candied Raisin Crispies (Raisin?), Imported Pepperocini, and just about anything else you can name in a pickle. It was an unusual and interesting stop.

## Rest Stop

About the time I groaned and moaned about not finding a rest stop, Vermont provided a nice quarter-mile, unannounced gravel pull out beside Lake Rescue. That's it, I was "Rescue'd," just in time to stifle my 10th yawn.

Not one to look a gift horse in the mouth, I settled in for a short spring's nap. I took out my table a long time ago and made the booth into a permanent couch with cushions all around and big stuffed pillows I bought heaven knows where. I snuggled under a blanket I bought on a beach in Mexico, and a faux sheepskin blanket I bought in another heaven-knows-where place. After a quick look at the scenery with May leaves unfurling, I was out like a light, coming awake once, just enough to realize it was raining.

What combinations - sleepiness, warm blankets, comfortable nest, and rain on the roof. It doesn't get much better than that. Kind of takes me back to when I was a kid sleeping on a Michigan summertime porch. We lived in a log cabin that must have been crowded with four boys and a girl plus Mama and Daddy. Summer days were hot and humid in those attic bedrooms. I don't rightly remember where we all slept when my oldest brothers were home. After I could remember, summertime found my youngest brother and I sleeping at opposite ends of the screened-in porch. It was nice when it rained. A gentle rain brought a fine mist through the screen justifying a deeper blanket snuggle.

I wish all kids could have that feeling of safety and warmth. I didn't know enough to appreciate it then. Also, one of my vivid memories is that daddy-long-legs used to crawl across my arms or face and wake me up.

But back to the present. I got up and turned on the heat. I don't like being cold. I never nap long. I don't know why, maybe this time it was that good Vermont Cheddar cheese I bought down at Weston's Country Stores that wouldn't leave me alone.

A bottle of *I can't-believe-it's-not butter* was in the frig. Have you ever tried squirting that on a Wheat Thin? Pretty soon there was *I can't believe it's not butter* all over everything, only I can, cause it was. I raised the stove lid to heat water for instant coffee but instead, a half-filled bottle of Yoo Hoo reared its chocolate head and I changed my mind. That goes great with Vermont Cheddar cheese, wheat thins, and *I can't believe it's not butter*.

The rain stopped except for what dropped from the trees. It was time to be on my way. From a wayside in Vermont, it's a wonderful life.

# New Orleans

The only time the world doesn't seem so small world is when I am lost - most of the time. Of course those are the times I meet nice people. I usually avoid big cities but sometimes in order to visit a friend or take part in a specific activity, I succumb to city driving. This was one of those times.

I wandered New Orleans with an Internet map sent to me by a friend who seldom drives. Residents were very nice, giving me friendly waves as I did St. Charles Avenue in the motorhome with the Little Lynx in tow. They waved, as well, the second and third time I went around. Obviously, they thought I was an early Mardi Gras parade. Too much traffic prevented me from stopping to ask directions. During this extended time in lostdom, my brakes were slowly disappearing, later diagnosed as a bad seal. New Orleans doesn't seem so big when you tie up to the Riverwalk on a barge campground and see the city from a streetcar or a horse and buggy as I had a few years earlier.

The Sprinter has always behaved with perfect decorum in our travels but this time he got caught up in some mirror arm wrestling with a bus and the Sprinter lost. His mirror went down, rendering it impossible for me to pull to the right lane because I couldn't see the traffic. Life is never simple. In sheer desperation, I finally edged my way to the only parking space in New Orleans that was long enough for our 50' entourage. A storeowner, seeing that glazed look in my eyes, said, "The Lord led you to the right place, Honey. We'll see that you get where you want to go."

Her partner said he was going within two blocks of my destination and I followed him. He stopped once and cautioned, "It's rush-hour traffic so you'll have to stay close as we go over the bridge." By then I had righted the mirror, but I didn't tell him that getting too close would be dangerous because the brakes were getting worse by the minute. Traffic sort of funnels onto the Huey P. Long Bridge but we made it.

This wonderful man stopped one more time explicitly directing me the last two blocks to my friend's house. I signed a *RVing Alaska* book and gave it to him, "You will no doubt have a good laugh at my having the audacity to instruct people how to travel through Canada and Alaska when I can't find my way through one large city."

Had I not gotten lost, I would not have met those two great people who went out of their way to help a stranger.

# Final Resting

If a special sign hadn't been erected on U. S. #89, you'd probably never realize Montana's Niehart-Pinehill Cemetery existed. It could be a cemetery anywhere, there are lots of them – there's an old joke about people dying to go there.

The dates spanned a century and a half. It sprawled along the roadside for a long way, tangled in the tall grass and wildflowers. A nearby stream lent the background music. I followed the path, human or animal I wasn't sure, and it didn't matter. It seemed appropriate that it wound through gravesites and the wildness of the woods before it crawled on up the mountain.

The large trees probably were seedlings carried through the air and dropped when the first inhabitants were returned dust to dust. It was unkempt by modern cemetery standards; but then again, who would mind their graves being decorated with purple fireweed and asters or wild pink roses. A few graves were well tended. Others that weren't, perhaps were among those whose family line had ended.

Several generations were wrapped in wrought iron fences; others inhabited plots behind white picket fences. Some headstones were elegant; others were simply carved wood, whose names were more often than not, wiped clean by wind and weather and time. Only those who have experienced it can truly know the pain and anguish of losing a child of any age. A boy and a girl, five and six years old, died the same day in 1902. An iron-posted, chain-draped black fence from which elegant black bells dangled, surrounded the

1910 grave of a 10-year-old boy. The gate was askew and rusted shut.

I listened to the stream, sipping hot coffee with my home on wheels beside me. Many stories resided in that hidden cemetery, but I left them there in the swaying white and yellow daisies and fragrant pine trees. I had places to go and things to do before I slept the eternal sleep.

# Tragedy

Five miles west of Glenwood Springs, Colorado, on Interstate-70, at the Canyon Creek Exit, a trail leads to a ridge-top observation point. In the distance white crosses stand out against the fire-ravaged slopes, one where each brave firefighter fell. The sign at the path bottom says, "*Leave only your footprints and your prayers.*" It was a talcum-powder switchback trail leading up through a thick forest. Every footstep created a brown cloud around my feet. The heat was stifling, the kind that wears you out almost before you begin. It was very likely a day like this in 1994 when there was no trail.

Fourteen men and woman fought their way through the thick piñon-juniper forest, almost straight up the side of that steep mountain, carrying exhaustively heavy backpacks and tools. I returned several hours later, fatigued from my efforts. They didn't return under their own power.

If I had not been moved to tears there, I would have been at the Two Rivers Park in Glenwood Springs. A monument of war is there, a different kind of war, a war against the elements. In July of 1994, a fire raged on Storm King Mountain. This monument has 14 circled evergreens and 14 matching boulders. A firefighter, biography, and picture is imprinted on each boulder.

I had followed forest fire progress in the newspapers as most people did. The mountain trek and seeing the photographs of these beautiful, brave young people and reading their biographies, brought it all up close and personal.

While that fire raged, I was visiting my kids. We experienced our own fire. The valley resounded with the drone of planes and helicopters. C130 cargo planes dropped red fire retardant from swollen bellies. Other planes were fire spotters. Helicopters dumped Wenatchee River water on the forest fires on three sides of us. The smoke was dense. We hadn't seen blue sky for days.

The Sprinter was parked at my daughter's house in preparation for a trip east together. On the last Friday in July, the tree-covered mountains, a backdrop to the Bavarian Village of Leavenworth, Washington, had once more failed to appear in what should have been the morning sunshine. Radio Station KPQ, Wenatchee, announced a possible Level I Evacuation.

Janet was calm and unemotional; then, I realized she was working at it. My hug brought tears, "I'm scared, Mom." Husband Bill was in Seattle. It would be her decision to leave or stay. Still she washed dishes, did laundry, picked up the living room and generally ignored the possible emergency. I repacked eight boxes of my photographs from their garage into my car. Janet made beds, watered plants and vacuumed.

In late morning, reality came knocking on every neighborhood door. A fireman in a bright yellow fire-retardant shirt, officially announced a level I evacuation. He asked occupants to prepare to leave and leave if possible. The request was a catalyst to more meaningful activity and a few more tears. I reminded her that Bill was safe, and we were leaving so we would be safe.

Janet packed a lock box of important records, files of computer discs, family albums, and photographs. As her world remained calm, she found new things not so important but still high on the list. Being its secretary, she packed Kiwanis Club information. Bill's treasured Viet Nam flight jacket was next and photographs from the walls. I was flattered to find one of my paintings among them.

She then did something that everyone should do in advance of an emergency. She took pictures of every room, the garage and outside equipment. It is impossible to remember everything destroyed in a fire, flood, or wind.

Bewildered five-year-old Rebecca collected dolls, toys, and her Barbie motorhome. She carried small items to the car and motorhome and held doors for us. It was Rebecca's duty to keep Sarah, the silver-haired, blue-eyed (just like Grandma Sharlene) Siamese cat, calm on her first motorhome ride. Our caravan proceeded to the high school and registered with the Red Cross as requested. The Salvation Army was set up with a food and comfort station (my favorite organization). Friends of Janet and Bill's invited us to park at their ranch and out of fire danger. All the way to Cathy's house, Rebecca repeated her mother's reassurances to Sarah, word for word. It is always a surprise to realize they have heard and remembered every word.

Bill arrived from Seattle. Another fire had started. Janet and Bill returned to their home and watched the fire progress down one ridge, cross the Icicle River, and on up the other side, a quarter mile from their house.

Meanwhile Rebecca bathed in Grandma's tiny RV bathtub and had her first lesson in conserving water (She'll make a great boondocker). When she was emulsified and wrapped safely in Grandma's arms, we discussed the fire and the safety of all Rebecca's loved ones. Sarah curled up at our feet and listened too, at least she "pawsed" to reflect. Sorry.

Since we could do nothing about the fire, we resumed our trip plans. As we traveled east, Janet called about fire conditions. The Rat Creek fire had gone straight for Blewett Pass, jumped the road and headed for Wenatchee, putting Cathy's ranch where we had stored the cars, on an Evacuation Level II which meant get out. The order was canceled before they had time to act.

Janet's reply to relatives who asked about her house, "I call my computer answering machine every day. If it answers, the house is still standing." Her sister suggested maybe it was only her desk and computer standing on a bare street. Sisters have a way with unsettling thoughts.

On our return a month later, lovely Leavenworth was untouched. The mountain above the house alternated green and blackened trees. The fires were considered "contained," but droning helicopters still dropped river water on hot spots, flinging giant ash clouds into the air.

It brought to our attention once more what is really important when reality comes knocking.

# Communication

A letter to Michigan friends Judy and Dick Richter, is very revealing of my daily life.

It is 6:35 a.m., I think. I'm not sure on which side of the time zone I am. I awakened about 4:30. My window was open. I listened to the Big Hole River babbling over the rocks. It's low this time of year. A full moon lit up the cottonwood trees along its edges as well as the mountain across the valley. At a 6,000'+ elevation, it was cold but I snuggled deep in my flannel sheets and comforters and thought about things in general and people in particular.

Of course the bathroom is always the first stop (or turning on the heat if I can wait!), then I check my traplines. Following my traplines isn't quite the job it was for Jeremiah Johnson. Although I can hear the wind has picked up, I don't think any snow accumulated, and my traplines are all inside. Yup, I had one. Out the door and into the dark went the mouse in the live trap until I could empty it later. Once again, a creature from mousedom fell for the fragrance of peanut butter. I know that if I park in the boonies, they will come. The word is out, Minshall carries a great brand of peanut butter.

Lewis and Clark passed through here in August 194 years ago (1805) on their way to the Columbia River. Chief Joseph and entourage had a big brouhaha with the U. S. Cavalry here in August 72 years later (1877). I'm glad it's not August. You never know what will happen!

I walked around Big Hole National Battlefield west of Wisdom yesterday (A lot of people mention that my wisdom has gone west). I'm east of Wisdom now and probably will head south again soon. I started down #93 from Missoula and sort of got sidetracked.

So you see, it isn't lonely here. The ghosts of Lewis and Clark and Chief Joseph are here, and hunters. It is hunting season and all the National Forest campsites are filled with hunters.

I left Janet's Wednesday morning. They are busy with the fall season and Janet's newspaper was putting out special bulletins for Leavenworth's fall festivities. I just returned from a month-long flying trip to Michigan for my class reunion and to Virginia to help Tom and Tracey and Will move into their new house.

Will was getting back to normal (and everybody else) by the time I left. He body-slammed into me so I would pick him up and "kiss him to pieces." He is both angel and devil. He is just putting words into short sentences. He had "Dahma" (Grandma) down pretty well.

I teased Rebecca about the condition of her room when I returned, cautioning her that the pack rats might come to claim her as their long lost daughter. She took that warning a little more seriously when one of their cats brought in a live rat. Janet got up in the night and on hearing a noise at her feet, she turned on the bathroom light and found the bloody (literally) creature running out of the room. They found him two nights later when Janet threw a shoe into her closet! She screamed. Bill caught him and threw him out in the alley. Life goes on.

# Washing

This is a subject that can cover a multitude of areas, washing dishes, washing the RV, washing clothes, or washing yourself. As a full-time RVer, I have learned to combine the natural with jobs that need to be done. Let's take this morning for instance. I am parked in a scenic stop overlooking Lake Superior, a stone's throw from Grand Portage, Minnesota, having just crossed the border from Thunder Bay, Ontario. Since this involved a journey across Labrador, Quebec, and Ontario, and traveling gravel roads, the Sprinter and I were a mess.

But first, food. I bought fresh strawberries somewhere in Quebec, fresh bread somewhere in Ontario, and now I'm preparing the fruits of someone else's labor. Fresh strawberries over fresh bread with Cool Whip and a cold glass of milk ain't all bad. It is raining, but back to the subject of washing.

It is really quite amazing how washboard roads and poorly patched pavement can rearrange your filing system, as in dumping the file box all over the floor. I wondered why some files were sticky. I place Damp Rid in the cupboards to keep photographs, negatives, and slides protected from the dampness. The containers have to be emptied every so often when the "stuff" has turned to liquid. I hadn't done it in a while. Those same washboard roads and poorly patched pavement pieces jounced the sticky liquid over the files that were on the floor.

After vigorously dusting everything including the computer (which thankfully, still worked), I took advantage of the rain. I was already a mess from cleaning the inside, so I got my long brush and washed the Sprinter. What better time? A rushing stream of rainwater ran alongside to clean my brush in; I was getting help from the Almighty as far as rinsing; and the Sprinter looked infinitely better though not perfect from the quick washing.

I stripped from soaking wet clothes. In my cleaning frenzy, I had put all the towels in the dirty clothes. All the clean towels were at the motorhome's opposite and open end. That would surely be the time someone would drive in to view the panoramic scene and I didn't want to be a part of it so I grabbed my winter coat and got the towels.

If you're like I am, the bathtub is a second garage and everything has to be thrown out so you can take a shower or bath. The sack of pop cans was lifted off the showerhead. You do recycle don't you? The tub is where all the good bugs go to expire. After cleaning the bugs out of the tub, ah, at last, a place for me. While I was washing the rig, my hair got so wet I didn't need much water when I washed it. I love it when a plan comes together.

# Kayaking

I visited my kayaking buddy, Art, who was working at Yellowstone National Park. He had just purchased a sail for his kayak. It didn't take us long to launch his 17' Klepper folding kayak in Yellowstone Lake for a shakedown cruise. If you question the wisdom of a sail on a kayak, the Klepper is an

**Art and the pre-flight folding Klepper**

ocean-going kayak with air sponsons along each side, making it extremely stable. Stability is, of course, directly related to the sailors gripping the paddles.

Yellowstone Lake, at 7,733' elevation, and with 110 shoreline miles, is the largest lake at high elevation in North America. At 22 miles long, 14 miles wide, and positioned along the face of the Absaroka Mountains, thunderheads form quickly. Winds arise quickly, too, and create thrilling whitecaps. An average of 3,100 gallons of warm thermal water bubbles into Yellowstone Lake every day, but July was still bringing snow melt down from the mountaintops and trickling its icy fingers into the warm bubbles. The water temperature averaged 45°.

We took off from Bridge Bay Harbor into a perfectly calm day. As we paddled the kayak, Art was philosophical, "The wind is metering itself to the talents of the sailors in charge." I should have taken that as a warning! I had become knowledgeable in RV jargon. Now I had to learn port, bow, tack, wake, and duck. He also mentioned something about a "clew," which I knew I didn't have any of. I soon learned it is a metal loop in the sail corner through which ropes move the sail up and down.

Then life got interesting. The thunderheads formed; the winds blew. We moved forward into the wind, tacking. Did I mention the lake's wide-open spaces? Suddenly the bow was parting the waters, and we were full sail into five-foot waves. Ahoy Mate! The wake of a passing speedboat sent waves of that 45° water into my lap. Yeow! Exciting, yesss! Exhilarating, yesss! Hypothermic, yesss!

When the kayak hit the beach, we were probably going only 680 knots. We would have made history as the first air-borne sailing kayak...if it hadn't been for the density of those trees.

And you thought the daily life of a full-time RVer was dull!

O.K., enough of this easy stuff, let's get to the wilderness.

# Forest Service Road

**Old Faithful, Yellowstone National Park**

After caravanning back-country Montana with Friend Steve, visiting Art in Yellowstone National Park, and driving through Grand Teton National Park amid a myriad of August tourists, I needed to get off by myself. I stopped in Alpine, Wyoming, to buy groceries and get gasoline. I asked the lady in charge about the Bridger-Teton National Forest Road from Alpine to La Barge.

"Are you driving that big thing?"

"Yes."

"It's rough and it gets really scary up there. I wouldn't do it."

"Why?"

"The roads get really, really narrow."

"I've been on narrow roads before, as long as they aren't less than eight feet wide."

"I guess you could always back up."

We agreed it was approximately a hundred miles so I filled up with gas. I bought bread from the cafe bakery and asked other people about road conditions. They weren't in the know. As the grocery clerk said, "You could always back up."

The Grey's River Road was bad in spots but the scenery following the river was great. I met a few cars, mostly camping and fishing people. About 14 miles in, a sign declared, "'RV travel beyond this point isn't recommended because of road conditions." Note it said, "Not recommended," not "Prohibited." The Sprinter and I had room to spare going through that washout. Others must have done it because I was still seeing people camped along the river.

The road eventually became narrower, windier, steeper, more washboardy, dustier and considerably smaller and rockier. My kind of road. The Sprinter wasn't sure. I drove slowly and stopped for the few passing vehicles. I had seen places for stopping and many campgrounds, a couple of which I pulled through and decided I didn't want that much company.

At dusk I found a reasonably flat area down by the creek, not too far from the road. I backed right over the stream. The last morning I was in Yellowstone, I had somehow wrenched my back doing laundry. I was very tired and hurting to the max.

**Wyoming Forest Service Road**

The stream's music running directly below my bed was lulling, but I turned on the fan so I wouldn't hear any mice. I didn't catch any that night but I knew that two critters still dwelled within my walls because they had run across my feet while I was driving. I set enticing new peanut butter-laced traps.

A sign explained that a pioneer was buried in the meadow. After parking the Sprinter in a daisy field, curiosity took me up through the meadow grass and flowers that waved in the morning sun. A two-foot monument marking the gravesite and a tall pine tree resided within a five-foot high wrought iron fence.

Elizabeth had died in childbirth on July 27, 1862. She was 32 years old. Her seventh child lived a week. Nothing was mentioned about where the child was buried but the sign revealed that the husband had lived until 1908. I wondered who followed their lives and erected the memorial.

My curiosity was further piqued when I saw something else. This was probably 35 - 50 miles from human habitation in any direction. It was mid-August so Memorial Day had long passed. On the grave were fresh flowers. They were not meadow flowers. Who was so thoughtful as to put flowers on that lonely grave. Did a several-greats granddaughter or grandson decorate it? Was it someone who knew the family and just happened to pass that way? On *that* road?

I stayed in the warm sunshine for a few minutes and wondered about the hard but short life she had lived. What were her dreams? What were her hopes for the six children traveling with her and the seventh she carried? I knew that the newest one died. What happened to the rest of them?

A fox ran across the meadow quite unaware of me. An owl hooted in the forest. Clouds crossed blue skies slowly and majestically, probably much like they had 136 years before. It was peaceful.

At times the road had only two tracks with grass and weeds growing between and I wondered if it was going to peter out. Around the next bend or over the hill or beyond the mountain it always became better, at least for a little while longer. I really hate to ever turn back unless the road is truly impassable.

Trees, boulders, and the mountainside pushed in, at times giving the Sprinter just enough room to pass through. Occasionally the road opened into typical western wide-open spaces.

It was freshly graded beyond the intersection leading to Marbleton/Big Piney. Sharp-edged rocks had been pulled out of the roadbed, not good news. I drove even slower but I couldn't miss any of it because the road was too narrow.

It was beautiful country, just bad road. I stopped several times to enjoy the lush green along the stream or to accommodate slow-moving cattle. Once I came to a dead stop while three cowboys on horseback and a small cattle herd filtered around me. The graded road ended and the road became a bit better. The last 15 miles were paved.

After reaching the main highway, I heard a tremendous bang. The Sprinter was immediately filled with blue smoke and dirt. I thought there was a fire. I pulled off quickly. An inner dual had blown up, destroying the wheel well and tearing the molding off the bathtub. It blew stuff from under the refrigerator out into the motorhome along with lots of dirt. What a mess. Fortunately, it didn't massacre the new refrigerator.

We limped 15 miles an hour on the shoulder, flashing the hazard lights. At I-80, a highway maintenance worker directed me into a little town where I stopped several places before finding someone who had tires to fit, immediately. A bubble was on the outer dual, too. I didn't want to buy only two tires so I bought four back ones and took the two best leftovers for my brother in Michigan.

The guy in charge was kind of prickly and I didn't appreciate it but as we talked, he softened a little and was downright friendly before I left.

"You should have a companion with you if you're going to travel the rough back roads by yourself."

"It might seem a bit unusual taking on a groom just for the purpose of traveling back roads."

That adventure was costly but now I've been there and I don't have to go back over that road again.

If I were a bell, I'd be ringing, but if I were these bells, I'd be as silent as they are.

# Silent Bells for All Seasons

The brochures claimed they were, "The most photographed peaks in North America, and maybe the most photogenic in all the world." "Yeah, right! Hype to the max, I thought. Then I rounded the corner and there they were, solid, massive, and awesome, the Maroon Bells, the silent ones, the focus of the Snowmass-Maroon Bells Wilderness.

In late June, the two "fourteeners," as Coloradans call anything above 14,000', were dusted with new snow. South Maroon Bell, 14,156', and North Maroon Bell, 14,014', painted in first-light pink, were reflected in Maroon Lake. From the Maroon-Snowmass Trail, I watched nature's engineers build a beaver lodge. A mish-mash of fallen aspen trees evidenced their labors.

Roly-poly marmots, the western version of a woodchuck, sunned themselves on meadow rocks, and listened respectfully to my greetings. Pikas, rabbit family members looking more like furry, overgrown mice, were not so brave. They squeaked and scurried to the safety of earth and hearth.

Ah, the land of the peaks and the pooped. I was the pooped. I paused, not only to admire the sun-sparkled snowmelt ribbons falling from the cliffs but because I couldn't breath. My physical condition in the thin mountain air was better than a desk jockey but not much. Five mule deer silently observed my "lowlander's" huffing and puffing. They deemed me harmless and went about their foraging.

A sturdy staff steadied my crossing of iffy rocks in swollen streams, a sometimes moving experience. My unhurried hiking was rewarded, a tiny fawn. She was well camouflaged against the shadows and orange rock lichen. Her legs were so new they hadn't gotten their walking papers yet. She sidled behind a fallen log. I was certain her mother was close by. Somewhere in that vast region were eagle, fox, porcupine, bear, goat, elk and big horn sheep, some of whom would find her baby a tasty morsel.

My destination was Crater Lake, 10,076'. Maroon Creek crashed wildly down the mountain on its frantic race to a far-away sea. Meadow strawberries blossomed alongside the inevitable healthy dandelions.

Crater Lake is a popular destination but June footing is tricky with snow patches adding to the necessity for sturdy footgear. The upper trail crosses rocky alluvial fans where avalanches violently ripped aspen trees out by their roots and scattered them like matchsticks among the boulders and snow. Power at work. There are no bridges, benches for resting, toilets, or snack bars. It is wilderness area. If you pack it in, you pack it out and if you can't wait, find a tree.

Primitive campsites are tucked inconspicuously into the trees, well away from Crater Lake. Campfires are not allowed within a half mile. Dogs must be on a leash and are only allowed while passing through.

The path divides and winds up through sub-alpine fir trees to an alpine environment where tree survival is impossible. Extreme temperatures, short growing seasons, and harsh, drying winds allow only the existence of specialized plants. One trail winds over Buckskin Pass, elevation 12, 462', and the other over West Maroon Pass at 12,500'.

It is wise to sign the trailhead register before continuing to more rugged elevations. When I hosted at Maroon Bells, clues to the whereabouts of several lost people were in trailhead registers. Maroon Bells attracts mountain climbers like moths to flame but the rock is loose and deceptive to even the most experienced climbers. Sometimes the rescue stories for both climbers and rescuers had happy endings, sometimes tragic.

It took three hundred million years for this land to emerge from a great inland sea to numerous rugged "fourteeners." For roughly 1,300 years, the Ute Indians used this valley for hunting and fishing. They still consider it sacred ground. During the 1870s, the Maroon Bells were named for their distinctive shape and the weathered iron-bearing mineral, hematite, that gives them a red tinge. Wind, water, and erosion continue shaping the valley, now part of the White River National Forest.

From Aspen, 11 paved miles lead to the Snowmass-Maroon Bells Wilderness. Because of its popularity and the environmental impact of its 200,000 visitors, the road is closed to private vehicles from 8:30 a.m. to 5 p.m. Shuttle buses operate from late June to mid-September.

Weather changes quickly at high elevations. One minute Sievers Mountain has a backdrop of white cumulous clouds billowing through azure skies and the next; thunderstorms roll in on a power extravaganza.

I often awakened at night, opening my screen to moon gaze or feast my eyes on a zillion twinkling stars. One restless night I crept through the meadow at 3:30 a.m., moon stalking with my camera. A beaver swam across the moon's silver path and there were no doubt a dozen animals sharing my clandestine hike but I couldn't see them. And of course the Architect who designed it all was there. I was so caught up in the wonder of it, I forgot that when the moon tumbled beyond the rugged Maroon Bells ridge, I would be very much in the dark. It was eerie and exciting and I loved it.

In mid-August, snow cornices still stretched across the higher mountain passes. Sometimes an entire mountainside of purple fireweed or yellow daisies waved in the breeze. If I wore red, hummingbirds flew within inches of my body, then in disappointment, shifted into reverse, and flew off to a more realistic sap sip. Deer munched through lush, shoulder-high growth around the campsites.

I saw the magnificent Maroon Bells in all their moods and in all seasons. The last gasp of winter snuck in on three inches of snowy feet on July Fourth. Dazzling colorful flowers sprang forth in rock crevasses and carpeted the meadow. Summer came on or about August 12th. Cool nights with pleasant afternoons slipped casually into "frost on the punkin'." Lush greens became autumn brown. Aspen leaves were inspired into gold and once again winter swirled around the mountain peaks. Full circle.

Visit our magnificent wilderness areas but follow the reminder from the National Forest Service, "Take only pictures, leave only footprints." I went one step further; I took powerful memories and left part of my heart.

Wanna take a leap with me, Baby?

# Higher than a Kite

Everyone's life should be liberally sprinkled with excitement and exhilaration. As a full-time RVer, I have had more than my share of both. The air balloon drift over Napa Valley, California; helicopter rides over Grand Canyon, Arizona, and Waimae Canyon, Hawaii; an ultralite flight over Quartzsite, Arizona; a bush plane soaring over Alaskan glaciers; temporarily having control of a Piper Cadet over North Dakota, none could top paragliding in Aspen, Colorado.

The brochure explained paragliding as "Not parachuting where you sink slowly earthward after jumping out of a plane...not parasailing where you're pulled a few hundred feet behind a boat...and not hangliding with a hard infrastructure that makes a huge kite for humans." It is, "Raw, exposed flying."

The instructions were "Be here by 7 a.m. Wear long pants, sturdy footwear, and a windbreaker." As we drove the windy, twisty road up Aspen Mountain, I remembered that the flimsy-looking 15 pounds of nylon or Dacron cloth sometimes "Flies forward at airspeeds of 30 mph and creates life with the same physics principles as a jet wing." My stomach had airspeeds of 190 mph.

Instructions were kept "Sweet and simple so as not to test the memory." They must have heard about my CRS. Warnings to soloists were a firm, "React immediately to instructions, don't hesitate." Others donned their equipment and took off. One aborted three times, another twice. A tiny lady aborted in a spectacular head over heals maneuver but made it on the second try. The sky filled with colorful butterflies.

My tandem partner was a tall Norwegian blonde with eight years of paragliding experience. He said, "We are waiting for the sun to warm the ground and create thermals." We were taking off from approximately 10,900'. As had everyone else, my partner spread the bright yellow "soft-wing" (canopy) on the ground and checked it thoroughly. He buckled me into the helmet, and a harness that resembled my granddaughter's jump seat. Lastly, he buckled us together. I told him I felt like a baby. He said, "Today, you're my baby." Whoa!

He told me I would have to run off the mountain, literally pulling him with me. "Don't worry, we'll stop if it doesn't feel right." I think that was comforting. He had said earlier, "Some people can't get themselves to run, so instructors get on either side and run them off the mountain." I took that to mean I was going off the mountain either under my power or theirs.

It was our turn. My knees were weak. He said, "Go on the count of three." I knew he expected obedience. I started running but I was momentarily stopped by his weight. I lunged out and into the sky. Wow! I laughed in the sheer joy of the moment. From then on, he was in control. I scooched my backside into the seat. My hands were free to take pictures. I felt his knees maneuvering the glider into various positions. I can't quite explain the feeling of complete freedom I felt.

Paragliding was a very intimate experience in that we were two strangers buckled together and running off a cliff. We were either going to soar with the angels or die together, dashed against the mountain (You can see where my confidence was!).

After my partner realized I wasn't going to get sick, he did a couple of 360s. My stomach did 660s. We gained altitude to 11,000'. He said sometimes they go as high as 15,000'. I wasn't surprised when he said, "Ladies are a little more adventuresome than guys. Guys have trouble trusting other guys."

"Will we come close to the treetops?"

"Under the right conditions, we could kick them with our feet." Fortunately, our conditions weren't right. We stayed up nearly 25 minutes. "This is unusual for a morning flight. Conditions this morning are better than average."

"Do you still get a thrill out of this after so many flights?"

"Paragliding is an 'Intellectual sport' (Certainly explaining my part in it). The challenge in doing it so many times becomes 'The where and the how.'" As far as I was concerned, the challenge in doing it once was having the "guts." "What is the average age of paragliders?"

"Mid-thirties" (Again explaining my participation).

Eventually we had to come down and he instructed me to run with it just as I had run off the mountain but I soon stumbled and we tumbled. He folded up the gear and we drove back to town.

Flying High

We shook hands and I said how great it was and that was the end. I didn't want it to end that way. I wanted to discuss the flight with other tandem riders and I was the only one. I wanted to extend the fun and it was over. I wanted to tell the world and nobody wanted to listen.

So, if you want the ultimate experience, try tandem paragliding. It is definitely the most exciting way to fly the friendly skies…and of course it never hurts when your tandem partner is a tall, good-looking, Norwegian blonde the age of your oldest daughter!

Now that we've stepped "off," let's step back…in time.

# Chaco Culture National Historic Park

It was October. My friend, Dan, whom I'd met several years before in Mexico, was visiting Albuquerque. The "It's a small world" syndrome allowed this full-time RV gypsy and this full-time world traveler, one of our rare contacts, to explore the Chaco Culture National Historic Park near Nageezi, in northwestern New Mexico.

We took off into a flurry of golden cottonwood and aspen leaves. The high desert terrain varied with flat-topped buttes and funny looking wind-blown rocks. Snow-dusted southwestern Colorado mountain peaks overlooked where New Mexico, Colorado, Arizona, and Utah were *"Standin' on the corner watching all the world go by."*

The park can be reached via I-40, but we preferred the longer, scenic SR #44. After turning south on SR #57, the last 16 of the 21 miles to the park were on a teeth-rattling washboard and dirt road. We descended into a dusty, hot, deserted canyon, much as the Anasazi Indians did nearly 8,000 years before us.

The "Ancient Ones," as they are known, at first lived an itinerant existence following food sources. By A.D. 400, they planted crops and settled in pithouse villages. Around A.D. 850, they constructed masonry cities, or what is called by archaeologists, the great pueblo architecture. So treasured are the ruins of these multi-storied "great houses," they were declared a World Heritage Site in 1987.

At the Chetro Ketl ruins, the booklet explains what we see as we follow the winding path through various levels and partial "great house" rooms. Using the science of dendrochronology (tree-ring dating), archeologists have dated "vigas" (primary beams carrying roof weight), and "Latillas" (secondary supports), in the A.D. 900's, with remodeling and additions, to around 1100. The Chacoan pueblos are unique from other southwestern pueblos due to their large-scale architectural pre-planning and engineering technology. While this pueblo was originally five stories high and had over 500 rooms, they believe that nearly 300 small one-story pueblos existed in Chaco Wash during the same time period.

We climb a narrow, boulder-strewn, ancient stairway behind a rock slice to reach the mesa-top road above Chetro Ketl. More than 200 arrow-straight miles of prehistoric roads have been found connecting north and south Chacoan pueblos, suggesting a "community of towns." The roads are 16' - 20' wide, filled with soil, and bordered by large boulders, or soil and loose rock berms.

One wonders, with no wheeled vehicles, why the roads? With no wheeled vehicles and no draft animals, how did they transport from forests 40 miles away, an estimated 200,000 ponderosa pine and Douglas fir trees, to build the canyon's great houses?

**Chetro Ketl**

Pueblo Bonito means "Beautiful town" and is the most thoroughly investigated great house. It was originally four stories high and contained approximately 600 rooms. Clues into room use were given via pillars, colonnades, firepits, grinding slabs, storage bins, and sometimes room size and configuration. Square ventilation holes allowed sunlight into the different levels. The plaza was separated into eastern and western halves by a dividing wall that aligned with true north.

So many construction features suggested astronomical significance, that a new word was coined for those who study these ruins, "Archaeoastronomists."

Great "kivas" were large, circular subterranean structures with low masonry benches around the room base, probably used for community-wide informal events, ceremonies, and political functions. The small Pueblo Bonito kiva-wall crypts were empty; however, at Chetro Ketl, beads, pendants, and ornaments were originally found in the niches.

The pueblos, built from stone quarried from the canyon's sandstone cliffs, were hand-carried to the building site and up log-carved ladders to build the upper rooms. The wash provided sand, silt, clay, and water for making the mortar and plaster used in finishing walls. Extensive irrigation systems diverted rainwater for storage and possibly they had hand-dug wells.

The pueblos were fascinating but I have only touched a few highlights. I didn't describe the corner doorways, pilasters, freestanding towers, or petroglyphs. I urge you to visit here and the other National Monument ruins in this "Land of Enchantment."

If you go, please stick to the trails, for your own safety in the unstable ruins, as well as to preserve history. It is important to disturb or remove nothing. Excavators have carted away charred dirt and charcoal, thinking it was useless. Now we have carbon dating that could tell us even more about these Ancient Ones. Unexcavated ruins remain for future archeologists (and our children) who will have greater knowledge and technology than we have.

But stop, before you climb into your 21st Century motor-powered vehicle and return to shopping malls and Ronald McDonald, listen closely. Doesn't that warm fall breeze carry murmuring voices? Do you hear the "click, click" of a "digging stick" cultivating corn? Is that fragrance something baking? Are there clues in the presence we feel?

During 300 years, possibly as many as 6,000 Anasazi Indians carved a unique existence out of this valley. They had families, raised animals, grew crops, made pottery, wove cotton, and traded with other cultures for turquoise, copper, shells, macaws, and ideas. By A. D. 1200, the Anasazi from Chaco Wash had disappeared without a trace. Why? Where did they go? What happened to them? Will you make it home tonight?

I have confidence we'll make it at least as far as the Mexican border.

# Memories of Mexico

Whether it was a long-term trip or a two-week jaunt, I always felt a terrific sense of freedom and excitement crossing the Mexico border, perhaps because it was an unknown, and trust me, Mexico is an unknown. No one knew me and no one knew where to find me, not that anyone was looking mind you. I have always felt perfectly safe anywhere in Mexico, but maybe it's that possible danger lurking in a foreign country that entices me.

In 1987, I lived three months at San Carlos, Mexico, and made subsequent brief winter visits. During winter 1987-88, I wandered three months in Old Mexico, as far south as Pueblo (below Mexico City), west to Acapulco, and north to Nogales, Arizona, a major Mexican adventure. I have had enjoyable times in closer-to-the-border Mexico as well. First, I'll tell you about my favorite, laid back

## Baja

In December of 1986, I followed Jan and Hoagie Carmichael into Baja. I probably wouldn't have made that first trip alone but with their experience and guidance, I learned the ropes well enough to be on my own for five months of Santispac beach living and a month at LaPaz.

In January of 1996, I revisited old haunts. I drove the 1,059 miles to Cabo San Lucas. Northern roads were pothole filled but southern roads were reasonably good. The only difference I noted from 1986, was an increase in desert agricultural reclamation. They were growing more tomatoes, chilis, corn, and citrus trees.

I boondocked in what I call God's Rock Garden at Catavina. I awakened to coyotes howling. It was a pleasant sunrise with fresh coffee and fresh strawberries crushed over fresh pancakes.

It is tiring to drive the Baja road. Mile after mile of it has no shoulders. The edge is jaggedly broken in many places and has anywhere from a 3" to 12" drop off. It requires concentration to miss the chuckholes and the vacas (cows) that wander, other vehicles, see the scenery, and still keep a reasonable speed.

I love San Ignacio. I stayed at a $7 no-hookup RV park close to the La Pinta Hotel and walked the dusty date-palm-lined road into town. It brought back memories of walking around the town square with its big trees and the inevitable cathedral.

A young lady offered me a $10 plastic bag of dates. I didn't want that many but I remembered how sticky and gooey and delicious they were when picked up sun-warmed from the ground. I finally felt the charm of Mexico again.

Cabo San Lucas had grown by leaps and bounds, much too touristy and crowded for my taste, but I couldn't resist another excursion boat trip to Land's End. Pepe guided the glass-bottom panga and offered to let us off at Lover's Beach. They can't pull the boats in far enough to land. We took off our shoes and socks and jumped off. I walked the beach and felt the salt spray in my face and the breeze in my hair. Rocks were smooth to the touch after endless kissing by the ocean waves. Yesss!

Near Todos Santos, north of Cabo, was Los Cerritas Beach. I parked the Sprinter's backside over a sand embankment looking out over the Pacific Ocean. Few people climbed the rock formations to the magnificent beaches beyond. Two beaches away, I was completely alone. I sat in the sun watching the great grey whales sliding in and out of the ocean and kept the tide schedule in mind. This wouldn't be a place to sleep without a planned escape route.

For six days, I parked beside a palm-thatched sun shelter at Santispac Playas, 17 miles south of Mulege, much as I did in 1986-87. It brought memories of questionable four-wheel drive roads to find cave paintings and cathedral ruins plus warm days bargaining with natives for trinkets. Ah, then there were the incredible moonlight nights.

This time I rented a kayak and paddled around the various islands in and near the lagoon. I walked on the old Baja Road and watched the sunrise light up the islands and peninsula. The air was so fresh. Would you believe I found some of the same people living on that beach who were there years before?

The Grey Whale Natural Park is near Guerrero Negro, the nursery where the gray whales have their babies. The approximately 15 miles through sand and ruts, beyond the salt ponds to Scammon's Lagoon, was as rough as I remembered it. I signed up for the whale tour and continued to the lagoon's end, boondocking in the moonlight with only the creatures of the night serenading me.

It was very cold on the lagoon but it was worth it to see new babies riding on Mama's back. They gave us a peek as Mama glided in and out of the water. Our American tour guide told us about the whale's evasive behavior. "They will either be curious and come toward us or turn away and leave. We do a whale count in the lagoon every two weeks. Up to 1,500 whales are here in February. They came in December this year, earlier than usual." After playing with the whales, it was time to cross the border again.

## *El Golfo*

South of Yuma, Arizona, I drove 90 miles through reclaimed desert farm country, then strictly desert, rather flat and uninteresting. Closer to towns, eclectic residences were scrapped school buses, stick and cardboard hovels, tiny scrap lumber buildings, among what we would call "real" houses. One area looked like it had been a town. The many one-story brick shells stood in emptiness, their doors and unfinished roof materials stolen, mute evidence of dreams gone awry.

Clothes hung on back yard lines. Prickly pear cactus gardens were well tended, but generally junk prevailed everywhere. One of my Colorado River Adventure's five campgrounds, El Golfo RV Resort, was beached at the road's end.

I love the sights and sounds of early morning. The locals' day began just before daybreak when deep-voiced trucks pulled fishing pangas across great sand expanses to bays deep enough to loose them in the water. They pulled the boats into the water as far as they dared and unhooked. If the boats still weren't launched, they were gently nudged from behind. The Sea of Cortez would have been as smooth as glass if not for the buzzing fishing boats. The last one bow-slapped across the wavy water playing catch-up. When they returned at sunset, Gringos gathered to buy shrimp.

My kayaking buddy, Art, arrived with his motorhome. We took the five-hour, 20-mile beach jeep tour. Enrique, the driver, pulled a rope across the lady in the front seat so she wouldn't fall out. There were no doors on either side. The mufflerless jeep produced a distinct Mexico sound. Enrique fastened the hood down with a rope. He unfastened it several times and opened the hood to cool the engine. It was getting a real workout. The windshield was wired to the roll bars. I knew we were in good shape for the trip though, two rolls of repair tape were slid onto the gearshift. Of necessity, our Mexican neighbors can fix anything.

The trip was tricky with the recent high tide but Enrique never wavered. He put it in four-wheel drive and always knew where to go through the thick dry sand or chance the still wet mud.

Curlews scouted breakfast with their long bills, and herons stood watch over the mud flats. Gulls scrapped with each other for food.

We passed a shrimp farm, several empty fish camps, and sandy roads coming from somewhere inland, leading to homes many miles from town. They wouldn't have won any architectural contests but obviously they were home sweet home to somebody. Ingenious watering systems tilted from above, and decks were built high enough for owners to catch the Sea of Cortez breezes.

At our destination, we all went our separate ways to enjoy the treasures of the sea. Art found a complete dolphin skeleton but opted to take only the vertebrae and a few teeth.

Outside the compound we ate dinner at Las Cabinos. We did this several times at sunset and never failed to have dolphins entertain us immediately offshore. Mexican music completed the ambiance.

We gathered our stuff for a Valentine's Day sandcastle sculpting competition. We worked fast and well together and finished a rather large castle. It looked great to us but obviously the judges weren't impressed.

It was fun riding Art's motorscooter into town, though it felt like we could go sprawling in the sandy road at any time. El Golfo is a very small village so it didn't take us long to explore it.

We wheeled Art's kayak across the wide beach. The tide came in and by the time we were ready to go, we waded in a foot of water which worked very well. He used the sail part of the time and we paddled when the breeze died. Well out into the Sea of Cortez, a school of dolphin came toward us. They soon surrounded the kayak. I was so excited; I hyperventilated each time they came out of the water, "Look at that! Look at that! Did you see that!" They were so close, less than five feet from the kayak. One shot across the bow, only a couple of feet from me. Wow! They were all around us, diving and swimming as we paddled. They were so huge up close and seemed to look us right in the eye. What a thrill. Neither of us had cameras in tow.

Art followed me back toward the border. In the middle of nowhere, young uniform-pressed Federalies with guns stopped us. I've gone through many such checkpoints through the years. Via CB, I told Art to play it cool. It was his first trip into Mexico. One came inside and walked through. That was it. He did the same in Art's rig. Art was impressed with how polite they were.

At Algodones, the narrow streets were crowded with Americans who walked in the middle as though they owned them. At the U. S. border, the guard requested that I step out and asked if I had any animals or birds. His dog walked through and right back out. When the dog came out, the guard leashed him and waved me on.

## Puerto Penasco
### (Rocky Point)

It has always been interesting crossing the border, finding my way around, and answering or asking questions in my "Limited Wounded Spanglish." This time it was disappointingly simple.

The friendly, smiling, spiffy uniformed border guards waved me through without questions or the usual little motion of thumb and forefinger signifying "Mordida" (bribe money) as they had while walking through the motorhome on former visits. Things had changed.

The 66 miles from Lukeville, Arizona, goes through a two-million-acre Biosphere Reserve that includes (a side trip) El Pinacate, a volcanic area dating back 30,000 years. This area was used by NASA to emulate "moon-like" settings for lunar exploration practice.

Originating as a small fishing village in 1927, Puerto Penasco became a major shrimp producing area. Now it relies more on the ever-growing tourist trade.

An English-speaking amigo at the airport assured me I would find Cholla Bay if I would "Turn at the tall rounded sign that lists many places (none of which said Cholla Bay)." A wide sandy road took me through the edge of town and past small stores with merchandise hanging from nearly everything, or laying on long tables, colorful and so typically Mexican, all outside in the dust.

Roads went every direction. It was impossible to know which was the right one. With questionable road conditions (Is there any other kind in Mexico?), I wondered about my route decision. Teenagers and lounging seniors watched the Sprinter's unwieldy progress through the sand, giving me big smiles and friendly nods. The Gringa was on the right track.

**Cholla Bay**

The road divided into sand troughs but the roadbed was solid and pure washboard. At 10 mph, the washboard was horrendous; at 35 mph, it was almost tolerable. Five miles on this teeth-rattling, possession-tossing road took me to a little village which varied widely from hovels to deluxe digs.

On a lonely side road I parked on a long stretch of magnificent beach. Only one other RV shared it. As I was thinking I had the entire "*World in my pocket, sitting on a rainbow,*" I learned I had no water. Removing the mattress and bed-pedestal plywood, I discovered the washboard road had dislodged a key water-pump wire. Soon fixed and my joyous atmosphere restored, I walked where the Old Man of the Sea stored fascinating seashells in rocky beach pockets.

It is amazing what the ocean covers. When the tide recedes, what a multitude of creatures and flotsam and jetsam it leaves behind, strangely enough, this time a number of lightbulbs. A lot of good ideas popping out of the Sea of Cortez?

Walking barefooted in the February surf, those long-ago Michigan winters didn't seem real any more. The water was icy cold the first time it hit my feet but after getting used to it, I crept in deeper and deeper and felt its soothing coolness while the hot sun fried my back.

Though it was a distance from town, two fellows tramped the beach daily, one with fresh tortillas and another with blankets. I bought a blanket. The first time I washed it, 15 pounds of sand escaped.

Walking the beach, climbing the dunes and rocky pinnacles, interspersed with a few idiot ATVers who felt it necessary to make their fellow Americans miserable with their noise until three a.m., ended with low batteries and the threat of a major storm. I moved into Puerto Penasco's Playa Bonita Campground. Although there were at least 10 RV parks in the vicinity, they were quite full. Those of us who did not have reservations played what we called "Musical RVs," switching from place to place for one or two nights. The problem was that reservations were made for specific sites, and as much as two years in advance.

Salespeople came through yelling, "Paper, paper" and "Tortillas, boletos, tamales" as well as others offering to wash RVs. Jewelry salesman carried attache cases filled with earrings, bracelets, rings, and necklaces for all prices. "Top dollar! Dangly silver, abalone, or turquoise earrings, $5 a pair. I geeve you bargain, ladee."

A severe sandstorm ruined one day with blowing so bad I didn't go outside. Afterward everything was coated with sand and salt, keeping the Mexicans busy washing RVs. Other days were hot but pleasant with a breeze.

I was invited to a GMC rally potluck by a couple I had met, as a more-or-less date for another single friend of theirs who had just arrived. Since I had met several others in the group, and I had no way to get out of it, I went. I feel very uncomfortable with forced companionship and I'm sure he did too, but he was gracious.

As the meal ended, a guest became distressed. Immediately, three CPR-knowledgeable RVers responded. They thought he was having a heart attack. A fellow in a wheelchair behind him, said, "Here, give him this." Handing over his own oxygen while waiting for the Mexican Paramedics and the ambulance, probably saved the man's life. I was quite impressed with the rapid Paramedic response and their expertise in handling the situation.

One morning I went over to look inside the rusted hulk of a big old beached ship. As I peered inside, a Mexican fellow crawled out of a bit of ship-shape shelter. He looked groggy from either sleep or drink.

A couple I met took me about five miles outside Puerto Penasco to the Earthship, a project of CEDO, The Intercultural Center for the Study of Deserts and Oceans, a non-profit foundation dedicated to research, science education and conservation in the northern Gulf of California and coastal Sonoran Desert. Since 1979 this has been a joint venture between Mexico and the United States.

The solar building was called an Earthship, a type of construction using waste materials - old tires and aluminum cans - plus sand and cement for low cost, energy efficient, and simple-to-build structures. They used grey water to irrigate plants and burned waste for bacteria-free garden fertilizer. They reused trash that would otherwise contaminate the environment. This was a demonstration project built with volunteer labor and donated materials.

One building was completed and used for a book and souvenir shop. Next door was a building in progress. Dirt was firmly packed into the tires which were layered. Where the wall ended and more reinforcement was needed, wire mesh was bent around the tires and filled with cement, one of the most costly materials they used.

A single invited me to a Wednesday singles happy hour at the Seaside Bar next door. Since I had someone to go with, I went. They all knew each other and were very excited about their own pursuits. I would have liked to ask questions about how they happened to be living in Puerto Penasco, but the smoke-filled, noisy room was not conducive to conversation nor was it my cup of tea. In less than an hour I was out of there with the excuse I wanted to walk before sunset. It was wonderful getting back on the quiet beach with the smokeless sea fragrance.

Mexico's bakeries are beyond description. The always ambiguous directions were, "Across from the escuela (school), down a narrow alley next to the railroad tracks between two buildings. If someone hadn't drawn me a map I would never have found it. Typically Mexico, the harder the place was to find, the better the surprise.

It looked like I might be walking into a chicken house. The door was crooked and sort of nailed together. It was clean but very sparse with more-or-less tables and shelves carelessly nailed together. The goodies came out of the huge red-hot oven on long boards. I couldn't get any fresher baked goods than that. Maybe it was the simplicity that made it taste so good.

Everything was 10¢ no matter what you bought. It came with a guarantee of high cholesterol and fat, and worth every gram of it. I was given a plastic bag and pinchers and picked whatever I wanted. They didn't even look to see if I had a baker's dozen. They just accepted my word. Who would be tempted to cheat at 10¢ each anyway? I can go to any of a dozen fragrant bakeries in almost any American town but somehow they lack the ambiance of a Mexican panaderia.

Departure day arrived. I parked along the palm-tree-lined sea wall in town. The fishmarket had many colorful stalls from which eager salesman hawked their wares, vying for my pesos. Every size shrimp, fish and clam were available with accompanying sights and smells.

At a seaside open-air restaurant, the smiling brown-eyed, dark-haired lady added a dash of this and a dash of that. Climato juice was mixed with another ingredient, all stirred together with a few spoonsful of something else to make it just so for eager customers.

She went to a fish market across the street for a handful of grandé shrimp for my order. A fellow came especially to bufferfly them, press them flat, pepper and garlic them, and drop them into a grandé frying pan. He put salad on a plate with all the shrimp and a container of hot corn tortillas. Yes! Yum! Grandé! especially while eaten overlooking the shrimp boats and other harbor activity. Unfinished stark white and Pepto-Bismol pink hotels sported sky-reaching steel rebar.

Some road construction had been finished and new projects started. It was a nice road and wide; a great deal of it is done by hand. The workers waved and a truck driver pulled over to let me by, tipping his hat with a smile. I had been gone two weeks but it was really nice to reach the border and be back on American soil.

While Baja will always be my favorite Mexican adventure, El Golfo and Puerto Penasco, for such short trips across the border, are both a nice taste of Mexico. Olé!

# *Various and Sundry*

## *Pioneer Christmas in Kentucky*

When the great wilderness of the west was still in the east, none other than Daniel Boone, with a little help from fellow frontiersmen, used axes and tomahawks to clear underbrush and trees to create the Wilderness Road. They went through Cumberland Gap tangles where a rabbit wouldn't go. Settlers followed. Fort Boonesborough, established in 1775, was a stopping point and trade center along the river.

In 1974, a replica of Fort Boonesborough was dedicated to all the pioneers who opened the doors of Kentucky and the western frontier.

On that note, let's step through the fort's mighty wooden doors on a misty November evening. Four blockhouses with projecting second stories dominate the rectangular enclosure. Twenty-six cabin walls form the fort sides. Candles flicker inside the cabins.

Costumed volunteers offer period conversation. A trader's store has sugar, flour, wool, and skins. In the weaver's store, nature's bounty, berries or roots or leaves, are used to dye the threads. The carpenter and pottery shops offer their wares.

As I continue along the torchlit path, the night turns cruelly cold with deep snow at my feet and flakes swirling above. I pull my cloak tightly about me. We are struggling with a hard winter in 1779. It will be a meager Christmas Eve.

Inside, a grand fire warms the building. Red-ribboned pine bough wreaths decorate the walls. I climb the balcony stairs to watch. Family, friends, and neighbors greet one another in a great swish of long skirts as they make their way to rough-hewn log tables. Buckskin-dressed men stack their guns against the wall.

Supplies are fast disappearing. We are grateful for our combined resources. We have chestnuts, vegetable soup, corn on the cob, baked potatoes, and roast chicken. "Johnny Cakes," corn bread, apple pie, and hot cider are shared. We eat with our fingers and the men use their sleeves for "wipin."

We are serenaded with solos and carols. A youngster tells about the Great Siege of Boonesborough in 1778. "We had a turrible fight with the Indians. Daniel Boone got shot in the shoulder. Blood was everywhere. It was wonderful!"

Beyond the daily life and death struggles, humorous tales are told of family escapades. A spinster sings, "There's a Man for Me." We listen with rapt attention as a neighbor plays the harpsichord. Suddenly the door bursts open. Daniel Boone arrives with his family and Cherokee friends. They bring abundant food and meat. Hallelujah!

The celebrating continues. Heavenly fragrances waft to my balcony table. The fire's warmth makes me drowsy. Wherever you are tonight, and whatever century you are in, I wish you a Merry Christmas.

## *Tinkertown*

After ridge hiking to the Vista Point stone house in Sandia Crest Recreation area outside of Albuquerque, I visited Tinkertown. Years before I had seen a TV program about this place. It went flying right out of my mind until I saw the sign for it on SR #536, the Sandia Crest National Scenic Byway. If I wanted a diverse collection of miscellanea, this was the place to find it.

Rock arches beckoned me through a fence made of roadside signs, wagon wheels, and gas pumps. What started as a four-room cabin, is now a 22-room showcase museum. Incorporating 48,000 assorted bottles with cement and other recyclable materials created the walls. Bottles were different sizes, shapes, and colors. Bottles and horseshoes were imbedded in the walkways.

Ross Ward, Tinkertown's creator and builder, started all this as a hobby in 1962, and opened the present Tinkertown in 1984. He says, "We did all this while you were watching TV." He is adamant that this museum is privately owned, "No taxpayer's money, no government funds, and no public grants have been used in building or maintaining this display."

It was obviously too cold, too early in the day, and too late in the season for other visitors, so I roamed Tinkertown's narrow hallways alone. They were covered with old photographs and signs. I loved the signs because I agreed with them,

"There's a race of men that can't fit in –
    a race that can't stay still –
    so they break the heart of kith and kin –
    and roam the world at will." Robert W. Service (Bard of the Yukon)

"There ought to be a law against anybody going to Europe until they have seen the things we have in this country." Will Rogers. "Welcome Charles Kuralt." I felt right at home following such good RVing company. "Dr. Coses barbed wire liniment. Money refunded if fresh wounds do not heal without blemish." This one made a lot of sense, "Think kindly of your undertaker, he's the last to let you down." But I liked this one best from Boot Hill, "Here lies an atheist – All dressed up and no place to go."

A rattlesnake recipe didn't do much for me but I loved putting coins in animated Otto, the one-man band. The fortuneteller, Grandmother Esmeralde, was ready to reveal my fate to me but I wasn't ready to hear it. She is originally from Chicago's River View Park.

The museum houses over a 1000 figures, many of them animated, a mad chef chasing a chicken, a donkey sipping beer in the Lucky Nugget Saloon, and construction crews building a house. Advertisements for "Velvet Tobacco" and "Smoked Salmon" were among 20,000 various miniatures displayed with insulators, coffee grinders and antique tools. Wedding cake figurines dated back to the 1840s.

Ross grew up in the Midwest, fascinated with wood-carved, animated farms, circuses, and whole villages he saw at county fairs or traveling carnivals. In junior high and high school he carved a miniature circus. It has been expanded and is now on display in the museum. He carves the people from wood or molds them from clay. He has given his miniatures the characteristics of friends.

A complete animated miniature 1880-1910 western main street with covered wagons, a pharmacy and an assay office, among others, stretches the entire length of a hallway. The glass case room is filled with dioramas of everything from Wells Fargo Express to Snow White and the Seven Dwarfs. I think I spotted "A spoonful of sugar" in there too. The General Merchandise store has everything from shoes to yard goods and the Monarch Hotel has a busy barber in the barbershop.

Antique stoves and hand-carved animated dioramas are tucked in with the bottle collections and old street lamps. A window was made of an old bike wheel. The cobwebs were authentic, too.

It is open April through October. With snow already falling in Albuquerque, it was extremely cold over 10,000' on the Crest. With no heat, and wandering slowly so as not to miss anything, it was cold in the museum, too. A leather sign with words attributed to Mahatma Gandi said, "There is more to life than increasing its speed." I agreed but it was so cold there on October 26th, I hurried back to the gift shop and the warmth of their pot-bellied stove.

I talked briefly with Ross and Carla Ward. She displays and sells the functional New Mexican clay pottery that she makes there in her studio. She digs and processes local clay into colors and designs inspired by the New Mexico landscape.

It was a fun stop and I recommend it but I was headed southwest and with snow sticking to the Sprinter's tires, I needed to move on.

## Virginia's Explore Park

If you happen to wander along the Blue Ridge Parkway near Roanoke, Virginia, and hear Native American drums beating, chances are you've stumbled onto Virginia's Explore Park.

We drove past the Brugh Tavern (circa 1800), an authentic 19th Century frontier tavern open for lunch and dinner. For 200 years, it was a popular landmark along the Great Wagon Road that is now US #11. Our first stop was the Arthur Taubman Welcome Center where we bought tickets, browsed the gift shop, and watched a movie. The "We" was Sue Norvelle (Daughter Tracey's mother-in-law) and Sue Hahn, another Virginia friend.

Everything the Rawanoke Trading Company sells is related to the living history program, dyeing kits, pewter jacks, clay marbles, tin whistles, and candles. During the summer months, we could have taken a wagon ride. We were soon tramping across the bridge and up and down wooded hills into this three-section period park.

Our first time period was in the 1850s. The warmth of The Blacksmith Shop and the roaring fire felt really good on that chilly, drizzly morning. He operated huge bellows, heating and dousing the irons as he shaped tools. He repairs anything in the village that needs it. The roads were not good in those days and blacksmith skills were often needed.

The Houtz Barn is a German double-crib "bank barn," a specialized architectural form still seen in Pennsylvania and in the Shenandoah Valley. This barn came from the Houtz family large-scale commercial farming operation on Mason's Creek near Salem, Virginia.

During a Fall Harvest Festival, Daughter Janet and I found the barn doors open and hay bales for seating. It was a foot-stomping good time listening to the Craig County Boys. The guy next to us amen'd and yes'd through all the hymns.

It was a good thing the "Sues" and I were prepared for walking because it was a long way around the loop. Good use has been made of the Roanoke River Gorge woods and hills, tucking the various historical cabins and activities into its nooks and crannies.

The Kemp's Ford School (circa 1860) is a one-room schoolhouse from the Franklin County Blackwater River area. A tall young lady in three layers of period costume was comfortable on this cool morning. All docents had cheerful fires going. McGuffrey readers and a small slate were on every bench. She explained that although they didn't literally teach from the Bible, it was usually the only book the pioneers had at home. Often the reading and other lessons came from the "Good Book." The school played a major role in settling and building new communities in rural mid-19$^{th}$ Century.

The three applebutter-making people were not in period dress and the sugar was poured from a store-bought 20$^{th}$ Century sack, small but obvious authenticity lapses.

The Hofauger Farmstead is a log cabin built before 1837. Samuel Hofauger was German but his wife came from a prominent English family on Back Creek. They raised four children on this Roanoke County farm near Cave Spring. A mid-19th Century "heirloom seed" garden had a variety of vegetables and herbs.

On the Loom House porch, a lady spun sheep's wool onto a wheel, portraying domestic manufacturing. She said it would then be washed. We saw demonstrations of natural dyeing and loom weaving via centuries-old textile processing methods. Commercial fabrics replaced this practice by 1850 but it was still used on farms until after the Civil War.

The Wray Barn smelled like the barn it was. Sheep, chickens and pigs occupied this circa 1850 building.

We entered the 1740s and the Longhunter Camp where we saw colonial woodsmen daily life. Daniel Boone was a Longhunter here during the mid-18th Century. We listened while the rain poured. They worked in the rain, as they would have 150 years before.

Stopping at a small log cabin, a French host explained the wearing and making of hats. She said the phrase, "Mad as a hatter" came from using mercury in hat processing. It caused the craftsmen to go mad.

The replica structures of the Native American village were unfinished. The guides told us this area dated back to 1671, and will eventually be a complete village with a Skills Work Arbor and a Horticultural Area.

The lodge was for a family of six to ten people. They bent green poles, stuck them 15" into the ground, and lashed them together around a smoke-escape hole at the top. The host demonstrated stone, bone, and shell tools, including a wood and stone hatchet.

As I was about to go outside, a young lad stuck his head in and said, "Mom?" We all laughed when every woman spontaneously turned to answer him. Once a mom, always a mom, answering to children of any age who call.

Virginia's Explore Park is a work in progress. I have visited three times and each time I find something new. They will eventually have a dugout canoe demonstration and offer canoeing and fishing on the Roanoke River. Different festivals are held throughout the year including Appalachia Folk Festival, Muster on the Green, and All Saints Day Celebration.

A new park entrance and a RV dedicated parking lot are planned. They are open April through October. It is a fun step back in time and very handy just off the Blue Ridge Parkway, one of my favorite drives.

## A Nice Déjà Vu

Tooling along US #50 near Rowlesburg, West Virginia, I rounded a corner into a narrow canyon, dark, and cooling rapidly at 4 p.m. I felt a déjà vu coming on. I haven't been able to figure out where or when but I know I have stopped at Cool Springs Park previously. I don't remember ever even being in that part of West Virginia before, but it was worth a look, curlicue US #50 doesn't have many places to stop and rest.

Beyond the picnic area a working water wheel methodically dumped water troughed in from the mountain. A covered bridge hovered over the stream. Goats and sheep grazed between steam engines and railroad cars.

The front sign announced, "Cool Springs Park, since 1929." They advertise lottery tickets and another sign proclaims them an "Official game checking station." The parking lot is big enough to accommodate cars, trucks, and RVs. They have fuel and propane.

Inside, a sit-down restaurant has counter stools where you can order a foot-long hot dog for $1.10. A Club Sandwich was $2.95. Coffee was 25¢ a cup with the second cup free (with breakfast only). A fresh hamburger was $1.00, tomato 15¢ extra. A breakfast of two eggs and toast was $1.40. A scrumptious-looking lemon pie was $1.00. This was a true country store with old-fashioned prices. Amazing! (If not déjà vu, maybe I had finally gone that "One step beyond!")

Surrounding the eating area was a combination grocery, hardware, and drugstore that sold everything from buckwheat mix to fresh fruits and vegetables. They sold Pennsylvania Dutch sanded cherry drop candy and Dry Cure Bacon in a bag, country ham, hunting supplies, clothes, tools, souvenirs, and ice cream. For what more could one ask?

## Weaver's Antique Service Station

Following US #50 through Burlington, West Virginia, an old filling station caught my eye. It wasn't your usual pay-a-fee organized museum, but any "regulation" museum would love to have his display.

A spruced-up 1923 Ford Model T truck was parked behind the antique gas pumps and under the roof. It sported a window sign that the owner belonged to the Upper Potomac Vintage Auto Club. The truck's flat bed was outfitted with a bag of chicken feed and a crate of chickens and chicks, the plastic kind that didn't make a mess or eat anything.

On the building were signs, "Square Snuff for a Square Deal." A certificate proudly announced this self-proclaimed museum to be on the National Register of Historic Places as of 12/7/92 by the National Park Service. The major headline of a Baltimore Sun newspaper dated Wednesday, December 6, 1933, read, "Prohibition Ended." The subheadline was, "Lindberg and wife on Atlantic Hop."

Two shiny black motorcycles were parked in front. The riders were asking questions of Ed Weaver, the owner and collector of this tiny but amazing storehouse of history. Ed, 68, told me that when he was in the eighth grade, he saw his first antique car, a 1909 Rio, "That charged me up on antique cars and parts. My first antique car was cranked from the side and kicked like a mule. My father made me sell it because he was afraid I would get hurt."

Through the years, Ed has bought everything from Crosleys and Fiats, to Sunbeams. Licensed to sell, he went into business, repairing and selling mostly off-brands like Singers, Helmers, and Saffires. "I sold off the microcars and the others through the years and I'm glad I did. I still have a 1920 coup with enough parts to get it on the road if I live long enough."

Seemingly docile Patterson Creek poked along its banks and curved around the back of Weaver's home and the old station. It flooded in 1993 and again in 1996. "Water was three feet deep in our house and up into the station as well. We still don't have all the bottom floor of our house renovated. Ed was a painter, then worked for the Rumley Chevrolet Garage for 23 years painting and repairing cars. He retired due to health problems.

"I've always been a pack rat, and always liked history. I used to go to auctions and pick up a whole pick-up load of antiques for ten dollars." He has gone out of business but still has a few model T parts for sale.

Ed inherited the building from his parents who owned the Amoco Station and a repair shop next door from 1929 until 1980. The gas pumps and underground tanks were removed in 1981.

Ed moved some antique pumps he already owned to the station front and then traded around until he found a few more. He furnished the building with what he had collected over the years. He doesn't charge anything to look around. I asked what his hours were and he said he comes over from his house whenever he sees anyone stopping to look. "I can't work any more because of back problems but I enjoy talking with people. They stop here from all over the world." He keeps a guest book.

An old coal stove was in the center of various styles of wooden cases filled with toy peddle cars, fire engines, and farm trucks. Bigger, sit-in type cars, tractors, boats, and scooters were under cabinets. Other cases held vintage tools of every description. Licence plates were tacked on the wall, along with old pictures, antique ads for everything from motor oil to drinks. A floor-base radio, desk, and a Coca-Cola machine were among the bigger antiques. Motor oil cans and other paraphernalia dealing with cars were on high shelves. Taillights were strung on wires overhead. A cowbell hung on a hook on the door back.

It would take days to really see all that was in that very small room. "I'm trying to get my grandkids interested. They'd like to keep it going. My grandson comes over once in a while."

We visitors admired the Model T truck. "It still runs. I used it in local parades until this year. I'll keep this going until they haul me up the hill. I'm not content to sit in the old rockin' chair yet, not as long as I have people stop that I can talk to and break the monotony. "Whether transportation runs with an electric engine or steam, I've always been interested." His business card reads, "Industrial Archeologist."

## *Memorials*

I stood to one side, watching Americans and world visitors make their way quietly and reverently along the wall. Their colorful clothes and solemn faces reflected in the highly polished black granite, broken only by the names grit-blasted into the Vietnam Veterans Memorial in Washington, D. C.

Bright flowers, a newspaper article, POW-MIA bracelets, small flags, and other momentos were propped against the wall. A lady, perhaps a daughter or granddaughter or sister, traced her fingers slowly over the letters of a name, a way of saying "I love you or you aren't forgotten." The 58,191 men and women who are dead or missing are listed in chronological order by date of casualty.

The National Park Service volunteers often do rubbings of a victim's name for the family. Reunions between buddies are held within view of the wall or near the companion statues also on the Mall. On the wall's 10th anniversary, in 1992, volunteers and family members read the names aloud continuously for 24 hours a day, taking nearly 56 hours to read them.

Across the Lincoln Memorial Reflecting Pool from the Vietnam Memorial, is the Korean War Veterans Memorial. The day was cold and somber and brown. The trees wore brush-cuts against the November horizon. We pulled our coats tightly around us against the wind. It could have been such a day for the real soldiers these life-sized statues portrayed. Nineteen soldiers trudge up a hill toward the American flag in their mud-clogged boots, carrying heavy weapons and equipment, looking infinitely exhausted.

An unknown Korean War Veteran said, "We knew that war through our feet...we walked every inch of that country."

Nearby, thanks to modern technology, actual enlarged photographs of soldiers and support people are imposed on a polished granite wall. The NPS guard said, "A few weeks ago, a guy got really excited because he found his own picture on the wall."

The memorial is inscribed, "Our Nation Honors Her Sons and Daughters Who Answered the Call to Defend a Country They Did Not Know and a People They Had Never Met. Korea, 1950 - 1953."

Our family wrote to a number of Viet Nam Veterans and my third oldest, brother, Leo, was one who "knew that war" through his feet. These memorials never fail to move me to tears.

I am often asked, "How do you find unique places?" Simple, you niq up on em! Sorry.

Consider a leap of faith – we're going to jump all the way to Vermont!

# A Taste of Vermont

Vermont was barely into springtime when I turned on US #17 and #22A to SR#7 at Vergennes. Immediately on opening my door at the Kennedy Brothers Factory Marketplace, I found a Canadian five-dollar bill. It was going to be a good day.

The Country Store was enchanting. As a full-time RVer, I was tempted by everything but any purchase would have to "replace" something already in the Sprinter. An old fashioned candy shop with hand-dipped chocolates nearly did me in but I hurried on to pottery, placemats, and potential kitchen gadgets that wouldn't cause me to acquire any more than the 25 pounds I gained just looking at the freshly made fudge. Did you notice how I hurried through that?

Although I have always appreciated antiques, they don't do much for me, and even less now that I live in a motorhome. However, my children both love antiques (It must be an every-other-generation thing) so I dutifully walked through the entire second level of The Antique Center. I admired until I realized how much of that stuff I recognized from my life! I may *be* an antique but I'm not ready to admit it yet.

The Craft Center featured Vermont craftspeople. That impressed me, but The Factory Outlet and Gift Shop got my full attention. This room was bursting with the handcrafted woodenware I love.

The Kennedy Brothers Marketplace is a renovated brick creamery housing over 95 Arts and Crafts and Antique booths plus specialty stores. What a great way to recycle an old building.

The spring scenery encompassed farm animals, sheep, cows, and babies of every species. Distant mountains were on one side and Lake Champlain on the other as I traveled north.

Teddy bears are soft and cuddly and wait patiently under trees for squealing toddlers on Christmas morning. Remembering that, I stopped at the Vermont Teddy Bear Factory. Mike, our tour guide, told about the factory's beginning, faking tears with his touching story. With little reaction, he threw a bear at a visitor and said, "Play with it until your attitude improves." Later he picked on the same good-natured guy again, "Sir, I've had enough out of you. I told you to play with him."

He showed us the hypoallergenic, fire retardant, and washable bear parts, ending with the distended stomach. "These are bodies by Ben and Jerry," referring to the Vermont ice cream makers.

Stuffers stuff the bears with the same stuffing used to stuff life jackets during WWII. Mike displayed a bear head on his fingertip and sang in a little voice, "*I ain't got no body.*" In the assembly room, he said people stayed focused on their work by singing, "*The bear head connected to the bear body, the bear arm connected to....* Workers were relaxed and smiling. He kidded with them and hugged several people in our group, a very lively guide.

"When a bear is born, it is whacked really hard. That puts everything in place and fluffs it up. If the family dog attacks your stuffed bear after you get it home, what do you do? Send it to the Vermont Teddy Bear Hospital." Mike played all the parts of the TV drama, ER, until he had the bear fixed again. "This service is free. The Vermont Teddy Bear is guaranteed to be a friend for life." Between tears, laughter, singing, and dancing, this was the most animated tour I had ever been on.

Jitney transportation is available every 15 minutes during the season, but I walked through Shelburne Museum during their "Limited winter schedule." Described as "An American Sampler," this museum at Shelburne, Vermont, is spread over 45 acres with perennial and herb gardens. I wasn't too early for their lilacs. Mmmm. I do love lilacs.

It's the kind of place to "meander" both the gardens and the art galleries. I didn't go through all 37 exhibit buildings but I gave it my best shot. Guided tours are available and the entrance fee covers two consecutive days.

Vermont historic buildings were dismantled and brought to Shelburne Museum with each piece marked, then put back together again. It now houses 80,000 pieces of Americana.

My only relief from the heat was inside air-conditioned buildings and the Covered Bridge. It was brought from Cambridge, Vermont, the last double-lane covered bridge with a footpath in the state. The Horseshoe Barn and Annex were constructed on site and were filled with horse-drawn carriages, Conestoga wagons, and sleighs. The General Store is 1840s Shelburne, Vermont, and fascinating. It is a barbershop, taproom, and post office, all wrapped up in a Country Store and Apothecary Shop.

The Colchester Reef Lighthouse seemed out of place, but I closed my eyes and pictured myself on stormy Lake Champlain in 1871 while waves hurtled themselves onto the boulders. The Ticonderoga, a National Historic Landmark, and the last vertical beam side-wheel passenger steamboat in America, is permanently berthed nearby. A film shows the engineering feat bringing the 220' steamboat overland two miles from Shelburne Harbor the winter of 1954-55.

Obviously they are working on and improving the museum all the time. I was especially interested in the Grandma Moses and Andrew Wyeth paintings in the Webb Gallery of American Art. Handcrafted weather vanes, cigar store Indians, and ship carvings fascinated me.

It would be much more lively during the season with demonstrations, activities, and theatre going full force and all buildings open. This is definitely a place to visit and would be of interest to all ages. Touch & Learn and Look & Learn symbols identify Learning Stations in exhibit buildings, a great place to take grandchildren. (Rebecca and Will are you listening?) To top all this they had a huge free parking lot – always a plus for RVers.

I cut cross lots east to US #116 and went south on a two-laner through the countryside, eventually connecting with SR #7 again. Stopping beside a creek to let the traffic go by, it started raining. It was a good time to eat lunch and take a nap. My short nap and the rainstorm finished about the same time. I love having my house on my back.

An eightyish charming and talkative couple gave me a no-hookup site for $8 at Elephant Mountain Campground near Bristol.

Vermont has places like the Smugglers' Notch Inn, The Mad River Inn, and The Nutmeg Inn. Magnificent gingerbread houses with cupolas are enough to make you take out even *more* stock in Kodak. I am completely charmed by dilapidated old barns, round ones and rectangular ones, still living with such character by the roadside. I always wanted to buy an old barn, fix it up, and live in it. Maybe if I continue to spend money at this rate, I'll get my wish for two out of three.

Everywhere in New England there is a maple syrup something. This was the New England Maple Syrup Museum at Rutland. I paid $1.50 to walk through the extensive museum, pushing buttons and watching a slide show for the inside scoop on sap to syrup in what they called the "World's Largest Maple Museum." The syrup tasting wasn't bad either. The only way to improve the light, medium, and dark amber syrup tastes, were to have a short stack to eat with them. IHOP where are you?

I was so intrigued with this procedure that I bought "*Making Maple Syrup: A Beginner's Guide.*" The information was for tapping only a couple of trees to where they lost me with, "At this point you have an investment of $20,000." Our family made maple syrup on a limited basis in southwestern Michigan but as with all the interesting stuff our family did, they did it when I was too young to remember. I still am!

The estate near where Jack and I raised our children had a "Sugar Shack." They boiled down the "sweet water" from the maple trees after collecting it in buckets. The trees were tapped in late winter and early spring when the freezing and thawing caused the sap to rise. It isn't any wonder that "real" maple syrup costs an arm and a leg when you realize that a single gallon of syrup requires 30 to 50 gallons of sap.

Of course the process has changed a bit since the settlers were taught by the Indians to drop hot stones into sap-filled hollow logs to boil it down into syrup.

The very helpful museum lady gave me easy directions to two covered bridges. Until she added, "You can't miss them," I thought I had a shot at finding them. They call the 1843 Hammond Covered Bridge, "The Traveling Bridge." It wasn't damaged in its 1½-mile float downstream in the 1927 Otter Creek flood. The 139' bridge was fastened to oil barrels and towed back upstream to its original site. Vermont boasts 114 covered bridges built with roof and walls to protect the wooden trusses from rotting.

As usual when I get lost (I didn't find the other covered bridge), I wound up on very scenic West Proctor Road, that took me all the way to I-4, passing the Wilson Castle. It is a mid-19th Century castle sitting on a 115-acre estate.

with parapets and turrets that would be perfect in a mystery story. It has 84 stained glass windows, 32 rooms, and 13 tile and bronze fireplaces, very little of which I could see from the road. It was closed until late May. Didn't these people know I was coming?

I was near Castleton where I had intended to stop. This just goes to show ya that you cain't always believe the printed word. In the Vermont Green Mountain Guide, I read that Castleton had "The oldest institution of higher learning in the state…plus the site of the one and only engagement of the Civil War on Vermont soil in 1777!!!" That made me wonder about their higher learning.

I ain't as dumb as I look and I got to thinking on how the Civil War that came along in 1861, had a battle in Vermont in 1777. After ponderin' that awhile I realized one o' two things mighta happened. Either they had the fust Civil War battle and it took the secon' one o'er three quarters of a cent'ry to git movin' again or they was referrin' to the Revolutionary War.

Regardless, driving through Castleton was a delight. Their houses had an inordinate amount of columns, archways, and porticoes, due they say to Architect Thomas Reynold Dake, a town resident way back in 1807. And that battle the brochure mentioned, it was a Revolutionary War battle fought on July 7, 1777, when retreating Colonial troops (from Ft. Ticonderoga) fought with British and Hessian troops. There warn't hardly no Hessians in the Civil War no how.

I had to do a little backtracking to find the Vermont Marble Exhibit at Proctor. I drove over a marble bridge to get to it. In the open-air Marble Market, people were discussing marble possibilities for their homes. I didn't think I'd better get into marble for the Sprinter even though they had "marble or granite to fit your budget."

The movie showed how marble formed over 400 million years ago, and the quarrying and producing of raw marble into finished products. The Hall of Presidents displayed life-sized white marble relief busts of all past U.S. presidents. After the Gallery of Modern Sculpture, I watched marble being hand-crafted into custom jewelry. The columns of Washington, D.C.'s Supreme Court building were made from Vermont marble. If you've ever seen those columns, you would be in awe of the talent that sculpted them.

On the second floor, I saw a fellow putting a big marble chunk on a pallet. He had marked on it and was preparing to sculpt. He said he was relatively new at sculpting. A completed angel didn't agree he was new at it. He would have been fun to watch but that might have taken a while.

They had many marble samples from other areas, and mentioned Marble, Colorado. Now that brought back memories. The whole marble quarry and village of Marble, Colorado, was very special, including the only marble dump station I've ever had the honor of using. Marble's marble was used in major buildings throughout the country also

I was actually able to follow a map to the Norman Rockwell Museum at Rutland. The brochure alone is a keepsake with a selection of the most popular Rockwell illustrations. They have 323 Saturday Evening Post Covers including one that showed a three-legged model. A divorce was uppermost on his mind and nobody caught the error. I wandered the entire chronological display of his career.

Norman Rockwell was born in 1894 in New York City and died at the age of 84. In 1939, the Rockwells moved to Arlington, Vermont, where many of his models were neighbors. While he was Art Editor for Boys' Life magazine, he took two illustrations to Saturday Evening Post. The rest is history. He also did illustrations for Look, McCall's and Ladies' Home Journal.

We relate to his paintings because they were "life in general." He did illustrations for novels, short stories and articles, but made twice as much money using his art to sell products as mundane as shaving lotion, wine, and socks. He created movie and war posters, greeting cards, calendars, and stamps. I remember an enormous stack of Saturday Evening Posts that my late husband's grandmother had on her front porch. A Sunday after dinner pastime was going through those old magazines.

For $17, I had a no-hookup night at Camping on the Bettenkill Campground north of Arlington. I continued south on US #7A, turning onto #313. I walked through the West Arlington Covered Bridge (over the Bettenkill River) to see the historic 1792 farmstead where Norman Rockwell lived from 1943 to 1954. It is now the Inn on the Covered Bridge Green. The picturesque church was built in 1804.

Then I turned east, crossed US #7 and up into the Green Mountains hunting for the Daniel Webster Memorial. There weren't any barriers or signs so when it turned into a gravel road, I continued. That lonely forest service road took me up through the trees with a little snow and a few fallen branches here and there but nothing the Sprinter couldn't handle. It was a pretty good road, not too steep or curvy, but the Sprinter brushed a lot of tree branches away from his windows. There was nowhere to turn around and I really wouldn't have relished backing down.

I thought I had missed the Memorial when the road started down the other side. Oh me of little faith. I pulled into a tiny clearing and listened to U. S. Senator Daniel Webster speak to 15,000 people in support of William Henry Harrison for president. (It's my story and I'm going to stick to it.) Back in the 1840s when this event really happened, people came on foot and in wagons, following, I'm sure, the same route I traveled, taking just a mite longer perhaps. The forest may or may not have been there and people may have been living closer, as in all over the mountain that is now national forest. At least they didn't have to worry about clearance.

As I pulled out again, I checked for possible traffic the direction whence I came and saw a sign, "Road Closed for the Winter." Ah well, so they couldn't afford to post signs on both ends. Less than a quarter mile farther, the road turned into a nice paved highway!

I connected with US #100 south to US #9 and west to the Bennington Museum and Grandma Moses Gallery. I had seen Anna Mary Robertson Moses paintings before but now I was in her territory, looking into her life, her paintings, and her memorabilia. I stood in the one-room 1834 schoolhouse that she attended, brought in from Eagle Bridge, New York, and related.

She is an inspiration to anyone but especially to women. She was a farmer's wife and mother and didn't become famous as an artist until 1940 when she was in her 70s! There is hope for me yet. An Edward R. Murrow video interview played while I walked around. How marvelous that I could see both of these special people who are now gone from this life's plane. She was a charming, sprightly, and bright-eyed lady. This nationally and internationally famous American folk artist lived to be 101 and didn't even hit her stride until she was 75. Even at that, she painted over 1500 known works. Wow!

The Bennington Museum housed Military, Church, Furniture, Glass and Pottery Galleries. My special interest beyond Grandma Moses was the Flag Gallery. Nathaniel Fillmore, a veteran of the Revolutionary War and specifically, the Battle of Bennington, presented the Bennington Flag to his nephew after the outbreak of the War of 1812. It is one of the oldest American flags in existence and one of the most unusual with white stripes for the outer bars, rather than red. It has a unique arrangement of seven-pointed stars with the number "76" in the center.

It traveled via time and relatives from Bennington to New York, Illinois, Minnesota, and back to Illinois before it was donated to Vermont's Bennington Museum in 1926. Dirt and dust have been removed and the fragile fibers stabilized. It is now protected within a temperature, humidity, and light controlled Plexiglas box.

A marble sidewalk took me to the Congregational Church. Between it and the Museum, I found Robert Frost's grave. We had a one-sided conversation. I sat in the shaded cemetery with spring flowers blooming and raindrops dotting his flat-topped gravesite. I told him he was one of my favorite poets. He accepted my compliment in grave silence.

On the hill above, the 306' Bennington Monument commemorated the Battle of Bennington, August 16, 1777. Brigadier General John Stark, his American forces, and the Green Mountain Boys, defeated British General John Burgoyne's invading army in their effort to take the Bennington arsenal depot. This British defeat along with their lack of supplies, were major factors in Burgoyne's surrender with his 8,000 troops following the Battle of Saratoga. This battle was the turning point in the American Revolution. The Battle at Bennington was the first time the American Flag was carried into battle.

Going back along US #9, I spent the night in a rest area that was separated from the highway by a tree-covered hill and overlooked the Harriman Reservoir. A Vermont car pulled in with a male driver and an in-arms child. I never heard a peep from that little one throughout the night. They got an early-drizzle start about the same time I did.

I continued east to Hogback Mountain and the 100-mile view, only it was fogged in. This was definitely ski country with nearby Mount Snow and Haystack Mountain.

In the edge of west Brattlesboro, I stopped at an all-night Laundromat. A fellow there said he had left Los Angeles 10 a.m. Friday and just arrived at 7 a.m. that day, Monday. That is roughly 3000 miles in 69 hours. I was glad I hadn't shared the road with him. He was a writer which gave us common ground. In the meantime, a fellow came in and asked to whom the motorhome belonged. When he discovered it was mine, he talked about his experiences RVing with his wife and another couple. He didn't have any laundry to do; he just wanted to talk about RVing. And they say New Englanders aren't friendly.

Brattlesboro was Ft. Dummer when it was established in 1724 on the bank of the Connecticut River that divides the bottom ¾ of Vermont and New Hampshire. It was Vermont's first permanent European settlement. A wee bit north is Dummerston where Rudyard Kipling wrote *Captain Courageous, Just So Stories* and two *Jungle Book* stories.

US #30 northeast was a beautiful route along the West River. A covered bridge was under construction. A worker said, "When it is finished, it will be the longest covered bridge in Vermont." It was a perfect place with the covered bridge and spring bursting its buttons. The rain had temporarily stopped and it was warm, sort of like living in poetry.

First at Newfane, then Townshend, I drove the back streets charmed by the historic buildings, ornate courthouses and churches, sometimes necessitating a turn around when the street petered out. Scott Covered Bridge was closed to traffic and as with most, the Sprinter would have been too big anyway. This 276' three-section bridge built in 1870, has been until now, Vermont's longest bridge. I intersected again with US #100 only going north this time.

At Weston I stepped back in time. The Vermont Country Store's history went back several generations in the same family. It had an old-fashioned candy counter and a vest in the clothing section that I couldn't resist. In the Weston Village Store, established in 1891, I walked on old wooden floors and under a tin ceiling, all the while listening to vintage radio programs. They had unique gifts like weathervanes and stitchery and not just a cheese counter, but the "Vermont Cheese Emporium."

The gas jockey at Ludlow was an inquisitive guy. I suppose he didn't have too many Texas customers. "Where are people the friendliest? Unfriendliest?" "Where have you been? Where are you going? Of all the places you've been, where would you choose to live?" When I could get a word in edgewise, I said the places I would choose to live would number at least 30 and that included right there.

At US #100A, I turned east to Plymouth Notch. The President Coolidge State Historic Site opening was two weeks later. I walked around the buildings following the brochure, reading signs and learning a whole lot about our 30th president that I never knew before. Except for a small official-looking group shaking hands and trying to look dry while having their pictures taken in the rain, I had the place to myself.

On July 4, 1872, Calvin Coolidge was born in the downstairs bedroom of a building attached to the General Store where his father was a storekeeper. He is the only President who was born on the Fourth of July. Did you know that? Also attached to the General Store is a U.S. Post Office still in operation. Above, is a room used by President Coolidge as a Summer White House office in 1924, but I'm getting ahead of myself.

In 1876, the family, including a baby sister, moved across the street to what is now called the Coolidge Homestead. He grew up in this house and vacationed there in his adult years. He was there when as Vice President, he heard of President Warren Harding's sudden death. His father, Colonel Coolidge, as a notary public, administered the presidential oath of office to his son on August 3, 1923, at 2:47 a.m. by the light of a kerosene lamp. At a later time someone asked Colonel Coolidge, "How did you know you could administer the presidential oath to your own son?" He replied, "I didn't know that I couldn't." That seems like perfectly good Vermont logic to me.

The Union Christian Church was built in 1840 and dedicated as a Congregational Church in 1842. Generations of Coolidge family members worshipped there and it is still in use. The Plymouth Cheese Factory, built in 1890 by the President's father and two other farmers, served as a milk outlet for their farms. It closed in the 1930s but in the 1960s, the President's son, John, reopened it. I took advantage of refilling my larder with mild Cheddar cheese and chatting with two rangers from Coolidge State Park. I asked when the campgrounds were opening, "Friday." Oh well.

The cemetery, less than a mile from where he was born, is on a narrow side road marked by a plain green "cemetery" sign. Encompassed by woods, it is on a multi-level, steep hillside. I walked along reading the Coolidge clan names, six generations resting with neighbors and friends. The plain tombstone wouldn't give a clue as to its occupant unless you happened to notice the presidential seal. It has his name, date of birth, and date of death, 1933. I stood there in the soft spring rain, sharing my umbrella with hungry mosquitoes. Tears ran down my cheeks. Why? I don't know. Somehow it seemed appropriate to shed a tear for our 30th president.

I connected with SR #4 and stopped at the Old Mill Marketplace at Bridgewater. I was driving the back street looking for a place to park when a fellow ran over waving his arms. "You don't want to drive that heavy rig through here. We've already roped off where the street fell in. Maybe the rest of it isn't too safe either." I wasn't going to argue with that. I backed up. It was better than digging the Sprinter out of Beijing.

The 1812 woolen mill was converted to a unique shopping center and living museum. I wandered through arts, crafts, antiques, gourmet food, and even a bookstore. They lay claim to having Vermont's largest ski and snowboard warehouse. All the shops were interesting and unfortunately, irresistible. I'm not sure what they're called but I bought a running stick with an elephant head for Will. He wasn't big enough at that time but he is now. With a little imagination, he can ride to all the places that Grandma visits!

I couldn't find my VISA card so I paid cash. I turned the motorhome upside down and shook it but still couldn't find the VISA card. I called the gas station. The talkative gas jockey had found the card. It was 25 miles back to Ludlow. I really hate backtracking but I didn't have a choice. After picking up my VISA, I took a different route, cutting across to SR#131 and 106, most of the time following a river or stream.

I continued on SR #4 to Quechee Gorge. They call it "Vermont's Little Grand Canyon." I admired the gorge from the bridge. I'm not quite sure I'd compare Grand Canyon's 7-9,000' drop to the Colorado River with a 162' drop to the Ottauquechee River but hey, who's counting feet. Quechee Gorge State Park was closed. I turned northwest again on I-89 to the rest area. It was closed from 11 p.m. to 7 a.m. just to prevent people like me from staying I guess. I found that all over New England.

At Sharon I took US #14 to a campground 3.5 miles away. When I got there, a double cow path led down a very steep hill where it looked like the gate was closed. It looked iffy and if I won't do it, you can bet it was iffy. I slept in an empty riverside parking area at Royalton.

US #110 had covered bridges crossing rivers to residences and leading to side roads. I roamed. I went through South and North Tumbridge and just plain Tumbridge. I went through Northfield Center, Northfield Falls, and just plain Northfield. I went north to US #65, then #12. Covered bridges were everywhere and I loved them all. But after a while you stop to see ones where it is really convenient to stop. It's a little like European Cathedrals or Oriental Temples, sooner or later…

I-89 to exit 10 at Waterbury and US #100 led to Ben and Jerry's Ice Cream Factory. Somehow in my love-of-ice-cream life, I had missed Ben and Jerry's marvelous, yummy, ice cream until only a few months previously. The walls had colorful, cheerful farm motifs. I felt they should somehow team up with Gateway 2000 because of all the cows.

My first question of the guide, "Are Ben and Jerry real people?"

"Yes. I've met them. They travel and are at the corporate offices in Burlington more than they are here." As we walked, I learned a lot about Ben Cohen and Jerry Greenfield. The philosophy they live by, "If it's not fun, why do it?" and "Business has a responsibility to give back to the community," sounded like good RVing philosophy to me.

Ben and Jerry met in seventh grade in Long Island, New York. The friendship continued through high school. They separated to go to college in 1969. By 1977 neither had zeroed in on what they wanted to do for a living. Since they both loved eating, they discussed restaurant possibilities, deciding it would more likely succeed if they had a limited menu. After fondue, crepes, kebobs and bagels, they focused on ice cream and took a $5 correspondence course in ice cream making.

They started in a refurbished Burlington gas station and soon people lined up for their delicious homemade ice cream. The rest is a struggling history that has taken Ben & Jerry's, Inc. into all 50 States and internationally.

This 30-minute tour took three of us through the ice-cream-making process. It was a fun tour but the three ice cream flavor examples at the end were best. Then I bought a bowlful as research for this book don'cha know.

Yawl know I'm the serious type, but I did get a kick out of Vermont Cow Pies advertised as "Pure chocolate (no doo-doo)." For $2.35 they promised, "Our Holstein plops are tops." Furthermore, they claimed them to be "udderly delicious." And rather than saying, "Have a nice day," their ad wished me to,

"Heifer good day!" Barnyard humor at its best.

The Sound of Music has always been my favorite story. The one place I intended to visit in Vermont was Stowe. I didn't spend any appreciable amount of time in Stowe itself because on May 12, it was already so busy that I didn't want to wrestle the traffic with the motorhome.

As with most RVers, I have taken up the lifestyle to escape from snow country, but just once I'd love to fly to Stowe for a winter week of moonlight nights, sleigh rides, buffalo-skin lap robes, fur muffs, and open-hearth fireplaces. Preferably, this would be with a tall, dark, handsome, romantic guy who has put a ring on my finger and will love, cherish and adore me for the rest of my life. Ooophs, guess I got carried away there but one has to dream occasionally (and they do perform weddings there on the mountain).

Johannes von Trapp was responsible for designing America's first cross-country ski center in 1968. They offer groomed trails for cross-country skiing (Yes, yes, this could be part of my dream). The Austrian style Trapp Family Lodge setting is against the 2,200 acre Mt. Mansfield State Forest. They have activities year around, maple sugaring, mountain biking, gardening workshops, and rock climbing, you name it. Other pursuits are concerts in the Trapp Meadow, theatre, sing-a-longs, and of course the festivals such as the May Tulip Festival going on while I was there. I understand it is not unusual for family members to make appearances at various activities.

After the family's escape to America and concert tours, in 1942, they built this delightful mountaintop home, now the Trapp Family Lodge. That lodge burned so this is a newer version. The gardens were magnificent with spring flowers blooming and that view, well, I was completely sold. It is just a neat place and people who worked there were friendly. It was one more place that I would return to in a heartbeat.

I returned to US #100 north to US #15 and turned east. I just had to stop at the Fisher Covered Railroad Bridge, built in 1908. In 1968, heavy steel beams were added to the bottom so it could continue to keep railroad cars from falling into the Lamoille River. It is a 103' bridge with a full-length cupola, an escape for steam engine smoke. It is Vermont's last covered railroad bridge still in use, and one of the most unusual covered bridges anywhere. It looked to be in very good condition with a few new boards standing out from the weathered ones.

A nice surprise was a tiny park from which to enjoy it. Two ladies picked something near the bridge. Curiosity prevailed.

"What are you doing?"

"Collecting fiddleheads for local restaurants."

"What are they?"

"The coiled tips of young fern fronds.

Turning south on US #215 took me through pretty country on a winding, hilly road to Cabot Creamery. They closed at 4 p.m. so I had 20 minutes to take the tour. First of all, I love cows. They are such gentle sloe-eyed creatures, although Jack's family had one that would take you out if you got too close. I love following cow paths through meadows. Cows wander aimlessly along streams, between trees, around rocks and eventually find their way back to the barn. Maybe it's because I can relate to them. If you look at my travels through New England, you'll see I've wandered aimlessly, although whether or not I will make it back to the barn is questionable.

I never really gave it any thought before but I have had three Gateway 2000 computers. Maybe in some other life I was a big gentle cow (no comments please) but then again, I can't believe I was part of a herd. But back to Cabot Creamery. This wasn't just any creamery. It is a dairy cooperative owned by 1,800 New England and New York farm families. They handle about 2.5 billion pounds of milk a year.

In 1919, 94 Cabot farmers bought what became the original Cabot Creamery plant. From the cost of $5 per cow, plus one cord of firewood each to fuel the boiler, Cabot and its parent company, Agri-Mark, grew into an $80 million business.

Among Monterey Jack cheese, cottage cheese, sour cream, yogurt, and butter, in the 1998 World's Championship Cheese Contest sponsored by the Wisconsin Cheese Makers Association, Cabot Vermont Cheddar was judged "Best Cheddar in the World." But taste says it all and they had free samples. Yummm. Well, you know I didn't get out of there without a supply of cheese and crackers. They gave me directions to Larry & Son Campground.

Morning found me going east on SR #2 toward New Hampshire. My last stop in Vermont was at St. Johnsbury and the Fairbanks Museum and Planetarium. An information sheet had the Fairbanks Family Lineage listed. It made a point of saying that they were listing only the male offspring of Joseph Fairbanks and their contributions to St. Johnsbury and Vermont. All well and good but how do they think that lineage continued? Women must have been involved somewhere.

Thaddeus Fairbanks, the son of patriarch Joseph, invented in 1830, an accurate weighing machine, the platform scale. This launched a global industry and put St. Johnsbury on the map. In 1889, nephew Franklin Fairbanks, who had a keen interest in the natural world all his life, founded the Franklin Museum and Planetarium to display the collections he had been preserving for years.

In the 1850s, just one of Franklin's many interests was gathering weather data. He kept concise records at his family home, Underclyffe. This represents the longest continuous account of daily weather patterns in the country. When the Fairbanks Museum opened in 1891, Franklin continued his work and in 1894, set up an observation station at the Museum and began to share his weather information with the National Weather Service Bureau archives. This same information station, more up-to-date, continues to gather basic, observable data.

After an alliance with Lyndon State College and its worldwide computer and satellite weather data service, the Northern New England Weather Center, located at the Museum, has a listener base of over three million people.

In the Civil War exhibit were Willie Johnston's drumsticks. He joined the

Civil War as a drummer. Willie, with the Third Vermont Regiment, joined General George McClellan's Peninsular Campaign. During a weeklong series of battles known as the "Seven Days," the Third Vermont Regiment experienced some of the heaviest fighting against the Confederates. During the retreat to Harrison's Landing, exhausted troops threw everything away that could hinder their retreat.

When the Vermonters reorganized under General William F. Smith, Willie Johnston was the only drummer left with equipment. He was given the honor of drumming for the division parade. On September 16, 1863, as a tribute to his courage, Willie was one of the first Americans to be awarded the Congressional Medal of Honor. He was thirteen. Nothing more is known about young Willie.

New Hampshire called to me. I was far enough north to see signs, "Moose crossing next four miles." After seeing that I kept looking for them...in vain. It's just like seeing the first mushroom of the season; you walk along with your nose to the ground hoping to see another.

"Watch for landslides" wasn't encouraging. I saw squeejawed cupola-topped barns still being used. These were a little like our bodies I guess, still being used but getting a little squeejawed.

Our family had crossed from Burlington, Vermont, to Lancaster, New Hampshire, many years before. Continuing east on SR # 2 into New Hampshire, I was retreading. Now I want you to "train" your thoughts on the next chapter.

**The Little Cog Train that Could**

# *New Hampshire, a Granite State*

South on SR #116 through the Easton Valley, I connected with I-93. At this point I'll explain that I did not yet have material on New Hampshire. Yes, in my "How-to" books I recommend getting material and making plans before you arrive. I write this, I do not always do this. I get lots of surprises but this is not a bad thing, it's just surprising, thus...

Suddenly I was on the Franconia Notch Parkway going through Franconia Notch State Park extending from the north at Echo Lake, eight miles south to the Flume Gorge. I could not figure why an Interstate highway went from major four lane down to two lane, then back to four lane as it made its way through a really spectacular mountain pass between Kinsman and Franconia mountain ranges. This was all explained in the Visitor Center movie.

As a starter, in New Hampshire, all mountain passes are referred to as "notches." The road was dangerous originally but the locals and environmentalists didn't want a big four-lane extravaganza ruining this beautiful area. Their concession was to build I-93 with two lanes where it compromised natural beauty. Off ramps were built accommodating stops for campgrounds, lakes, and special activities such as the Cannon Mountain Tram II, Ski Museum, and the Flume Visitor Center.

What I discovered with a little frustration was that you could get off but you couldn't necessarily get back on at the same place. It took a few trips back and forth to learn the system. The speed is 45 mph all through the Notch, great for me.

In this region you hear about four things almost immediately, the Kancamagus Highway, Mt. Washington and the Cog Railway, Franconia Flume Gorge, and the "Old Man of the Mountain," who represents New Hampshire.

Hanging 1,200' above Profile Lake, this chiseled-looking 40' Old Man of the Mountain profile is made up of natural boulder rock layers that formed about 200 million years ago. Profile Lake, the headwaters of the Pemigewasset River, is known as The Old Man's Wash Bowl.

Indian legend has it that Chief Pemigewasset, awaited the return of his Mohawk wife, Minerva, from visiting her dying father. He stayed the winter in a clifftop shelter watching for her. In the spring his braves found only a pile of bones. As they returned to their tribe, they looked up and saw Chief Pemigewasset's face molded into the cliff peak.

The Old Man of the Mountain and I nodded to each other as I drove south to a gas station. Others were also impressed with this mountain profile. Daniel Webster wrote about it and Nathaniel Hawthorne wrote, "Great Stone Face."

The gas pump cut my credit card off at $35. It also didn't give me a receipt. I was not a happy camper. I had experienced having the credit card cut off at $50 but never at $35! While I was keeping my cool because I knew this poor clerk had nothing to do with the problem, he explained that the company could shut off credit wherever they wanted to. He gave me a receipt. Since I was already complaining, I expounded on the area's lack of campground facilities for early visitors.

"Do you need hookups?"

"No, I just need a place to park."

"If you wouldn't mind, you can park in back."

"Are you sure that would be all right?"

"I'm the manager. I can give you permission."

Then I felt bad about griping so after I parked, I went in and bought a few groceries and spoke briefly with the manager again. He and his wife and son had briefly lived in El Paso, Texas. His wife was born in Maine but he said New Hampshire didn't have income or state sales tax so they settled there.

"I'm retired and I want to buy a motorhome and do what you're doing." I refrained from telling him to get with it because none of us are getting any younger. He was so nice and I felt so guilty at my impatience (See, that's where being nice all the time is an advantage), I went out to find one of my books.

I saw "Harry" written on his shirt. He looked a little puzzled when I asked his wife's name.

"Edna."

My *RVing Full-time: How to Make it Happen* was autographed to Edna and Harry, saying one kindness deserved another. He looked at it and said, "Oh, wow." He was already flipping through its pages when I went out, closed the curtains and read all evening.

I was up and moving by 5:30 so as not to impede delivery-truck progress or other business. I walked around the Flume Visitor Center circumventing the unbelievably late 9 a.m. opening and a locked turnstile. If I'm hiking, I want to do it before half the day is over. I found the bike path and a side trail to the gorge.

The first interesting thing I found was the Flume Covered Bridge built over the Pemigewasset River in the 1800s. Pemigewasset means "swift or rapid current" in the Abnacki Indian Language, and they knew of which they spoke. Trail signs explained the natural features. Table Rock, a huge smooth rock forms a bed for Flume Brook to cascade over. It isn't deep but goes over the edge and down to meet the river above the

Flume Covered Bridge. At first I thought that area was The Flume, nope.

The boardwalk and stairs led into a natural 800' gorge. The chasm had 12' - 20' wide walls allowing a close view of ferns, flowers, and mosses growing on the Conway granite rising nearly straight up to a height of 70' - 90'.

Just imagine that this magnificent natural wonder discovered way back in 1808 when 93-year-old Jess Guernsey went fishing. Nobody believed her story but time took others there, confirming her find. When "Aunt" Jess, as she was called locally, found The Flume, there was an enormous egg-shaped boulder suspended between the walls. A mountain rainstorm in 1883, known as, "The Great Shower in the Mountains," dislodged the boulder via landslide, forever changing The Flume's configuration, and adding two waterfalls. That's what you call a really moving experience!

I won't go into how The Flume was formed at the base of Mt. Liberty; you have to have some reason to go there other than the scenic value. It stands to reason, however, that erosion had a whole lot to do with it. The various types of layers are labeled as you walk through. A small section of boardwalk is wet with spray from Avalanche Falls but that way you are again, very close to what is around you.

The elevation sign at the top said I had reached 1,600'. I sat on a boulder overlooking Avalanche Falls and down into "The Flume." It was remarkable but even more remarkable that I had just climbed it!

Trees surrounded everything in New Hampshire and they were wearing fresh green leaves. Flowers were blooming. I especially noted the trilliums because they are favorites of mine. Pemigewasset Mountain was in the distance. The sun was up but hadn't quite penetrated the trees. I would say it was peaceful and quiet but quiet wasn't an honest description sitting on top of the roaring Flume.

Continuing the loop trail away from the falls, birds chirped but birds weren't the only ones out and about. Just above Liberty Gorge and its fast-rushing cascades, I went around a corner and found myself nose to nose with a yearling moose. We both froze in our tracks.

Since moose have a reputation for being easily antagonized, their attacks are at least as dangerous as bears, and it is the better part of valor to ask their permission to pass, I let her make the first move. Granted she was not a full-grown moose but have you seen a yearling lately? She was a big hummer! We eyed each other for what seemed like an eternity, then she went back the direction whence she came. I was able to breathe normally again after only a few hours.

No way would I have wanted to be any closer but it was quite a thrill. I get goosebumps just thinking about it. She probably asked her Mom later in the day. "Mama, why is it that we stay away from humans? That lady was just a tiny thing compared to me and she was so scared her hair turned white."

By this time I was back to the Pemigewasset River, a bit north of where I had crossed before. In September of 1938, a hurricane successfully extracted a 175' giant pine called Sentinel Pine from the forest ground. It fell into the gorge. A year later, with the help of mules, blocks, tackles, and lots of manpower, it was wenched up and across the river chasm, forming a base for the Sentinel Pine Bridge. The view off both sides of this covered footbridge is great. The south view is of the cascading river diving into The Pool, a 40' deep basin.

After viewing The Pool from several locations, I returned to the Visitor Center. Along the wide, well-graded gravel Wildwood Path, were several rain shelters and lots of inviting benches where one could sit and contemplate nature. They were freshly painted but with all those boulders, I always had something to rest on.

I returned to the Sprinter about 8:30 and wrote a short story about hiking The Flume. I went into the Visitor Center a little reluctant to confess I had bypassed the turnstile and hiked The Flume at 6 a.m. without paying. They didn't seem particularly perturbed. The single lady who was so curious about my lifestyle, said a lot of people do that but they never come in to pay afterward. They wouldn't let me pay but wanted to read the story I wrote. I watched the movie and later while I was snacking, the ranger, Bill O'Connor, came in to visit.

"We were curious. How did you get this written up so quickly?"

"My motorhome is my office and it's solar powered." He asked who I worked for and about my travels.

"My wife and I have a 20' motorhome and have traveled across country three times in the spring and fall when I have had time off. We'd like to do what you're doing some day...or a degree of it."

Later in the day at the Lincoln Information Center I was looking through information and a couple walked in. He waved at me. I said hello and wondered who they were. They came over and she said, "She doesn't recognize you." That's when I realized it was Harry, the station manager from the night before. He wasn't in a white shirt and tie and I didn't recognize him. He introduced me to his Edna. She said, "I've already read a lot of the book and love it!" That's always good to hear.

"We were driving around and Harry said, 'That's Charlie's rig.'"

Harry said, "You can come and stay there anytime you want to."

"I came to see Harry last night and he said he had something to show me. It was your motorhome. My son and I came over to look at it but you had the curtains closed and we didn't want to disturb you."

"I wish you had. I wouldn't have minded a bit. I was reading a Mary Higgins Clark book and couldn't put it down." We discovered we were reading the same book. Small world.

As a writer who uses the dictionary a whole bunch, I figured it was only fitting to visit the two-room house where Daniel Webster was born in 1782. You guessed it, the Franklin Chamber of Commerce confirmed it wasn't open until late June.

This knowledge changed my route to SR #175 through the countryside to US #3, SRs #11, 28, and 109 around Lake

Winnipesaukee. This is New Hampshire's largest freshwater lake with a 283-mile shoreline following its many bays and deep coves. It is another gift left behind by the Pleistocene ice sheet.

**He looks pretty good for almost 14 years, doesn't he?**

I stopped at Weirs Beach to bask in the "Smile of the Great Spirit" as the lake's name is thought to mean. During the season, various cruises are available. There are 274 islands and boucoup vistas from which I could view them as I traveled above this major resort area. All this with an Ossipee and Sandwich Mountain backdrop.

On the southeastern shore of Lake Winnipesaukee is Wolfeboro, the oldest American summer resort. To the northwest is Squam Lake. A sign informed me *On Golden Pond* was filmed there.

I turned north on SR #16 until I came to the Davis Family Campground and no hook-up camping ($15). The screens were covered with Alaska-sized mosquitoes and I really didn't want to go out. I was parked in a nice grove of trees with no lights except the moon and I could hear the stream through the trees. Ah yes.

Mail retrieval took me up through Pinkham Notch to Gorham and back into the White Mountain National Forest. Pinkham Notch was named after Joseph Pinkham. In 1790, Joseph and his followers carved a rough road through the wilderness mountain country to build a new home. Legend has it that he transported his possessions via a pig-drawn sled. It took me about an hour to drive SR #16 to Gorham following his trail. I wonder how long it took him. Boggles the mind doesn't it?

Each Notch has its share of stories, some happy, some tragic. Willey Mountain is named after Samuel Willey, Jr., his wife and five children. With many landslides in the area, they built a cave-like shelter above the inn their family operated in the heart of Crawford Notch, a place they felt they could go for safety.

In August of 1826, a violent storm hit the mountains. The parent's bodies, two Willey children, and two hired men were found nearby, probably on their way to the shelter. The slide split and the house was left untouched. Three children were never found.

The Notch itself was discovered in 1771 by Timothy Nash while he was tracking a moose. He found his way through the notch and on to

Portsmouth to tell the governor of his find. The Governor said he would grant Nash a large parcel of notch land if he could get a horse through it from Lancaster, and build a road to it from the east.

Nash, a friend, and a good-natured farm horse they pulled over the boulders with ropes and ingenuity, made it through the notch. The governor kept his word and the trail through Crawford Notch was opened in 1775. It kinda oughta seems like it shoulda been called Nash Notch.

I backtracked down to the Kancamagus Highway. I really didn't mind all the backtracking because it looks different going the opposite direction and SR #16 north from Glen is a designated Scenic Byway. I was in hog heaven with all the mountain scenery. At the Saco Ranger District Information Center they not only filled me in on the Kancamagus Highway (SR #112), but also some needed information about Maine.

It takes a long time to build a road in New Hampshire but when they get it done, it is worthy, at least that's so with the Kancamagus. In 1837, it started as a town road in Passaconaway. A 122 years later, it was extended eastward to Conway and westward to Lincoln. I'll just bet it started even earlier as an Indian path considering their known history begins with Chief Passaconaway in 1627. He was a peace-loving chief who united 17 Indian tribes of Central New England into the Panacook Confederacy.

This two-lane blacktop highway is named after his grandson, Kancamagus, The Fearless One. He attempted to keep peace among the Indians and the pioneers. Due to English interference, this turned to war and bloodshed. Around 1691 Kancamagus and his followers moved north. I finally got a handle on pronouncing it. It's Kan-kuh-MOG-us.

Moving back into the White Mountain National Forest, I followed the Swift River past the Covered Bridge and Blackberry Crossing NF Campgrounds. For a late Friday, the traffic was light, giving me plenty of time and space to gawk at the Rocky Gorge Scenic Area and 3,000'+ mountains.

I settled in at Jigger Johnson Campground. I thought I had it all to myself until I heard a radio's loud base beat. No way did I want to listen to that in the midst of a forest. I moved to the other side of the campground. Nearby is the Passaconaway Historic Site and Visitor Center in the Russell-Colbath Homestead. Austin George built it in 1832. During the season costumed docents fill you in on unusual stories. One is that in 1891 Mr. Colbath told his wife he would be back soon. She placed a lit lantern in the window for the next 39 years. When he finally came home, she had been dead for three years.

I was up and out by 7 a.m. I like being out early but today I had a special reason, to hike to Sabbaday Falls while it was cool. The story is that these 25' falls were discovered by early explorers while looking for a mountain pass on the Sabbath.

The sound of rushing water is always soothing unless you are in it, in which case you are too intimately involved to be soothed. It was a series of cascades plunging down through a narrow flume. Rock

Potholes evidenced bigger falls once upon a time. Cushy-looking moss grew on roots and rocks. Trees of all sizes ingratiated themselves to boulders in a "help me help me" attitude as they leaned precariously over the rushing stream. Their thick tentacle-like roots traveled many feet across those rocks to find nourishing soil.

The morning mist was fast disappearing with the rising sun. I parked at an overlook. Birds were singing. A stream cascaded somewhere below me. I found myself a boulder seat to listen and feel. Something was moving in the woods. Big animals abide here, including mosquitoes. I experimented with someone's suggestion of stuffing fabric softener sheets in my headband to keep them away. I didn't have any mosquitoes but maybe they weren't flying that high or maybe they already had their fill of sugar.

It was nice parked in the overlook corner, out of the way, not that anyone was moving yet. Mountains were blue in the morning haze. The spring leaf fairy hadn't visited the hard woods yet. I opened the window to the cool air while I ate breakfast. I figured the loon on the pond a mile down the road was eating his breakfast, too.

I drove slowly when there was no traffic and let them by when there was. At the top of 2,855' Kancamagus Pass, 4,000'+ mountains were all around me. The Kancamagus Highway is only 34 miles long so I ambled down the other side of the mountain and was soon following the East Branch of the Pemigewasset River to connect with I-93 at Lincoln. I had come full circle. There were lots of campgrounds, hiking trails, and other stopping spots. It must be even more spectacular in autumn color.

I continued across I-93 on SR #112 and up through Kinsman Notch with Mt. Moosilauke, 4,810' and Mt. Kinsman, 1,814' on either side, headed for Lost River Reservation. Not too many States claim to have lost a river. Discovered by the Jackman brothers in 1852, in the usual way kids discover things, one of them fell 15' into a cave. They explored the one-half mile ravine where the Lost River plays hide and seek with the sunshine. Eventually one brother, Royal, blazed a trail and gave guided tours.

Informational signs were good, especially about the creatures, wiggly red efts, toads, frogs, bears, deer, and moose. Newts to efts, water to land, and back again when they want to reproduce. The sign ended, "Is one watching you now?"

Families explained to children what was happening or what they were seeing. Big tooth aspen, red maples, mountain maples, paper birch, balsam fir, red spruce trees were all in attendance. Water coming from who knows where trickled under a convenient bridge. It came through tree roots and rocks bent on starting a new gorge. A tiny baby fretted in a backpack, probably too small and too bug-bothered to be here but in order for the others to learn, he was here too.

It was a warm day but coolness won out as I descended 300 vertical feet into the gorge via a boardwalk and steps. Gorge view platforms let me see what I was getting into and it looked fascinating.

This unique gorge came about thanks again to that ice sheet mentioned in conjunction with about everything natural in New Hampshire. "They" say the melting northern glacial water with its pebbles, sand, and silt, poured through the notch for a short few 100 years, causing erosion of the Lost River Gorge. When the ice melted far enough to the northwest, the meltwater began to go a different direction, leaving only the small brook that flows through the gorge today. Speculation is that the spring and fall frosts widened joint cracks and forced blocks off the cliff face and into the gorge bottom. In their chaotic tumbling, caves were created.

I walked boardwalks, climbed ladders, crossed bridges, and hung on to handrails designed to withstand 1,000s of visitors, flash floods, and winter snows. Paradise Falls drops 35' into an irregularly-shaped granite pothole. It has done this forever and will forever, always changing yet staying the same. High above the gorge, white clouds roamed and a breeze stirred the treetops. Stairways narrowed to accommodate going between boulders. On shady sides snow hid behind boulders on May 15.

I went down two levels inside the Devil's Kitchen. It sounds like a big bowling kettle under there. Going into the Cave of Silence felt like going into a deep freeze. I ducked down and stayed low. It is the only case where you cannot see or hear the stream. "Closed due to high water" signs covered some cave entrances.

At Parallel Rocks, I went down a ladder between two granite slabs. To get out again, I had to climb down a ladder to a platform, pass through a small opening, walk over some small rocks, crawl through another hole and climb the ladder back to the platform.

The Giant Pothole is 60' high and 28' wide, possibly the tallest granite pothole in the U.S. I passed on the Lemon Squeezer (originally called "Fat Man's Misery"). Not only did I not want to be embarrassed by being caught in the Squeezer Gauge to make sure I could fit in the cave, but I had no desire to go feet first into a pit or negotiate the Lemon Squeezer by going head first. Then you have to crawl along the boardwalk and crawl up over a rock, or you can choose to go in the Lemon Squeezer Pit, another difficult cave.

Guides Scott and Beth were stationed nearby to answer questions or help people out of the cave.

"How often do people get stuck?"

"About once a year I have to go down and encourage someone in backing out."

I was tempted with the waterfall and pool, but I skipped The Dungeon for much the same reasons as the Lemon Squeezer, doing the stomach crawl to get inside.

Other interesting formations included the Triphammer, the Hall of Ships, and of course, the Guillotine. The plants and trees, explained on informational signs, were very interesting. It is a bird-watchers paradise, too. The Lost River Reservation has a mixture of "northern" and "southern" in both plants and birds. The last stop before coming out of the gorge is Look Off Point. The riverbed was 48' below me. In the distance were Kinsman Ridge, Mt. Tripyramid, Mt. Osceola and Mt. Tecumseh.

Lost River Covered Bridge took me through the Nature Garden and eventually to the main building where I pigged out on chocolate milk and a cookie, enjoying the terrace and the view. I would encourage anyone to stop there if you have no problem with ladders. Wear sturdy shoes and old clothes, especially if you intend to wallow through the caves on your belly.

I awakened to a beautiful Sunday in a Zeeland National Forest campsite but it was raining by the time I got to the Mt. Washington Cog Railway.

The wife of a couple ahead of me decided the train trip would exacerbate a back problem so she stayed behind. When I got on the train, the husband graciously consented to my sitting with him. Chuck and his wife were from Cleveland, Ohio. They had been married 54 years and were taking several weeks traveliing this part of the country. He was as curious about my lifestyle as I was theirs.

When they said this train would take us to the top of New England, they weren't kidding. Mt. Washington at 6,288' is only a little shorter than the highest mountain east of the Mississippi, North Carolina's Mt. Mitchell at 6,684'.

They said it was steep. They weren't kidding about that either but I didn't realize it would be that steep! It is one of those feats they said couldn't be done. When you think about it, some pretty amazing things were done back in the days when they didn't have as much to work with. They certainly didn't have the technology. What they had was an "I know I can make it work" attitude and they did.

Think about what has been accomplished in your lifetime alone, and then go back to 1869. In those days they only had man and beast power, the water wheel, and the steam engine. In the same year this was built, the golden spike linked east to west at Promontory, Utah, with the first transcontinental railroad. Railroading was young but it was moving!

However, like anything new, Sylvester Marsh who was pursuing this amazing enterprise, was nearly laughed out of the New Hampshire State Legislature with his idea. They told him he might as well take a train to the moon. He only wanted to go three miles up a steep mountainside. A 100 years later Neil Armstrong did land on the moon. Thankfully some people believe in the impossible!

This was the world's first mountain climbing cog railway, and the second steepest railway track in the world, only surpassed by one in Switzerland. It is still the only one powered entirely by steam. Cog railway personnel create all the engine parts.

The thing you are the most aware of is how steep the track really is. When you sit in the cars, you are forced back against the seat. The little engine sits level which means the back end is high off the track while the boiler looks like it skids its nose along the track. The passenger car is pushed via a bumper. The engine and car are not fastened together so that the passenger car can independently brake during its stops and descent. I'm not sure if that was a comfort or not.

Our first stop was at Waumbek Tank on Coldspring Hill where the engine's water supply was replenished. It looked like we were going over the horizon to that great railroad station in the sky, then another section of track appeared.

It took Ethan Allen Crawford a little longer than an 1½ hours to make his way to the top of Mt. Washington in 1820. While his paths are long since gone, the steep rocky crag where he carved his initials is still there. He named it "Jacob's Ladder."

While the track rises 1,320' per mile with an average track grade of 25%, the steepest grade at Jacob's Ladder climbs over a 300' curving trestle at 37%. This trestle is 25' above the ground at its maximum height. The train climbs 37' up for every 100' it moves forward. As Chuck and I were sitting in the front of the car, the people sitting in the back of the same car were 14' feet below us!

Heights and steepness didn't really bother me but let me tell you that as safe as I knew it had to be, that trestle looked mighty iffy. The brakes were noisy but who is going to argue with noisy brakes at that angle, right? Going through clouds was eerie but we knew the train knew where to go (we hoped).

Sixty thousand hikers climb Mt. Washington each year. You can see the Lake-of-the-clouds Appalachian Mountain Club hut where the Appalachian Trail crosses the mountain just above Jacob's Ladder. Rock cairns mark the trails above timberline, especially helpful in stormy weather or fog. Though the time went fast, as people got acquainted, more than one piped up with, "Are we there yet?" At last we arrived at the summit, now Mount Washington State Park.

We went from forested mountainside to grotesque stubby thickets, then beyond the timberline to grass and rocks. On a clear day, you can see three States, Canada, and possibly even the Atlantic Ocean, 70 miles away. If it's foggy, you at least know you are standing on one of the Presidential Range peaks.

The other big difference was going from full-bloom spring with fiddleheads and flowers growing alongside the track, to snow in the mountain crevasses. With only a 20-minute stop, we boogied to see everything.

The concrete and steel Sherman Adams Summit Building houses the Mount Washington Observatory, Museum and Shop. Since 1932, weather has been observed and researched in this place that holds title to the highest windspeed ever recorded on Earth, 231 miles per hour on April 12, 1934.

They claim that some of the world's worst weather occurs on Mt.

Washington's Summit, a confluence of three major continental storm tracts. Here where hurricane wind forces occur on two out of every three days, temperatures can change drastically in a matter of minutes. Permafrost containing ice from the last glacial period extends 200' below the summit surface. No wonder they limited our stay to 20 minutes.

By the time we boarded for our return trip, the seats had been turned around. Ethan said it would take us 45 minutes to go down, although the record was approximately two minutes and 45 seconds. That was on a 3' X 1' slideboard called a "Devil's Shingle" that maintenance men used to inspect the tracks. This was discontinued in 1906 after an employee was killed and another injured.

When we got off, we went out to meet Chuck's wife who was writing letters in their van. She may have embarrassed him a little by bragging on the way women were always after him to fix something. We chatted a couple of minutes and said our goodbyes. I have heard from them a couple of times since.

I watched the cog train fill with passengers and head topside again. It was a living museum with a mournful whistle that told of a "journey through time." I watched it wind its way out of sight. The little steam train that could was going up the mountainside into the middle of a cloud.

I connected with US #3 north, crossing back into Vermont and north on SR #102. After passing a few more covered bridges, and being within 10 miles of Canada, I turned east into New Hampshire on SR #26 through Dixville Notch State Park. I didn't stop anywhere but I saw some fantastic scenery through one of the most dramatic mountain passes I had been through yet. I passed into Maine on SR #16 with at least five New Hampshire Notches added to my belt.

All of a sudden I went over a hill and there it was, just for me, the prettiest mowed campground right on a river, Aziscoos Valley Camping Area. Full hook-ups were $12.50; no hook-ups were $8.50.

The mosquitoes were horrible but then it was late enough I didn't need to get out. It was a magnificent grassy spot overlooking the water, and a perfect place from which to launch my third trip into Maine.

# Magnificent Maine

Yes!!! A magnificent day in magnificent Maine. I didn't want to leave too early and waste that beautiful river spot. I worked until about 9:30, then made the mistake of going outside to visit the state-owned covered bridge over the same Magalloway River that helped me sleep through the night. Out of the original 120 Maine covered bridges, only eight remain. When I came back in, the mosquitoes came with, to share my orange juice. Muriel and Norman Littlehale, the campground owners, warned me about moose but I didn't see any until late afternoon.

It was a great day for traveling through the Rangeley Lakes Region. Maine has a lot of *big* lakes! I wound around the southern end of Aziscohos Lake, and the northern end of Umbagog, Richardson, Mooselookmeguntic and Rangeley Lakes, before I reached the first big town. Rangeley was my kind of big town; the population was around 1,100. I wouldn't want to be in a spelling/pronunciation class in this area.

Fishing ranges right up there in the same category with touring major cities as something I am interested in doing, but just in case a fisher "person" is reading this...this area is "famous" for trout and landlocked salmon fishing.

I let someone else cook breakfast. It was a great one for $3.58, two eggs, hash browns, *homemade* thick toast smothered in butter, and coffee. With that kind of breakfast under my belt, I felt like a logger, an occupation on top of the list in this country. I hoped for a little conversation and that's just what I got, very little.

Still, people were helpful, coming into the street to point out the grocery or post office. It was a town where I'd like to wrinkle my nose and for a Bubble in Time, have a tiny main street house with a picket fence, blooming flowers and a porch swing from which to watch the world go by. I listened to the locals kibitz while I mailed books and bought groceries. Although they didn't notice, I was a part of their lives for a few minutes.

SR #16 made a big curve north to the Bigelow Preserve and Flagstaff Lake. I made a southern curve on SRs #4 and #142 to US #201, crossing the Appalachian Trail twice. At Kingfield the Stanley Steamer Automobile Museum was closed. The 4,150' Bigelow Mountain, part of the Bigelow Range, was to my left as I headed north along the Kennebec River. The Kennebec, if I had jumped on it going south, would have taken me all the way to the Atlantic Ocean.

In my third life I want to continue north into the Allagash Wilderness with my four-wheel drive RV, or better yet, go to the top of the state and kayak down through it. Driving would take a lot of permission, as the roads are private with locked gates. The Waterway is a 92-mile lake and river corridor connecting large public reserved land units surrounded by a privately owned, vast commercial forest. I think I was meant to be an eastern Jeremiah Johnson.

Not everyone would choose traveling this isolated Maine backcountry but I wanted to see Moosehead Lake. I turned east on SRs #6 and #15 and got my wish. Rockwood was filled with fishing people in pickups and baseball caps. Rockwood is *the* place to at least view Mt. Kineo if you aren't taking a boat across to hike it, which I wasn't. It sounds like quite a dramatic hike to the top. It is Moosehead Lake's major landmark, rising 800' out of the water, and possibly going below the surface as far as 300'. This cliff contains the world's largest amassment of hornblende. It has such a flintlike hardness it was used by the Indians to make implements and weapons.

I continued through Moosehead to Greenville at the end of the lake. This was still May. Very little was open to explore the lake short of canoe rental. I didn't cotton to going alone into heap big water where instant weather changes can leave you stranded or upended.

The S/S Katahdin, fondly referred to as "Kate," a restored 1914 lake steamboat, provides various cruises. Steamboats were the main transportation until roads were developed to Moosehead Lake. The Katahdin was active until 1975 as a pulpwood-hauling towboat. In 1985, after being restored, she once again became useful for tours combined with education, as the mobile Moosehead Marine Museum. Being so close to the Canadian border, Greenville (pop-1600) even has an international airport.

I snapped a picture and talked with a lady while her husband was buying pizza. She told me about free boondocking five miles away. Squaw Brook Campsite was state maintained but "landowners providing public access" was by the S. D. Warren Northeast Timberlands people. It was across from 3,267' Big Squaw Mountain where the first United States firetower was built in 1905.

Mosquitoes were thick. My acquaintance in Greenville said, "They just came out. It won't be so bad in another two weeks." So much for being an eastern Jeremiah Johnson. Actually the mosquitoes did me a favor, they forced me to stay inside and take care of the mail I had picked up earlier.

Several units were parked there but from observation, I surmised they were all empty. When I finally turned the lights out, I realized I wasn't alone. A faint light glowed in the end unit. It was very quiet, very dark, and after spraying for mosquitoes, I slept like a log. The next thing I knew it was daylight.

During the nine-mile ride along Moosehead Lake's eastern shoreline to Lily Bay State Park, I stopped on Blair Hill. It overlooks Moosehead Lake all the way to Mt. Kineo. I'm not sure if Lily Bay was open but its gates were and men were working. I questioned a fellow who drove up to the office for information just as I did.

"Hi. Are you by any chance from Maine?"

"No, I'm from Massachusetts but I come up fairly often."

"Do you know anything about Baxter State Park and whether I can drive through it with the motorhome? I've heard conflicting reports."

"I know there are restrictions but I don't know what they are. You should definitely go up that direction though, it's really pretty."

He was kind enough to look in his car for some Internet information but he didn't have it with him. After talking a few minutes, we exchanged business cards and he said if I was ever down in that area to stop. He was a Drug Prevention Safety Officer with the Ipswich, Massachusetts, Police Department.

Park maintenance men with chain saws were cleaning up the horrendous mess from the January ice storm that had "steamrolled" across New England, leaving widespread power outages and extensive tree damage I had seen along the way.

I was determined to reach Baxter State Park and walk the last bit of the Appalachian Trail at Mt. Katahdin. It was not to be. After stopping at a ranger station in town, the official word was, "Narrow roads prohibit travel with large trailers." They further stated that meant "any vehicle over nine feet high, seven feet wide, or 22' long." My next best shot was to fly over it. At Currier's Flying Service, I found a flight over Moosehead Lake that would take me within a pebble throw of Baxter State Park and Mt. Katahdin.

The trip was normally $55 per person but this early with no one else going, it was double. I could understand that and agreed. I rather liked the idea of having a personal guide and be able to ask questions without interruption. The problem was that her husband, the pilot, was involved in shooting a movie with Paul Newman about three hours from Greenville and he wasn't sure when he would be back. I offered to pay triple to go on the shoot with him but alas…

Moosehead Family Campground called to me. It wasn't on the lake, which would have been my preference, but it was in a blooming apple orchard and I had it mostly to myself. In the morning we got into a lengthy discussion about the area, business, and family, discovering we both had daughters in Virginia. Before my grandson was born, Tracey had sonograms at the Roanoke hospital where his daughter worked. Small world.

Being in Maine is a little like being in northern Canada and Alaska, flying to your destination is not unusual. Currier flies people pretty much wherever they want to go, and everywhere the brochure mentioned, I wanted to go, the Allagash Wilderness, Mt. Kineo, Rainbow Lake. They even take you, plus gear, and set you down where you can take off canoeing. Yes!! I must go back.

Roger Currier was tall, lanky, and very much at ease with flying. The first thing he said was, "Are you sure you want to do this? We could be lost for days."

"I have lots of time."

He winked at the girl, "We'll be back in three or four days."

"Be careful to whom you're talking. As far as I'm concerned that would be another adventure to write about." I didn't exactly want to crash in the wilderness but the prospect of being lost for several days sounded like fun, and also quite unlikely given Roger's knowledge of flying and Maine.

He walked the 1964 Cessna 180 to the end of the pier. We climbed aboard and with an initial push, we were off into a beautiful flying weather with only an occasional bump. I love flying and as I write this, it takes me back to how excited I was that day. In addition to tours and other charters, Roger flies extensively with the Department of Inland Fisheries & Wildlife doing land surveys and animal counts. He has a vast knowledge of the area.

It was a boundless study of water and trees, not too strange considering Maine's 6,000 lakes and ponds, 32,000 miles of rivers and streams, and 17,000,000 forested acres. It took on a bit more personality as he pointed out landmarks such as the 10,000-acre burn from the 1970s that Mother Nature reseeded. We flew near 2,647' Elephant Mountain, the site of a 1963 B-52 bomber wreckage, and 2,890' Number Four Mountain. Both have trailheads off Lily Bay Road. Number Four Mountain has a fire tower.

A moose fed in the lake. Two dark forms stood in what looked like a field. Roger didn't know what they were either so he circled around. They were moose probably standing in a bog.

"Does circling make you sick?"

"No."

"Let's see how sharp your eyes are."

As he circled around, still keeping his distance, I saw an eagle in her treetop nest. We flew across lakes and ponds and waterfalls that he said would be very hard to reach. There were roads in and around, all belonging to lumber companies.

The Appalachian Trail meandered through the trees making its way to Mt. Katahdin. I took note for a future life as a backpacker. Baxter Peak is the northernmost point of the 2,160-mile trail that starts on 3,782' Springer Mountain in northern Georgia.

Pemadumcook and Millinocket Lakes were off to the east of us. I waved to 5,267' Mt. Katahdin and Baxter State Park. It was as close as I was going to get.

Former Maine Governor Percival P. Baxter purchased and donated this 201,018-acre wilderness dedicated, "To be forever left in its natural wild state." Maybe this was why my oversized vehicle wasn't allowed.

O.K. I could handle that. The park has 175 miles of trails to and around 46 mountain peaks, 18 exceeding 3,000'. Summer brings approximately 85,000 hikers and visitors.

We turned toward home and Moosehead Lake. Below us was Ripogenus Dam holding back Pemadumcook Lake, also reached via Lily Bay Road through a fee gate. Now I knew all the places Lily Bay Road would have taken me if I had continued after the pavement. From the air the roads looked passable.

Down there somewhere below the dam, in the Ripogenus Gorge on the West Branch of the Penobscot River, were Abol, Nesowdehunk Stream, and Pockwockamus Falls. I love those Indian names.

We passed 3,230' Big Spencer Mountain, also a local landmark. We were soon over Spencer Bay. Mt. Kineo was a distance away on our right. The home stretch was over Moosehead Lake, the northeast's largest freshwater lake. It is publicized as "40 miles long and 85% underdeveloped," (but developing fast) with 420 miles of shoreline.

I had seen ads for snowmobiling and Roger said they did a lot of it in Maine. "I don't like the noise and perfectly nice people get on those things and become idiots. They get hurt and the hospital patches them together again… sometimes." I could relate to not liking the noise.

When he was ready to land, he said, "I'm not sure I can remember how to do this."

"It would take a lot to scare me."

"Is that a challenge?"

"Definitely not, but I've enjoyed every minute of this." Somehow I knew he could do it. His seaplane landing was as smooth as butter.

The flight was an hour on the nose and not nearly long enough. I had flown many miles over places the Sprinter would not take me, not because it couldn't but more because they were behind locked private gates. I didn't know the ropes as far as getting permission. I love the Sprinter but maybe in the next life, I'll take up flying.

Moose number almost as many as mosquitoes in Greenville. Thankfully, they don't fly, bite, or try to get inside RVs. Residents capitalize on this proliferation with a month-long spring celebration called MooseMainea. It had just started. I was too late for the canoe race and too early for their Tour de Moose, a mountain biking event. You can't have everything. So far I had seen only four Maine moose, not that I was, you know, wanting to run into one, at least not literally. I did expect to see more considering they are the state animal.

I continued south on SR #15 to Bangor for major shopping, laundry, and a VISA advance. I carry very little cash with me. I backtracked a short ways to Kenduskeag and a few days sanctuary with Sue and Jim Wadlington, my son-in-law Bill's parents. Sue had just had surgery and wasn't moving too fast.

We shared coffee, delicious meals that Jim cooked, and pleasant afternoons reminiscing about our travels. They are former RVers.

Naturally, we also discussed the good points and bad points of our kids and grandkids but ultimately decided to keep them.

Jim creates jewelry boxes, end tables, and other small pieces, woodburning and painting them with various scenes. I left, the proud recipient of a five-inch-in-diameter, one-drawer, flip-top jewelry box with a covered bridge on top, an apropos New England souvenir. I gave them a copy of *RVing North America: Silver, Single, & Solo.*

The Sprinter was scheduled for an oil change in Bangor. While that was being done, the mechanic discovered a crack in the exhaust pipe. It was getting louder and louder so I wasn't surprised. They sent the old piece out to have it rebuilt which meant it had to be taken off first. I asked if they thought the propane should be shut off. Suddenly they were quite aware they were working with a blowtorch!

It was Friday, Memorial Day weekend. I was thrilled that they and the company that created the new piece, were able to get everything done. Two hundred and thirty-five dollars later, I left exhausted.

Big cities, although they assuredly offer a great deal, are not places I very often choose to spend time. Bangor was no exception. I had traveled Maine's 3,478 meandering coastline miles on two other trips, and stood on the easternmost point of the continental United States at West Quoddy Lighthouse. I watched the sun come up and as the only one there, I must have been the first person in my country to see the sun that morning.

But this was my *northern* Maine tour. I headed north on I-95 into Aroostook County. Everything in Maine is done in a big way. The state is as big as all of the other New England States combined, and this county is actually larger than Connecticut and Rhode Island.

I thoroughly enjoyed Maine but I have to end this chapter on a sad note. One of my nine sisters-in-law, Dorothy, my brother Dean's wife, was dying of cancer. I had said my goodbyes to her when I left Arizona in March and kept in contact by telephone.

I called for messages just before crossing the Canadian border. Dorothy had died the morning before. It was Memorial weekend and Houlton, Maine, was far too remote to get back to Arizona for her funeral. I didn't try. My eyes watered the countryside for many miles into Canada, not for her, she was no longer in pain, but for Dean, and the rest of us who would miss her so very much.

But as with others who have passed on since I have gone on the road, I took them with me in my heart. Together we crossed the border into New Brunswick Province, Canada.

# New Brunswick

The border guard asked me to go inside and speak with immigration. A Pennsylvania father and son were going bear hunting and into Canada for the first time. They were nervous. With a full house on my back that includes innumerable grandchild pictures, I don't carry them in my purse. I was at a disadvantage but I was appreciative of this proud grandfather's progeny.

"My granddaughter is 10 and she catches bigger fish than I do."

"My granddaughter is 10 also and she catches fish a whole lot bigger than I do." (I didn't tell him I don't fish but I figured my granddaughter of 10 could catch bigger fish than his granddaughter of 10!) Then he talked about how fast she skinned something out. Rebecca probably hadn't skinned anything but her knees lately (not that she couldn't, mind you).

"O.K., you win, hands down."

On a previous trip, I entered New Brunswick from Québec's Gaspé Peninsula. After visiting Prince Edward Island, Nova Scotia, The Hopewell Rocks, and Bay of Fundy National Park, I crossed the border into the States again at Calais, Maine. That was October and the fall colors were so glorious it was almost too bright to handle.

Now it was glorious spring. It took all of five minutes to answer questions and I was soon perusing information at the Visitor Center that the border patrol had told me was closed. After discussing singledom, RVing, men, and New Brunswick with the single clerk, I was well fortified with how to find New Brunswick delights (places, not men!).

The Maritimes do a great job with their information. In New Brunswick they had Fundy Coastal Drive, Acadian Coastal Drive, River Valley Drive, Appalachian Range Route, and the Miramichi River Route. Map routes are all color-coded with booklets for each section.

I hardly realize I have crossed into a foreign country when I enter Canada, except I have to adjust to seeing dual signs in French and English. There is no fear or apprehension involved, ever. It is a highly civilized country, extremely clean, and though I have been told that people are unfriendly, I have not found that to be true.

I drove northerly back roads that had no names so I'm not sure how I got there, but at Hartland I parked next to the World's longest covered bridge. It is 1,282' long and spans the St. John River. Improvements through the years included removing the 3¢ toll, and constructing the boxed sidewalk. At a fast pace, I walked the well-scuffed wooden sidewalk in five minutes. Church bells peeled in the distance. The Visitor Center on the other side was closed on this Sunday afternoon. It was still May and a month early for touristy activities.

I had no reason to cross the bridge other than it beckoned to me, and it was spring, and they are known as "kissing bridges," and hope springs eternal. Alas, there was no one to kiss, and I guess they would have been pretty startled anyway.

Hartland Covered Bridge was built in 1921, an engineering wonder in its time. Because the timbers were covered, this type of bridge was expected to last at least 80 years. It looked pretty healthy considering it only had three more years to go. Space-age cars raced beside me on the single lane span. They wouldn't have fared well in the days when "20-dollar fine for driving faster than a walk" laws were enforced.

Highway #103 traffic was fast-paced for a one laner. Impatient drivers waited at either end. They were a bit out of touch with the history they were driving through. The highway was what they called a "Collector Highway" or Community or Local road in my thinking. I'll just refer to them by number.

**Hartland Bridge**

I couldn't say much for road conditions going south on #105 following the St. John River, but I was in no hurry going through this scenic valley. A motorcyclist passed me as I pulled off the road for a map check. He stopped, turned around, drove back, parked across the road, and came over to my window. "Are you guys lost?" he asked, and for once I wasn't.

After his recommendation that I continue on the same road for the prettiest St. John River view, this young fellow said he had been born on Prince Edward Island. He was really ticked about the new Confederation Bridge. He liked the ferry better.

"I guess the bridge is more practical than romantic."

"I ran out of gas in the middle of it recently. It doesn't take as much gas to ride the ferry."

He must have more time than cents and run on the tank bottom sometimes, like I do. I eventually crossed the river and found a campground for $15 Canadian. I wasn't tethered by sewer or electric so he let me park on a grassy river overlook.

Fredericton, New Brunswick's capital and one of North America's oldest settlements, straddles the St. John River. Their Christ Church Cathedral is said to be the first new cathedral foundation on British soil since the Norman Conquest in 1066.

If I could have waited until the following weekend, the Kings Landing Historical Settlement was opening with a Wool Washing Bee.

New Brunswick isn't a place I've ever heard much about and I don't know why. It has everything, mountains, beaches, fishing villages, history, and it shares the world's highest tides with Nova Scotia on the Bay of Fundy.

I followed the northeasterly Miramichi River Route, Hwy #8, from Fredericton to Miramichi, through farming country and, so I've heard, a great salmon-catching area. It was the everyday life that fascinated me, rich brown plowed fields, green pastures shared by cattle and horses, and the fragrance of lilacs floating through the window. Mowed and trimmed lawns wrapped neatly around freshly painted, shuttered frame homes where clothes hung on backyard Monday lines.

Big cathedrals and small churches were abundant in their elegance or simplicity. Cars lined both sides of the road near a country church where on that sunshiny morning, neighbors and loved ones bade farewell to a friend.

The Miramichi area is noted for lumbering, fishing, and shipbuilding. Joseph Cunard, founder of the Cunard cruise ships, lived here. They boasted of producing some of Canada's best square-rigged ships in the 1820s.

If you ever wondered where Old MacDonald's Farm is – it is north of Mirimichi overlooking Mirimichi Bay. Actually, it is a Historic Scottish-style stone farmhouse built in 1815. I turned on #117 at Loggieville. It was a charming route through small picturesque fishing villages. At Baie-Ste-Anne, I watched the fishing fleet come in with their catch. They have one of the largest wharves in New Brunswick with a fleet of a hundred boats. The sea air and the gulls calling to one another were exciting. I hadn't been near big water for a long time.

I continued on a gravel road to Point Escuminac. I found not only the Gulf of St. Lawrence, but also a grassy site in the Escuminac Family Campground. A short walk took me to gazebos, picnic tables, boardwalks crossing the dunes, and a sandy beach overlooking Miramichi Bay. The beach pulled me along to a small restaurant, Le Coin de Pêcheurs (Fishermen's Corner), beside a big lobster cannery and fish market. It was cannery break time. The place filled with French-speaking employees, glad for a few minutes to chat and chew.

The waitress spoke French to them and thankfully, English to me. When

I ordered a Pepsi with my halibut dinner, she asked, "Do you want a can or a long neck?" I must have looked blank because she showed me a glass Pepsi bottle with a long neck. I sat at an outside table and watched their world.

I walked back along the road, wishing I had chosen the beach again. A magnificent huge new house seemed rather obscene among the fishing cottages. An old vacant house, probably no longer fixable, looked sad with its windows knocked out. What was its history?

The fishing fleet was out in force the next morning. As the sun rose over the sand dunes, I counted 45 boats bobbing on the horizon,

I asked the campground owner, Joseph McIntyre, about the fishermen's memorial I had seen near the restaurant the night before. He said, "My father and I were out jiggin' cod that morning (Catching fish on hooks dangling near the bottom with hand-held lines). We caught fish with rocks in their stomachs, some as big as eight inches in diameter. My father said that meant the fish were trying to anchor themselves to the bottom, using the rocks as ballast, the sure sign of a storm coming." Joseph and his father returned home. The memorial is to the 35 fishermen who were killed in that tragic 1959 storm.

Joseph and Mary were spring cleaning and watching the grandchildren. This was their third season as campground owners. I loved hearing Joseph talk in his slow way, probably an Acadian accent. He was definitely a storyteller. He had been in the military 35 years but in his old clothes and boots, he really looked like he had spent his entire life as a fisherman. In reality, he worked with his father as a fisherman for only four years. They were so helpful and friendly, I hated to leave.

Lilac fragrance floated through the window. I drove along the beach for a while after passing the Pointe-Sapin Lighthouse, eventually going into the Kouchibouguac National Park. Joseph pronounced it "Kushibushua." Officially, its "Koush-e-boo-gwak," a Micmac Indian word meaning, "River of long tides."

After watching the movie about the shoreline seasons, I drove to the campgrounds. Very few campers were utilizing this huge park with such nice sites. During the season, it is probably jammed. This park has rivers, dunes, marshes, bogs, lagoons, fields and forests. Canoeing and kayaking is allowed along its waterways and great biking trails wind through the park. They have miles of white sandy beach, as does the rest of this coastline.

I hiked the Salt Marsh Trail boardwalks and Kelly's Beach, talking with other hikers. It felt good to swing along the shoreline and back along the long stretches of boardwalk that protects their dunes and fragile grasses, and an endangered species, the piping plover. Although it had rained in the night, it was a beautiful sunny day with white clouds wisping through it. This area boasts "the warmest saltwater beaches north of Virginia."

On the way out, a porcupine waddled along, seemingly oblivious to the six-ton vehicle with a woman behind the wheel that was rolling along behind him. The forest is also home to moose and deer.

Although this was definitely not the tourist season, Highway #134 beyond the national park and through many tiny communities, was extremely busy. I missed the turn to La dune de Bouctouche. It is a white sand dune that stretches across Bouctouche Bay in the Northumberland Strait. Its existence since the last ice age, is attributed to constant wind, tides and sea currents.

For hundreds of years, this sheltered fishermen and their boats with roughly seven miles of natural sand; now it shelters wildlife. As with other dune areas, a curved boardwalk allows people to observe without disturbing sensitive areas. J. D. Irving of Irving Oil developed this area, also called the Irving Eco-Centre. It is staffed by biologists and interpreters for on-site research and provides learning opportunities for all ages, but especially school children.

LePays De La Sagouine, "An island of legends, music, and theatre," is a theme park in Bouctouche Harbor. It is the mythical community of La Sagouine, created by Antonine Maillet, a native of Bouctouche. This "Village that never really was, is a recreated historical settlement from the early part of the century, showing people enduring hard times with humor in a simple, brightly colored world." Acadian cuisine is served in its restaurant. Special events and activities are scheduled all summer.

While this appealed to me greatly, it didn't open until June and the performances are all in French! Even the pictures of it with musicians walking through the village, well, they say you should "come to experience the Acadian joie de vivre." O.K.

I hit #15 at Shediac, "Lobster Capital of the World," and took a picture of an enormous lobster permanently posing for tourists. Although he would certainly give you a belly full, I hope not all of them are that size! The Shediac Lobster Festival is held in mid-July. Behind this enormous lobster were gathering equally enormous black clouds. I was fortunate that I didn't find La dune de Bouctouche because I would probably have been at the wrong end of that long boardwalk when the storm hit.

It moved in big time at Cap-Pele. The wind blew furiously. The sky was so dark it was like night, and then the rain came. I hunkered down for a couple of hours close to a building, eating dinner and reading. So nice to have my dry cozy house on my back for emergencies.

It was raining lightly but the sky was much lighter as I continued through pretty farming country to #16. This took me over the Northumberland Strait on the new Confederation Bridge to Prince Edward Island (PEI) just as the sun came out from under the storm clouds. I had a spectacular sunset and the storm was over, but the high, nearly nine-mile-bridge drive, provided a gusty-winded, white-knuckled drive. The Confederation Bridge has the distinction of being the world's longest bridge over ice-covered waters.

Major construction was taking place at the Visitor Center, the future Gateway Village. It was well beyond closing time. I snuggled in for the night. ZZZZZZzzzzzzzz, dreaming of bonny Prince Edward (Island).

# "Land that Cradles the Waves"

When I last visited Prince Edward Island in 1988, was the first time I had taken the Sprinter on a "big" ferry. The Confederation Bridge was quicker, beautiful during the sunset, but still controversial among the PEIers I was to learn. It was now accessible for "Sunday" visitors, those who "Come for the day just to look." Others were thrilled because they could get products to market much faster and cheaper.

The last time, a friend whom I had met in San Carlos, Mexico, was my personal guide and great woman company. This time I was on my own and determined to see uncharted (by me) territory. I made a valiant effort. The back roads were almost as busy as the main roads, but then again, I'm not sure they were back roads. They were main roads, just not as main as their main roads.

PEI is divided into sections for tourist ease but that didn't do me much good. I started on TransCanada #1 but shortly turned on to Blue Heron Drive #10. I should have stayed on it. In an attempt to drive the outer island perimeters, I ended up on a red dirt road. It was well packed, easily driven, and why not. After a few short miles, it became a two track with no place to turn around. I continued on to the water. If you get lost, you can find water in any direction! Two farms lived at the lane's end. There had to be a turnaround, right? For once I was right. A lady and her daughter were exiting in a farm truck. I pulled over to let them by.

She was so sweet, "Are you lost?" I wondered how she could tell. I suspect she was taking the daughter to the school bus stop. My motorhome just might have been the subject of discussion under, "You should have seen what was in my driveway this morning!" The little one waved to me several times as I drove behind them. I should have asked her where I was. I think I was either at Seacow Head or Salutation Cove. It didn't matter.

PEI is referred to as "Canada's Million-Acre Farm," with 30% farming. Potatoes, just one of their crops, was evident in the Quonset-hut storage barns. Farm fields newly plowed, were the deep rich brown against the lush green of everything else. The well-groomed farmlands surrounded houses that all looked newly painted. Not a blade of grass was out of place.

The next road was paved. Safe, right? The repair crew was out. I asked the sign lady, "Does this road go someplace or will I wind up on another muddy dead-end road?" She said it deadended shortly. I asked if I might turn around in the nearby field access. She replied rather doubtfully, "You may, but it might be better if you go to the next farmhouse." That was a ways down the road and beyond the repairs. I turned around right there. She said, "I guess you can!" I think she was glad to see me. We chatted a while. It was interesting that they had workers holding stop and slow signs on a road that probably had two people per hour if they were lucky, on a dead-end road leading to nowhere.

I still wasn't sure where I was but I found Bedeque and it had a corner store. I bought a detailed map.

Prince Edward Island is Canada's smallest province but considered to be the place where Canada began. It is only 139 miles long and 40 miles wide. At its narrowest, the island is 1.8 miles wide. It is connected by three isthmuses that are only three miles wide. I was into my second isthmus and riding hard for the third, all areas I had not explored previously.

Fields and pastures stretched down to the sea. Cliffs, Coves, and inlets snuggled up to lighthouses guarding their coastline, almost always visible from the road. Birds followed plowing tractors, looking for wormy tidbits for eager birdlings. Green pastures sprouted new grass and new babies wobbling on new legs. Logs and wood stacks lived in back yards, awaiting the next cozy winter fire, hopefully a ways off from this perfect spring day. Fishing boats rested in nearly every yard like airplanes in Alaska or RVs in the lower 48.

From almost any high place, I could see a steeple reaching toward the heavens. Churches that dotted the countryside were both quite small and impressively large.

I curved along Bedeque Bay to Summerside. This brought memories because the Sprinter was broken down a couple of days there on my last trip. Summerside's wharf embraces large ships that transport PEI potatoes to tables around the world. Summerside is so named because, well, it is on the "summer" side of the island.

Following Lady Slipper Drive to Cap-Egmont and the Bottle Houses, somehow I knew they wouldn't be open. I admired from a distance, the chapel, the six-gabled house, and a third structure, all built with bottles. Various sizes and shapes make up the 25,000 bottles used in creating these buildings.

The Sprinter bounced along the red sandstone cliffs on Lady Slipper Drive and some really bad roads on Egmont Bay, with only an occasional break with good highway #2. At Tignish, I hoped to get out to the North Cape lighthouse and the northernmost tip of the island but alas, I slipped unknowingly into lostdom. By the time I realized it, I had rounded the west side of the island and was on my way east.

Of course it isn't any wonder I got lost in Tignish. It was the biggest city since two isthmuses ago, with a population of 800. I just wanted to touch bases with explorer Jacques Cartier. He arrived on North Cape point in 1534. I suppose he didn't wait.

PEI was waking up from winter. It didn't matter if I was on a dead-end road, farm road, or main road, the cars sped by. Every kind of farm equipment, extra wide and extra slow, was ahead of me. They were my acceptable excuse for dawdling. Tractors pulled trailers filled with seed potatoes. Repairmen were held precariously in little airborne buckets while they fixed broken lines. Red, white, and blue garbage trucks picked up their bounty in my lane. A trucker had lost his log load onto the road. He sat in the truck, probably quite disgusted with affairs in particular and everything in general. I couldn't blame him.

I leisurely enjoyed the "real" Prince Edward Island in the slow lane because I wasn't leading the pack. At Kensington I followed #6 into "Anne's Land." If not so slowly moving, I probably wouldn't have noticed the Blue Winds Tearoom near New London. It was a renovated old island home turned tearoom, with an outstanding view, and equally outstanding fresh rhubarb pie with ice cream.

Soft-spoken Terry Kamikawa waited on me. She and her husband, Mark, had lived there about 10 years and opened the tearoom four years ago. They did major foundation renovation and furnace work. If they had already been there 10 years, they will probably still be there if you go. Try that rhubarb pie; it is outstanding.

Sidonia, my Mexico friend, and I had visited Basin Head, Charlottetown, art galleries and churches, but my favorite place was Cavendish, the stomping grounds of Lucy Maud Montgomery, author of "*Anne of Green Gables*." I am a tried and true fan. The magic of her books helped me visualize her Haunted Woods and Dryad's Bubble. From New London through Cavendish, I walked the paths of the childhood that she turned into such delightful stories. Though she died over 50 years before, I still felt I was one of her "Kindred Spirits." I didn't have time to revisit her special places but the area brought back great memories.

I ducked to the beach. Prince Edward Island National Park is a very long stretch of beach interrupted by North Rustico Harbour. The park had opened a few days before, although the campground wasn't open yet. I walked the dune-protecting boardwalk, wandering lost in thought at the water's edge.

As I left the park, a young fox blocked my way. I slowly approached and stopped. He was settled into his Delicacy de Mouse. I was so enthralled that I didn't get a picture. This was O.K. On reflection what would one do with a fox-mangling-mouse photograph? It might make me feel better when I have one running around in my rolling house. There's an idea. I'll get a fox for company and to keep the mouse population down. Traveling is so educational.

On the cliffs were benches and big rocks that invited sitting for an afternoon of crashing seawaves, raucous gulls, cloud watching and dreaming. The Micmac Indians believed that when the Great Spirit created the world, he had red clay left over. He shaped it into an island and laid it in the Gulf of St. Lawrence. The Indians named it Abegweit, or "Land cradled on the waves."

I talked with a couple and their daughter from Massachusetts. Later I realized the mother and daughter had disappeared with the car. He looked a bit grumpy. I wondered if they had abandoned him.

Visitors from Newfoundland gave me the scoop on my next port of call. After I climbed around, took pictures, drank a Pepsi, and encompassed the magic of this place in the sun, the fellow from Massachusetts was still sitting on a bench, by himself, with his partners still missing. The Newfie lady came over to say goodbye and said, "You have the most incredible blue eyes." I think it must have been the ocean reflection but grateful for any compliments, I just said, "Thanks."

When I left a couple of hours later, the bench sitter was still looking out to sea. It's so interesting to watch people. Who knows, maybe he is still sitting there.

At Orby Head overlook, two gulls nested on a large boulder below me. She seemed appreciative of her mate's sharing parental duties.

North Rustico Harbor also brought back memories. The Court Brothers offered Sidonia and me a chance to go lobstering but with an eye to the weather and the wind chill factor that October day, we declined. As I drove through this fishing village, I wondered if I would find any of the people I had met before. Nothing looked familiar. I parked at the closed Court Brothers Establishment. A young man on a bike looked at the Sprinter with great interest. It was obvious I was the new guy in town.

"Do you live here?"

"Yes."

"Does Emard Court still live here?"

"Yeah, right across the street."

I found my *RVing North America, Silver, Single, and Solo* book and autographed it to Emard. My new friend, Gabe Gamauf, the young fellow on the bike, accompanied me.

Emard's brother, Quintin, was outside on the porch.

"Is Emard here?"

"Yes." He brought Emard out.

Showing him the picture in the book, I asked if it was him.

"Yes."

"I'd like you to have this." Emard, with his long white beard and twinkling eyes, seemed quite pleased.

We were soon chatting on his front porch with brothers Quintin, and later Vince and his wife, Alice, while he showed everyone the book. Gabe and his bike joined us as well.

Emard didn't like the new bridge, "It brings so many people on the Island who just drive over for the day and don't stay to become a part of things." The four Court brothers still live in the family home, land granted to their great grandfather by Queen Victoria for the sum of one peppercorn a year. The fifth brother and two sisters live elsewhere. Since I visited in 1988, the four bachelor Court brothers, had become three.

Alice came from Ontario as a tourist, loved it, stayed to work at a B & B, and after dating Vince for five years, they were married. Obviously she was very fond of all the brothers and took them under her wing. She took Emard's book and said she couldn't wait to read it. Charming lady (and not just because she said that).

Vince and his stepdaughter, Alice, (as opposed to his wife, Alice) now do all the lobstering. Nothing would do for Emard but that I be on the family lobstering boat the next morning. I'm not sure Vince was pleased with taking a landlubbering female out lobstering but he graciously went along with it. I really thought strongly about refusing considering the time of day involved, but then again, that's why I do what I do, to write about it.

Emard invited me to park for the night in front of the Fish House that since 1820 has been the nucleus of their business. After I parked, Quintin, who was very shy and sweet and had little to say, showed me the lobstering boat and introduced me to young Alice. I asked if she was the First Mate since I was going with them the next day. She didn't know about it and I'm not sure she was pleased either, but then she was on the shy side, too.

Gabe asked if he could see the Sprinter. His family lived behind the Court family in a large home overlooking the Ocean. When Quintin and I returned from our tour, Gabe brought his folks and little brother to see my home on wheels. I felt like a fraud because everyone expects it to be as luxurious as most motorhomes are, but they seemed to understand that I had made it to fit my lifestyle in particular.

The boys did their share of pretending, attracted to the engine end to sit and drive. They invited me to their house to shower or park and plug into their electricity but I explained I had solar. That interested Gabe. He had to hear all about it.

Gabe had written a recycling story with another boy for the local monthly paper. He brought it over for me to read. Several people wandered by looking at the motorhome – We were definitely a curiosity.

Duly warned about possible seasickness and hypothermia, I laid out my warm clothing layers for a 3:00 a.m. alarm.

We took off with the comforting hum of the 175 HP diesel below us. I wondered what I was getting into. Alice munched a sandwich breakfast while Vince confidently swung the boat around and took off into the first glow of a rosy sunrise.

Alice, no bigger than a minute, was in banking for 17 years in Ontario. When her mother married Vince, she came to visit and eventually exchanged her dress-up clothes for thermals on a lobster boat. This was her second season.

With everything well under control, I asked Vince, "What is the little TV-type machine?"

"I use it to watch cartoons," but then he explained it was a depth finder. "It shows exactly how many feet to the bottom and what kind of terrain we are going over. If there are rocks, it shows on the monitor as a thicker line. Another electronic gizmo tells us where the traps are situated."

**Dinner Time**

Alive leaned well over the side, snagged the first trap line with a long-handled hook and pulled it in. Vince fastened the line over an electrically-operated wench and pulled the 80-pound lobster trap of wet wood and cement sinkers, up and onto the boat ledge in a line of salt-water spray. He slid the traps to Alice. During all this, he guided the boat and kept it on an even keel in the ocean swells.

I commented on the difficulty of lifting them on board. He said, "I just tip them onto the side." But his kind of "not lifting" looked pretty difficult to me. I wouldn't want to arm wrestle either one of them.

Alice opened them, pulled out and replaced the old fish bait, threw the lobsters into a crate, and tossed freeloading fish, crabs, and sea urchins back into the ocean. She aligned the traps and waited for Vince to pull around. When he yelled "O.K.," she shoved one trap off, went back and threw off the first buoy and line, then shoved the rest of the traps into the harbour one at a time, every 42 feet, picking up the second buoy last, turning around with it and throwing it overboard. It may sound easy and she did it efficiently, but while this was all going on, she had to make sure she didn't step on a rope, or get caught in it, and go overboard with a trap or buoy.

While waiting for his O.K., and in between traps, she quickly measured lobsters. Undersized critters went flying back into the ocean to grow and be trapped again. It was quite a routine, and she had great aim. I asked Vince if he had tried her on a basketball court. He laughed and repeated that to her. They both wore protective suits, but as the sun came up and they were busy, they both removed the jackets and put on "sleeves" as protection against the wet and the lobster claws. She eventually abandoned the sleeves but she paid for it by getting nipped by cranky lobsters. In between trap areas, they grabbed a bite to eat or drink.

This was repeated all day long until they had retrieved, emptied, and replaced 300 traps. By law, they could have no more than that. Each trap has a numbered tag. If they were found without that number, they were in trouble.

It was definitely a work boat, painted on the outside but unfinished and unpainted on the inside, just as you might expect a work boat to be. Clean, but bare bones. He said a lot of the lobsterers had 250 HP boats and bigger but, "This 175 gets me where I want to go."

"Do you ever have trouble sleeping at night after a day of lobstering?"

"Yes, sometimes my arms ache." Alice had very short dark hair and was quite attractive. If you saw her on the street, you'd never dream she was a lobsterman (lobsterperson?).

Vince asked, "Where did you buy the book that had Emard's picture in it?"

"I wrote it."

"Did you write all of it?"

"Yes."

"Alice! You'd better watch what you say. She writes books!" A well-placed spit went sailing over the side as he kicked the rope down toward Alice.

Vince is the youngest brother and without any children, the last of the Court line in a business started 150 years ago by their grandfather. After 50 years in the same harbour, this was his last lobstering season. He acknowledged he would miss it but he wasn't giving up the charters, "That will keep me on the water." They make three fishing charter trips a day with Captains Vince, Emard, or Veard (the third bachelor) Court.

Vince said the fifth brother lives in Alberta with his wife, who had also come to North Rustico as a tourist. I said if enough tourists came along, they'd all be married yet. Vince was tall and the spitting image of Walter Mathau and had a break in his voice when he talked. He was 65 and as with his brothers, he still had dark hair.

I asked Alice if lobstering was a permanent career move. "I'd like to be 'second man' for another lobstering boat after Vince stops, but crews are usually family members so I'm not sure."

Some of the inadvertently trapped fish were huge ugly things that gave Alice quite a battle before she could fling them into the ocean. Vince called them "cobbler fish."

"Have you ever caught anything really unusual?"

"No. We've been catching the same stuff for 50 years."

"Have you noticed any difference in your catches through the years."

"No." That surprised me.

Alice banded the larger lobsters, depending on what kind of market they were going to, then threw them into a cooler.

When they came onto a buoy at not quite the right angle or too fast, he said, "If you don't get it, we can come 'round again.'" She missed it once and ran down toward the other end of the boat and finally brought it in. He watched her with great pride.

"She's really something isn't she? She had to lower her standard of living and makes less wages but she's happy." Why would anybody want to work that hard if they didn't love it.

It was pretty coming through the channel and into the harbor by the lighthouse. Alice dumped the old fish bait and the gulls came in for dinner. They were quickly out of their slickers and off to dinner.

Shy Quintin came to greet me. He told me what he was doing and wanted to know how I liked the trip.

Vince's wife, Alice, was quite pleased when I gave her an autographed *RVing Alaska!* book. They talked about going some day. Vince shook hands goodbye as I thanked him for giving this Midwesterner a fantastic adventure I wouldn't have had otherwise.

When I was ready to leave, Quintin took my hand and I asked for a hug. He is so sweet. I found Emard and gave him a hug, too.

It was only 1:30 in the afternoon. I hadn't done a thing all day but watch. I was exhausted. My message service brought me the bad news that my husband's step brother-in-law had died. Two very ill family members gone within five days of each other. Loved ones to be missed.

I drove as far as Brackley Beach Visitor Information and crashed for three hours. After calling my friend, Sidonia, we met at Adventureland Campground, splitting the difference between her place at Charlottetown and Brackley Beach. She brought the pizza. We had great fun catching up on 10 years of news (minus the occasional letter), reminiscing over our Cabot Trail trip, and even greater sillier times in San Carlos, Mexico.

Her view of the Federation Bridge was that it made PEI "An appendage of New Brunswick."

We looked at old photos of Mexico and Canada, laughed a lot, and decided to get together when I went back through Nova Scotia. Unfortunately, that was not to be. Somewhere I flipped a coin and changed directions.

By morning it was raining lightly. I walked a little on the PEI National Park beach but drove through the rest of it, connecting with #6, #219, and #2 taking me east. Sidonia and I had been to Souris and several of the east side PEI beaches. I turned south toward #4 and the Wood Islands Ferry. The last ferry for the day was leaving in two hours.

This took me cross lots through more pretty farming country and down to the ferry. I had just fallen asleep in line behind a camper and a guy knocked on my window with tags for shutting down the propane.

They don't charge you for crossing from New Brunswick to PEI on the new bridge but they get you either returning over the bridge or taking the ferry. It was $53 Canadian (for RV's from 20' - 40' including passengers) or $36.68 American, which wasn't bad for the 75-minute trip to Nova Scotia. It is also possible to drive to Nova Scotia from New Brunswick via the Isthmus of Chignecto (easy for them to say). I did it on the return trip last time.

I bought groceries and continued until I saw a Provincial Park sign. I paid my $10 Canadian, parked next to a stream, opened my window, and for all intents and purposes, died until morning. Then I discovered things were a bit damp. It had rained in the night. Even that hadn't awakened me!

**Prince Edward Island Beach**

# Nova Scotia

On a previous trip to Nova Scotia, PEI friend Sidonia, had accompanied me around the Cabot Trail. Other friends I met in Sayulita, Mexico, had toured me around the mid-section of Nova Scotia. Nova Scotia is also "tourist-sected" (I think I just coined a new word!) for ease in seeing its various parts. This time I started on Sunrise Trail #104, and was shortly into Truro and the Glooscap Trail on #215, headed around the southwestern loop of Nova Scotia. Are you with me here?

As a Michigoose (as opposed to a Michigander), I am fascinated with tides. The only tide we had in Michigan was what we put in the washing machine. I guess the water that goes up and down in the stool was sort of a tide, too, but we didn't have an inside toilet until I was 12.

Chignecto Bay, bordered by New Brunswick and Nova Scotia, and the Minas Basin, all within the arms of Nova Scotia, share the world's highest tides. They are both at the end of the famous Bay of Fundy.

I followed #236 and crossed the Shubenacadie River on the Clarence Gosse Bridge. This is supposed to be a great place to watch the tidal bore but Shubenacadie's mud bottom was shamelessly exposed. I turned on #215 following the river. It is quite startling find a naked river bottom. Rivers literally empty out, leaving boats and docks wondering where the water went. The real drama happens approximately 12½ hours later, when high tide returns 14 billion tons of water to hearth and home. This is most dramatic during a tidal bore, usually the highest during a springtime full moon.

Fascination with the tide drew me in to the Shubenacadie River Runners Ltd, at Maitland, on the mouth of Nova Scotia's longest river. They take people in 16' Zodiac rafts to ride the tidal bores, which are generally about 40'. They advertise, "You'll feel the rush of riding the tidal bore and up to eight sets of rapids as the tide thunders up the Shubenacadie." Yesss! I wanted to go!

Kim explained the tide was on the wane at the moment and not as dramatic as usual. She suggested waiting until around June 19 or so. My always mercurial plans would probably bring me back about that time. They put my name down.

Maitland is an interesting 200-year-old village. It is lined with 19th Century homes and Nova Scotia's first Heritage Conservation District. At one time it was a shipbuilding empire. Canada's largest wooden full-rigged sailing ship was built and launched there in 1874 by William D. Lawrence. His home is now the Lawrence House Museum.

A hike over a small bridge led to a wharf and beach at Anthony Picnic Provincial Park. That gave me a good view of Cobequid Bay and the still receding tide. I turned on Point Road thinking it would lead to a beach or lighthouse or something. Ha! It led right into a farmer's barnyard. A two track went over the hill but I wasn't certain if it was private property. The cows watched me turn around and didn't say a thing. I suppose at milking time they told the farmer about this strange white box on wheels...

A loop road led to Burncoat Head Lighthouse and a little park honoring the highest tides in the world. During the 1869 Saxby Tide, the high tide reached 54'. The first lighthouse was built in 1858. The tides eroded the land away leaving just enough land to drive a horse and wagon across. After that eroded too, lighthouse keepers climbed the bank to the lighthouse via a ladder. A second lighthouse was constructed in 1913 on the mainland. This was destroyed in 1972 as unrepairable. The interpretive center is a full-scale replica but not a working lighthouse. A narrow, steep sideless ladder led to the cupola. What a view.

I went down the new stairs and deck built across from the island and watched the tide for a couple of hours. I expected high drama but it seeped in slowly. It was peaceful and I had this three-acre interpretive park all to myself.

Up the road a piece, the restored Walton Lighthouse is not a working lighthouse and not manned. I wondered what four teenage boys in a pickup were up to but maybe they weren't up to anything. They left when I came. From the top I looked across the Minas Basin to Cape Blomidon. This huge headland is the home of the legendary and mighty Glooscap, whose trail I followed. It is he, according to the Mi'kmaq legends, that controlls the great tides.

At Brooklyn, I took #14 and crossed to the Evangeline Trail #1. I had already been in this area so I didn't linger but for you winter athletes, I'll tell you that Windsor is the "birthplace of hockey."

When I previously visited the Grand Pré National Historic Site of the great 1755 Acadian expulsion, I was told the statue Evangeline's face regresses from happy to unhappy as you walk around it. Someone had asked me about this and I didn't remember it. I went back to check. I still didn't see it. Perhaps one has to believe it to see it.

Our own Henry Wadsworth Longfellow wrote the poem, *"Evangeline,"* in 1847. It tells the tale of Evangeline and Gabriel her betrothed, being separated by the expulsion.

Beginning in the late 1600s, the Acadians reclaimed over 3,000 acres of rich level lowlands from the tides by building over 28,000' of dykes. Grand Pré means "Great Meadow." The French Acadians were deported and their lands confiscated because they wouldn't swear allegiance to the British Crown. A large number of them settled in our Louisiana. Others returned later to re-establish the Acadian Coast.

The church, built on an original Acadian village site, has expulsion exhibits. There is a Visitor Center and formal gardens as well.

The fertile Annapolis Valley is known as "Canada's first breadbasket." It was the end of May and its apple orchards were blooming. Kentville was celebrating with an Apple Blossom Festival. I stopped for some of the festivities but overcrowded conditions soon had me on my way.

Nova Scotia is varied. Not only is it famous for its apples, they also have dairy farms, "freezer beef" livestock, lumber, blueberries, balsam fir Christmas trees, and boat building. They have rocky shoreline, sandy beaches, and picturesque fishing villages tucked into their curlicue seashore. They pack a lot into their 55,490 square miles. With rising directly from sea level, their Appalachian Mountains seem higher than the 1,745'+ elevation. Add to the mountains, the rugged coastline, bogs, marshes, and over 3,000 lakes, and they have awesome scenery.

**Bear River, Bare Bottom**

I had followed #1 most of the way, interchanging with #101 when necessary. On this last day of May, I turned left toward Bear River and a deadend. It is called Nova Scotia's "Switzerland." Having seen Switzerland, I felt it's other title, Historic Tidal Village on Stilts" fit better. The waterfront buildings were all on stilts to keep them from drowning during high tide.

Parking in a bank parking lot, I took a bath. Doesn't everyone? Small trucks were parked side by side with baseball-capped guys talking to each other. I didn't know if something was going on or whether these were typical Sunday morning chats.

Though the past history of this arts and crafts community includes shipbuilding and trading, its more recent claim to fame, and seemingly a major tourist attraction, is their unique wastewater treatment facility. It is Canada's first, a Solar Aquatics Treatment in a greenhouse. Effluent is cleansed within an environment of biologically balanced ecosystems of aquatic plants, snails, and other creatures. I missed the tour by a day.

Hunger drove me from the flowerbeds and boardwalk to a tiny café. A Minnesota couple had flown into Pennsylvania, rented a car, and was touring the Maritimes.

"I'm meeting my kids at International Falls for July 4 weekend."

"That's beautiful territory. It's about 60 miles north of where we live, Grand Rapids."

"Isn't that Judy Garland territory?" They were surprised I knew that but I had gone through there a couple of times. They came over on "The Cat," the new ferry from Bar Harbor, Maine, to Yarmouth, Nova Scotia. I hadn't heard about it so I was fascinated. They said it was great and with only a 2½ hour trip, it was possible for them to come up much quicker.

The café was so tiny; you couldn't help overhearing other conversations. Locals at two tables were discussing tandem parachuting. My eyes twirled uncontrollably. As I was leaving, the fellow's companions had already gone so I asked him about it. He invited me to sit down while he finished breakfast. We discussed why I wanted to know about parachuting and he explained he was making arrangements for an upcoming festival. He lived there in town with his wife but she was doing her business taxes in Digby that morning.

All of a sudden he asked,"Where do you go to church?"

"I'm Presbyterian but I go to whatever is available as I travel."

He invited me to his church and told me how to get there.

Bear River Advent Christian Church Sunday School was just letting out. Eddie sat with me in the back row and introduced me to people as they arrived, his uncle, his brother, etc. It was a small church in a small community and everyone was related. There were many children and overall, a good mix of ages. He told me the pastor was very laid back but very emotional. During one song and several readings, a different kind of sermon was happening. The minister's wife, who had a three-week-old baby, couldn't restrain their little girl who was probably less than two. She ran to her daddy who picked her up and held her.

She looked him in the eyes; she leaned her head on his shoulder and she rubbed the back of his head with her hand. She was very good and seemed to realize although she wasn't allowed to disturb his talking, it was perfectly all right to love him up. The minister was a bachelor until age 42 and never dreamed he would ever get married, let alone have three children under five.

I was invited to the church dinner 30 miles away in Digby, the direction was going anyway. Eddie told me later that as I was following him in the motorhome, he called his wife on the phone. She couldn't come but she wanted to know how old I was! Apparently she deemed me a safe date!

They apologized because dinner was leftovers from a Mission collecting dinner the night before, but it beat my one-dimensional meals. We chatted about my travels and Eddie's interesting business. He bought and sold wrecked airplanes and airplane parts all over the world. He called someone about CB channel #19 I was using. He said that was for West Coast Canadian truckers, the same as in the United States, but in the Maritimes, it was #1, a good thing to know in an emergency.

Eddie had been to Labrador and knew there was a road connecting to Québec but he didn't know the particulars. Others eventually came in and we chatted briefly. It was a lovely dinner with lovely people.

I was already on Digby Neck so I continued on down. This is a long "spinal column" of land plus two islands, with the Bay of Fundy on one side and St. Marys Bay on the other. It wasn't the place for a motorhome. I saw red cliffs, a bird sanctuary, quaint shops and inns, beaches, and places to hunt for precious gems, but big-vehicle parking was nil even on the off season.

At the Long Island ferry, the guy asked,

"Are you over or under a ton?"

"Way over."

"O.K., just for today I'll charge you $2 (About $1.20 US)."

On the Brier Island ferry, the attendant asked, "What did the first ferry charge you?"

"$2"

"O.K."

On Brier Island I parked on the ferry dock and walked to D & B café for a take-out hamburger. While I ate my burger in the motorhome, a lady tapped on the window. She saw my Texas license plate and wanted to speak to another woman who was crazy enough to drive all the way from Texas alone. Brier Island is the westernmost point of Nova Scotia, on the mouth of the Bay of Fundy.

Exploring led to a very limited deadend with no way to turn around except in a narrow driveway with no room for error. I did it but I'm not sure how. Sandy Cove was the prettiest spot on the drive.

I could see Digby Neck for hikers, bikers, and walkers and I didn't have time for any of it. Digby was a cute little seaside-fishing village that has the world's largest inshore scallop fleet. They did offer interesting food, Dulse and Digby Chicks. It was getting late. I was tired, and somehow neither purple dried seaweed nor smoked herring appealed to me.

The sky was black with rain when I stopped at a private campground near Grosses Coques. It was $20 for no hookups from my first real grouch, but I wasn't going to argue with the storm increasing in intensity.

It lulled and rocked me to sleep, an altogether amazing day. Grosses Coques means "large clams." These are the big bar clams found on the tidal flats that provided life-saving food during the deportation and for early settlers.

The next morning I was guided through "The largest and tallest wooden church in North America," Église Sainte-Marie, by a lass in native Acadian dress. St. Mary's was constructed in the form of a cross, 190' long and 135' wide. Originally the steeple was 212' but in 1916, it caught fire when lightning struck. The church was saved when a rainstorm put out the fire. Divine intervention? The spire is now 185' high.

The church is so large, 40 tons of rock ballast was put in the steeple to keep it from swaying in the hurricane force winds off St. Mary's Bay. The church is all wood. The huge columns are actually tree trunks wrapped in sailcloth and plastered. The marble columns along the top of the church, aren't. They are wood. Painted canvas covers the walls and ceiling. My young guide said it took 400 gallons to paint the outside and 300 gallons for the inside. St. Mary's is on the University of St. Anne Campus, Nova Scotia's only French-language University, and the center for Acadian culture.

In Meteghen, a huge ship was an interesting work in progress. I drove through the village but with the motorhome, I really felt like a bull in a china shop. I dwarfed everything and there was no place to park. Perhaps I would have been just as obvious had I been walking. It was a very busy port with all manner of scallop, lobster, and fishing boats.

At Smuggler's Cove Provincial Park, the beach stairs had fallen away from the cliff. The natural cave at the cliff bottom was supposedly used during U. S. Prohibition to store contraband rum.

The entire Evangeline Trail and Acadian Coast are quite beautiful. The colorful houses are bright blue, salmon pink, dark and light green, shades of yellow, aquamarine, and red.

I chatted with two young French-Acadian fellows in Salmon River. One struggled with French and the other struggled with English. Everything in Canada is kilometre, metre, and take me to your litre, and gasoline was running 52.9 to 60.9/litre. One fellow pumped $120 of gasoline into the Sprinter. They were curious and when either of them wasn't doing something else, he followed me and asked questions. They admired the Sprinter's black guard.

"What's it for?"

"It's a moose catcher."

"That wouldn't hold a moose!" Then I explained it was a rock guard for traveling Alaska's gravel roads. They laughed at my explanation but warned me that Newfoundland was full of moose.

I found the candy factory in Port Maitland but they weren't doing anything but wrapping candy. I bought some. A mistake. It was good but not good enough to be worth the calories.

Except for the Trans-Canada and congested sections of the Provincial Arterial Highways, the main roads are two-lane with slow lanes on long hills, usually in good condition and posted at 80-100 km/h (50-62 mph). The view is basically trees. The lesser roads follow the scenic routes. Unfortunately, they are really not in very good shape and it isn't wise to drive the posted 80 km/h.

My experience in May, June, and October was cool mornings and evenings with warm afternoons. Layered clothing works well. Mostly what you need to pack is a smile. Nova Scotians are very friendly. With few exceptions, Visitor Centers, Provincial Parks, and tourist attractions do not function until mid-June.

I parked at the Yarmouth ferry dock, a city of roughly 8,000. The big news this year was the "Cat" that the Minnesotans told me about in Bear River. Ferries cross from Portland, Maine (858 driving miles), and Bar Harbor, Maine (630 driving miles), to Yarmouth. The new 64 million-dollar jet-powered catamaran "Cat" takes 2½ hours from Bar Harbor, as compared to the previous 11-hour crossing. As the fastest ferry in North America, they are calling it the "Concorde of the Seven Seas."

It is supposed to be a much smoother ride because it cuts through the waves; it doesn't ride the tops. The four 9,500 horsepower engines run the four water jets actually propelling the Cat. The water jets can pump the equivalent of two Olympic-sized swimming pools *per second*.

It carries 240 cars, four buses and 900 people. It maneuvers quickly and can stop suddenly within two vessel lengths. (I don't think I'd want a cup of McDonald's coffee balanced in my lap!) It has no propeller but the jet engines make much more noise than their predecessors. The environmentalists are concerned about how the fast ferry will affect the endangered Atlantic right whale.

After a lot of frustration with desk clerks and making phone calls that didn't get me anywhere, I finally got a reservation to go on the Cat to Bar Harbor, Maine, when I returned from Newfoundland, but they wouldn't guarantee them. I made the Cat reservation anyway, then called for a Sydney ferry reservation to Newfoundland. I felt very "reserved." I called Escapee RV members in Glace Bay and received permission to park Saturday night and have my mail forwarded via two-day Fed-Ex service costing me $26.

I had seen the Cat just before walking around town but by the time I came back, it had disappeared in fog. When it cleared somewhat, the Cat had slipped out. Cats are like that. No doubt it slipped out past Cape Forchu where the Yarmouth Lighthouse lives on a rocky point. The original was built in 1840 and replaced in the 1960s. It is approximately 76' high and has a million-candlepower light that can be seen 30 nautical miles away.

Beyond Yarmouth, I traveled the Lighthouse Route, on and off #103 and #3. At times I took a loop trip following the water, other times staying on the main highway.

With friendly instructions from a native, I drove through Islands Provincial Park twice, looking for the perfect spot. It was a nice hiking area with bridges, piers, trails, trees and rocks along Shelburne Harbor. The village of Shelburne was on the other side. As I wandered and dreamed, a woman and her daughter and a dog came along. She asked if I was the one who had just turned around in their campsite. They were impressed I was able to back out.

After talking a bit, we naturally got on the subject of nats. I was keeping them at bay with dryer sheets tucked in my headband. Since I have my house on my back, I offered to take some to their campsite. They had a fire going so we chatted for a few minutes. She cleaned houses and did other odd jobs. He was a lobster fisherman so I told them of my PEI experience.

Working until noon, I then drove around Shelburne and on to Lockeport, a historic fishing centre. The Visitor Center was on magnificent sandy Crescent Beach. The water was clear and blue with beautiful whitecaps. I walked along the causeway to the island and Nova Scotia's "first officially designated heritage streetscape." The five historic houses were built in the 1800s, all associated with the Locke family.

I hated leaving that perfect beach but life goes on. This mile-long beach is so impressive that it was once on the back of the Canadian $50 bill. And of course, where there is water and sand and islands, there are lighthouses. Carter's and Gull Rock lighthouses can be seen from Lockeport wharf.

Samuel Champlain really got around didn't he? He landed in 1604 at what is now Liverpool, but it wasn't established as a town until 1759. He is honored at the 1855 Fort Point Lighthouse Park.

Also honored are the town's privateers, whose raiders inflicted devastation, destruction, and downright nastiness on our shipping during the American Revolution and the War of 1812. In the Liverpool Packet's career, it was responsible for capturing over a 100 enemy vessels. They are considered North America's most successful "government-sanctioned pirates." Pox.

Lunenburg's Old Town has been declared a UNESCO World Heritage Site. A salt-bank schooner and a steel-hulled trawler live at the Fisheries Museum of the Atlantic, but I knew that from Visit #1.

What I learned from the helpful Visitor Center lady at Lockeport was that by a fraction of a day, I missed riding on the Bluenose II, a replica of the famous undefeated North Atlantic fishing schooner depicted on the Canadian dime that was built in Lunenburg. Now that would have been exciting. So far I'd missed the Cat and the Bluenose II. I wondered what I would miss next.

The town of Mahone Bay was settled in 1754, 200 years before I graduated from high school but I suppose that isn't historically important in the giant scheme of things. It was pretty neat. The Tingle Bridge

TeaHouse where I had eaten with Anne and Trevor in 1988, was still serving baked apples and cinnamon sauce.

It was an altogether quaint area but what caught my eye, as they had millions of photographers before me no doubt, were "The Three Churches." St. James Anglican, St. John's Lutheran, and the Trinity United Church of Canada were cozied up beside each other on the bay, ecumenical and spectacular, on reflection.

Grave Islands was one of the most beautiful Provincial Parks I had seen. Groomed with trees on a hilly island surrounded by Mahone Bay, I found a great spot where I could look out toward the islands. The volunteer camp host, Brenda, was an Anglican Priest on health leave. She wanted a part-time position and loved campground hosting. Being close to nature appealed to her so her volunteering was from a 10'-in-diameter dome tent that she shares with a Dalmatian dog. I was glad to hear she had a tent heater because it was really cold that night. However, she had been there since March so I guess she was used to it. She was hardier and braver than I.

She was a kayaker, certainly not it in the wimpy 17' ocean-going one I occasionally share with friend Art, but one of those tippy things. She hikes, loves wolves, and asked about Alaska. After swapped stories for almost an hour, we exchanged hugs and said goodbye, a warm, delightful lady.

I awakened to fog and mist but it cleared as the Sprinter and I wandered the headlands. I had forgotten how rugged it was with enormous granite boulders in a sea-carved and barren existence.

Nova Scotia has its own Treasure Island. They call it Oak Island. In 1795 tunnels and shafts were discovered that were thought to be hiding places for treasure hidden by none other than Captain Kidd himself. A museum gives Oak Island's history but the island isn't open to the public.

Road construction stopped me just before Peggy's Cove. I was next to a lady who was fascinated when she saw I was traveling alone. She wanted to do exactly what I'm doing. I didn't ask her if her mechanical abilities exceeded mine.

Though the famed Peggy's Cove Lighthouse no longer serves as a beacon, it is now distinguished as Canada's only lighthouse post office. Walking across the uneven granite and windy headland to the post office, I found their warning to use extreme caution on the rocks well taken, but strange. "Injury and death have 'rewarded' careless visitors to Peggy's Cove." That didn't sound so much like "be careful" as "we'll gitcha if you aren't." I wouldn't think of taking that warning for granite!

I was hungry. The Sou'Wester Restaurant lurked there on the windy rock overlooking all this beautiousness. They advertised a special – lobster. I had tasted bits of it but had never actually eaten a lobster. I always advise people to open their arms to adventure. It was time to put my money where the lobster was.

The waitress brought me the lobster-eating utensils and an instructional placemat on *how* to do it. Good thing, cause I didn't know. Since PEI, I knew how to catch 'em but I didn't know how to eat 'em. The picture showed them as green before cooking and red afterward. That helped a lot. I think I was green before and red afterward, too.

First I twisted the claws off. I tried to forget that just a few short minutes before, this huge lobster was alive and could fight back. I cracked each claw with a nutcracker. I separated the tailpiece from the body by arching the back until it cracked. Then I bent the back and broke the flippers off the tailpiece. By that time its juice had flown everywhere and I knew for sure why I was wearing a plastic bib.

I pushed that poor lobster's insides out with a fork. The next instruction had me unhinging the back from the body. All that yucky green stuff inside was the "tomalley." That was supposed to be the best part. I wasn't convinced I wanted the same thing for breakfast that he did, considering he grabbed whatever was handy on the ocean bottom.

Well, I bent and broke and cracked and pulled and prodded and dug until I finished it. It was o.k. but I'll never be persuaded to wrestle my food before I eat it again. The waitress knew she had a greenhorn on her hands so she did an occasional progress check and said I was doing great. I was kind of glad she was there in case the thing decided to fight back. So much for opening my arms to adventure!

William de Garthe's 100' sculptured granite monument to Canadian fisherman is now a Provincial Park. For models, he used Peggy's Cove residents, plus a guardian angel and the legendary Peggy after whom the Cove is named. Since I was there last, his wife donated his paintings and sculptures to the deGarthe Gallery.

At Halifax, I followed the Visitor Center signs that led me directly downtown with no parking whatsoever and none within a several-block area. I gave up on that but saw a Mail Boxes where I could send out an on-deadline article. I was upset by the time I found an unreasonable parking space. When I walked in and they said, "How are you today?" I replied, "That's not a question to ask right this minute." They were so kind that we were soon all joking. With their explicit directions, I still went the wrong way and drove #102 back to Truro and then toward Cape Breton Island on #104, instead of the coastline. Cities are definitely points in favor of having a car.

The Sprinter's appetite was assuaged for $121 at the Big Irving Station. It was late so I asked to park for the night. Salt Spring Provincial Park where I had stayed on the way down was across the street but I decided for $121, Big Irvin could save me $10 and they kindly did.

It was overcast and spitting rain the next day, a good time and place to take care of "stuff." At a New Glasgow Wal-Mart (I hadn't seen one for months!), I left 10 rolls of slide film, thinking I would come back through about the right time to pick them up.

I crossed the Canso Causeway to Cape Breton Island. It is the world's deepest causeway at 217'. With the French influence in western Nova Scotia, there's a "wee bit 'o Scotland" in the Highlands of Cape Breton Island. If you listen carefully, you'll likely hear bagpipes playing. If you're interested in showing a "bit o the leg," you can even rent kilts. The Cabot Trail skirts (so to speak) three sides of Cape Breton Highlands National Park, a place not to be missed. Supposedly in Nova Scotia there is more Gaelic language spoken than in Scotland!

My views of St. Georges Bay and Bras d'Or Lake (pronounced Brador), were through the rain but none-the-less beautiful. When Sid and I came back through Baddeck, the Alexander Graham Bell Historic Site was closed. I made sure I saw it this time. It was split into seven sections of "The Amazing Worlds of Alexander Graham Bell." Each one, from his homelife to his dedication to the deaf, his inventor's mind, to aviation and building the world's fastest boat, I was totally overwhelmed. It was wonderful. I had no idea he was responsible for so many innovations.

A huge portrait of him brought me to tears. He was a really big man with soft brown eyes and a full white beard. He reminded me of a good friend. He was a compassionate man very much in love with his wife. I bought the book, *The Sound and Silence*, written about their relationship and thoroughly enjoyed it.

She was deaf from an illness and he spent his whole life finding ways to help the deaf. The guide pointed out the huge house across the bay that Bell and his wife built. It was to be a cottage but became a castle, "Beinn Bhreagh," still owned by the family, and private.

The weather wasn't cooperating. I went directly to Mira Lake Provincial Park. On Friday, it was still overcast. I took a roundabout way to the Fortress of Louisbourg National Historic Site through the lobstering Main-à-Dieu area. A bus took us to the island fort. Two-day passes are available, but I had only one day so I buzzed around and saw it in brief form in five hours.

It is one of Canada's largest national historic sites with 16,549 acres, one of the world's largest restorations. Parks Canada has taken public buildings, fortifications, private homes with yards and gardens, and rebuilt a quarter of this 18th Century town.

After its founding in 1713 as a cod fishery, this French colonial seaport had three peaceful decades. Then it went back and forth between the British and French. By 1760, the British, who had it last, destroyed it and left town. To encourage local economy and commemorate its history 201 years later, the Canadian Government began reconstruction.

Through chilly drizzle I did a fast self-guiding tour through the most interesting buildings which included the King's Bakery where soldiers were baking bread. I vowed to buy some on my way out but I didn't make it before they closed. The buildings were somewhat more cheerful with fires going. Costumed docents gave talks and answered questions.

At lunchtime I thawed out, and shared a table with an interesting young couple from Boston, Massachusetts. They were renovating a 130-year-old house. The Grandchamps House provided delicious pea soup, homemade bread and coffee, as they would have in 1744.

In the afternoon I took a tour. *Bienvenue au lieu historique national de la Forteresse-de-Louisbourg. Nous vous invitons à retourner à l'époque où les nations européennes établissent des colonies prospères en Amérique du Nord et luttent*...oops, that was the French tour. I expected more activity but it was early in the season. We did see a firing demonstration and there were other places to visit including Lighthouse Point, the site of Canada's first lighthouse and the Royal Battery interpretive walk.

Saturday morning I drove the back way to Glace Bay along high cliffs. I stopped to drink in the ocean scenery. Just as I realized an eagle was sitting on a rock jetty, a man walking a dog came along and pointed him out to me. It was a narrow road and a young kid standing beside his car, moved closer and hid his face in his arms as I passed. Smart aleck!

The most interesting thing at the Marconi Center was the volunteer who ran their wireless. He showed me all the places he had talked with that morning, Russia, Japan, Australia, Spain.

I walked the high cliffs outside to read Guglielmo Marconi's history and see the photographs and models on display inside. He sent the first west-to-east trans-Atlantic wireless message on December 15, 1902, from Table Head, on the outskirts of Glace Bay, to Cornwall, England. Many radio experiments were conducted at this transoceanic wireless station, the first on the North American continent.

The volunteer, having read the business card I gave the receptionist, became very excited about my RVing experiences. He lived alone since his mother's death, and now wanted with a passion, to go traveling in an RV, but obviously not passion enough, as he was still in Glace Bay.

He went out the door to see what I was driving and thought that was wonderful so I asked if he wanted to see it. Of course I had just come from the laundry and damp pieces were hanging helter skelter. He loved it. I think if I hadn't left the minute I talked him back out the door, he would have been a passenger.

I visited with Escapees Karen and Ron Gillis who graciously allowed me overnight parking in their driveway and took me with them to the grocery store.

On Sunday morning, June 7, with the wind howling and blowing, I left the Gillis home at 6:30 a.m. I was first in line for an 8:00 loading. A military convoy from Ontario was lined up along with trucks, cars, and a couple of RVs. Then tanks moved in. What was I getting into? Had the world declared war on somebody while I wasn't watching TV or reading the papers? A soldier flirted with a little girl in the car next to him, probably had a daughter like her at home and missed her already.

One of the loading guys had a long clean mane of reddish brown hair and a beard. He was very attractive. Well, there's nothing wrong with looking! I know, just another romantic ferry tale.

There is something exciting about waiting for a ferry - going somewhere I'd never seen was part of it. Newfoundland and Labrador, even the name excited me. All announcements were given first in English and French. Anticipation.

Thoughts cross your mind while you're waiting. How can that hull that is pointed skyward, be watertight when it is put back down? What will the wind that was blowing the RV all over the road on the way here, do on the high seas? With disclaimers many paragraphs long, do these people really know what they're doing?

It was an uneventful, reasonably sunny trip with only a few jolts and high swells. As we came into the harbor at Port aux Basque, I saw a big snow ridge hanging on the distant mountain. Yesss! New territory! Up close were Newfoundland's rocky shoreline and high headlands. The sign said, "Welcome to the Rock."

**Gros Morne National Park, Western Brook Pond**

# Newfoundland and Labrador

This island is on Newfoundland Standard Time, the farthest east zone I could be in and still be part of North America. I was a half-hour ahead of Atlantic Standard Time. Yes, a half hour. I knew it would be a fun place, it is pronounced, NewfunLAND.

It was new territory to me, much bigger, and with many more places to visit and things to do than I realized. I arrived in Britain's first colony and Canada's 10th and last province, on June 7, and they do not open their tourist eyes until after mid-June.

Port aux Basque was a fishing village with narrow streets, colorful houses, fishing piers, and a church that dominated the town. Mountains had sizable niches of snow. It was sunny with frigid winds.

I nursed a toothache all day. I stopped for a hot meal thinking coffee would feel good on the tooth. Wrong! I nearly went into orbit. A couple of aspirin calmed it again. Barachois Pond Provincial Park beckoned me for $11. A pain pill and two aspirin got me through a short walk and the night.

A brief morning hop and Cornerbrook, Newfoundland's second largest city, came into view. At the Visitor Center, I explained my dental plight. A call was made to a clinic and *within an hour*, I was in a dental chair. The diagnosis was an abscessed tooth and a hairline-filling crack in another. They pushed together causing my excruciating pain. She ground out the filling, put in a new one and declared it a temporary fix, along with Amoxicillin 500 mgs every six hours for seven days.

Gros Morne became a National Park in 1973, and a World Heritage Site in 1987. It includes Newfoundland's western highlands and the Gulf of St. Lawrence lowlands.

I drove through The Tablelands, where rocks, originally beneath the ocean, were pushed to their present position when Europe and North America collided. Gros Morne is also called the "Galapagos of Geology." At Trout River Village, friendly residents assured me I was welcome to spend the night in a picnic area since the campground wasn't open yet.

What we call lakes and streams, Newfoundlanders call ponds and brooks. I could hardly sleep with looking over a slightly foggy Trout River Pond, a landlocked fjord between "The golden Tablelands and the huge cliffs of the Gregory Plateau," painted in full moonlight.

Although you might see black bears, it is more likely you will see whales, caribou, eagles, and fox. You most certainly will see moose. Speed bumps are not necessary. The possibility of a moose walking in front of your vehicle keeps traveling speeds reasonable. The next morning I counted 17 moose on my return to the main highway.

Hiking trails along rivers and into the mountains beckoned at every point. I finally succumbed and hiked the two-mile boardwalk through the coastal bogs and tuckamore (stunted trees) to Western Brook Pond and the magnificent billion-year-old cliffs rising 2,250' above it. A 2½ hour boat tour explores fjords and waterfalls in this northernmost part of the Appalachian Mountain Range.

Driving north through the Great Northern Peninsula revealed tidy fishing villages with the ocean hurling spray over rocks on one side and boggy marshes and freshwater lakes to the other. Big hauling sleds rested on wood stacks being added to for next winter's fires. Some stacks were arranged in tee-pee fashion, and others this way and that way as somewhat of a cutter's signature. Each yard had its wood stack and fishing boats.

I pulled to the side to take a village picture and realized someone was standing there. I opened my window and waved to him. He took his glove off and grinned with a big wave. A part of me wondered why on earth anyone would live in so bleak an area, and then I realized that in its very bleakness, it was incredibly beautiful.

Five moose were within a few miles of each other. Two crossed in front of me. They didn't pay any attention to fast moving cars but when the Sprinter slowed down, they looked up and moved. Imagine what a "daring do do" entrepreneur could do with all that possible moose poop jewelry.

At St. Anthony, I first walked the boardwalks ending at a deck overlooking the iceberg that nearly blocked the harbor neck. I was properly awed and thrilled with my first major iceberg. Picnicking teenagers told me that it had been twice as big, then it flipped and started to break apart. It was stark white. They also said isn't so unusual to see springtime polar bears in St. Anthony's. Wouldn't I have been thrilled? I didn't think I would ever see one.

I ate clam chowder and a roll at the Lighthouse Café above the iceberg, watching the fog roll in. My tooth was hurting again and I was feverish.

On the northernmost peninsula tip, L'Anse aux Meadows, a National Historic Site, wasn't officially open but people were walking through it. This first authenticated North American Viking Settlement is also a World Heritage Site and may have been used for a base camp to repair boats and lay in supplies. The few restored huts were made from thick peat layers sandwiched with sand and gravel. Ceilings holes provided smoke escapes.

With winter winds blowing, one can only imagine how bleak it must have been in that wide-open space where nothing grows but stunted vegetation. It hasn't changed much in a 1,000 years since this hardy group of Norse men and woman landed at what they called, "Vinland." The ranger, who had lived and played on the mounds as a child, said everyone at that time thought they were Indian mounds.

**L'Anse aux Meadows, Newfoundland**

I asked him about all the neat little gardens I had seen along the roadside. "Before we had a road, we needed to be self-sufficient and always had gardens. When the road came along, we started buying from the stores. We realized it didn't taste as good so we started planting gardens again."

The bog land is rich. They plant gardens beside the roads on what he called "The Queen's land," because of easy access. Some were enclosed in wooden fences, others with wire fences. Still others had no edging, just there, growing in their fertile ground.

I stayed in Pistolet Bay Provincial Park for a couple of days to work on taxes, sleep, take aspirin and get rid of the fever. I shared the park with one other RVer. The drive to Cape Onion was pretty and I could see icebergs that must have been enormous because even in the distance they were big.

A local traveling ahead of me hit his brakes several times, perhaps as a warning to me. He didn't stop but I saw twin moose beside the road. They were good-sized but this year's babies. I had seen four caribou and two other moose already.

People often ask if I get lonely, and for the most part, I don't. Even writing about this, I remember how exciting it was driving south from L'Anse aux Meadows very early on that desolate drive along the St. Lawrence Seaway. However, all of a sudden I realized I was singing this ditty over and over as I drove, no doubt influenced by all the moose I had seen since arriving in Newfoundland.

"I'm a Michigoosey,

And I'm on the loosey,
Lookin' for a moosey, yes I am.
Yes I am." I thought to myself, "You've been alone too long!" It makes me smile to remember how I couldn't stop laughing. Good thing no one could see or hear me. They would have locked me up for sure!

There are two opportunities to visit Labrador. After giving it a minimum of thought, and realizing I might never be there again, I decided to take the ferry to Labrador at St. Barbe. The friendly gas-station fellow directed me to the hotel for information. They had a direct-line ferry-service telephone. It was an early June Friday and I didn't need a reservation, "Just get in line." But first things first, the local restaurant where I had breakfast had only one other patron. It was neat as a pin and if I had been so inclined, I could have eaten off the floor.

I had to laugh, on the ferry brochure, they refer to "Winnebagos" as synonymous with motorhomes. As with any ticket line, I talked with two fellows ahead of me. They were on their way to work on a fishing business refrigeration unit. We discussed places I should visit. One of them sat with me and asked questions about RVing and my travels. It is sometimes easier to tell a stranger your troubles so I was soon hearing about a painful separation and the two teenage sons involved. And you listen because you want someone to listen to you when you are troubled.

After the 1½-hour ferry ride from St. Barbe and across the Strait of Belle Isle, I spent two days exploring a small portion of Labrador and Québec. It was a breathtaking view leaving Blanc Sablon, Québec. Waves crashed into shore on a sandy crescent beach. In higher country, windblown trees and bushes clung to whatever earth they could find. Freshwater lakes reflected blue skies from massive boulder nests, their overflow cascading through the last pockets of springtime snow. The good paved road had grades from 6 to 15%. A spectacular view overlooked the St. Paul River and the town. The mist rolled in. The wind howled. The camper rocked.

I was getting dangerously low on gas. Down the mountain and beyond the one-lane, wooden-bottomed bridge across the St. Paul River, I found an open Visitor Center. Wow! They said the road continued for another 10-12 km. I couldn't stop before the end of the road could I?

I traveled the last dusty gravel miles. It was worth it for the grand smile elicited from a fisherman carrying gasoline jugs down a hill. They were obviously empty because when I waved at him, he grinned and lifted one can high in response to my greeting. His enthusiasm made my day.

The Labrador end of my exploring took me through mountains with tall trees, a herd of sheep, and along the Pinware River that forged its way through the valley. The scenery became more like Québec's rocky side as I neared the ocean and the northern end of the road.

At the Whaler's Restaurant in Red Bay, I found talkative locals and a waitress who kindly phoned the guide to open the Visitor Center and Whaler's

Museum. In the late 1500s, Red Bay was the whaling capital of the world.

It was the opinion of this group that even Cornerbrook (pop 22,400), had too fast a pace. They really liked being in Red Bay (pop 300) where it was quiet. My on-call museum guide was a girl who attended college in Cornerbrook. It was her first experience away from home. As with the restaurant group, she felt the pace was too fast and really liked coming back where it was quiet.

At Pinware River Provincial Park, eight boys and girls knocked on my door. The spokesgirl said they wanted to say hello. They were sixth, seventh, and eighth graders who lived in nearby Pinware and came to the campground evenings to visit with (and question) campers.

I asked why one girl's hair was wet. A fellow said, "She went swimming," then added, "in the water." I couldn't help myself, "In all my travels, I have found it extremely difficult to swim outside the water." They thought the American was hilarious.

We chatted for 15 minutes. I think they would have liked to come inside but I thought eight kids of any age were a few too many to invite inside. I commented that "Newfies" were very friendly. They set me straight, "*We* are Labbies!"

On the way to L'Anse Amour Lighthouse, the tallest in Atlantic Canada, was the Maritime Archaic Indian burial place of a 12-year-old child dating back 7,500 years. It is the oldest dated human burial mound in North America. The lighthouse was built in 1857 when all equipment and supplies had to be brought in by schooners.

Too late I discovered two ferry crossings on Saturday instead of three. I was on mainland North America but I had traveled as far as I could in either direction. I boondocked until I could ferry back to an island! My afternoon/evening home was on a Labrador gravel spit high over the Strait of Belle Isle, overlooking Blanc Sablon, Québec. I shared it with sheep.

I still felt a bit feverish but with a little extra sleep, tax work (which was what put me to sleep), and enjoying the view, the time passed quickly.

At the ferry station, my Alaska sweatshirt sparked conversation with a retired Florida engineer and highway builder who grew up on a Texas offshore island. Being the oldest of six children and too often having the responsibility of caring for them, he made the decision to never marry or have any "rugrats."

He had traveled via freighter (with his boxed Honda car) from somewhere above Québec City. It had taken a week because the freighter stopped at every port along the St. Lawrence Seaway. As motorcyclist, pilot, and military, he had traveled the world except for the Canadian "Providences" as he called them.

His job had been as a three-piece suiter but with his uncut hair and a full-untrimmed beard, he no longer looked the part. He was seeing everything in his path and doing it as fast as he could. He spent four weeks in Alaska and figured he covered all of it. I mentioned several places he hadn't been, and then he said he had driven the circle. Ah well, another one who would no doubt travel Europe in a weekend and think they had seen it all.

The cute guy who directed traffic aboard the Northern Cruiser Limited at St. Barbe, was directing here at Blanc Sablon. He said he might not be able to get the Sprinter aboard because of its height but eventually he directed my backing on board. I usually have no problem with backing but I was backing from bright sunlight into a black abyss and I couldn't see where I was going. I think he was pulling my leg mightily when he said this was his first year directing ferry traffic because I backed the Sprinter into a spot that looked like it would require butter smeared on either side.

At any rate, he was even more talkative this time. He was born in Halifax, Nova Scotia, and though quite proud of being French, he neither spoke the language nor knew his heritage. He wasn't even sure if he was Acadian or not. His dream was to be a Master Mariner and captain of his own ship, but then again, with a family in St. John, he wasn't sure he wanted to be gone that much. He had worked some of the great ports around the world, Seattle, Los Angeles, Tokyo, but with each job, he was getting closer to home. He didn't look old enough to have done all that but then again, maybe that was the product of my being older.

Back in St. Barbe, Newfoundland, I stopped at the gas station and grocery store where the owner had been so helpful. He filled the Sprinter and we talked of my Labrador visit and the fact I had never seen an iceberg until this trip. When I paid my bill, the gentleman gave me a lovely, matted photograph of an iceberg dwarfing a village.

Since I had spent so much time seeing the western side of Newfoundland, I scrambled to see the rest and barely scratched the surface.

At a Provincial Visitor Center, Louise said she had just talked with two guys that had driven the Trans-Labrador Highway, "Better gravel was being put on it and they seemed to think it was quite driveable for cars." I surmised it would be o.k. for the Sprinter, too.

The plans for the Cat trip from Yarmouth to Maine; the Shubenacadie River tidal bore ride; and the stop to pick up my Wal-Mart slides (a big headache for me later), were ditched. I cancelled and made ferry reservations for Goose Bay, Labrador, leaving on Wednesday, June 17.

Gander International Airport had a very interesting air museum with a sad video on the 1985 plane that crashed at the end of their runway right after takeoff. All 259 members of the U. S. 101st Airborne Division, the "Screaming Eagles," returning from peacekeeping duties in the Middle East, were killed.

The video was a 10-year perspective on what the families were doing and whether they felt it was sabotage and if the government was holding back the truth. A few miles away, The "Silent Witness Memorial" to the soldiers and crew at the crash site, now Peacekeeper Park, was impressive.

The trip to Bonavista took me through part of the Terra Nova National

Park. Costumed interpreters showed me through the three floors of the 1843 Cape Bonavista restored lighthouse. This was also the spot where John Cabot sighted the New World in 1497, 501 years before. His statue and memorial were outside on the rocks. Side roads took me above the shore. Sheep grazed along and in the gravel road and on the green carpeted cliffs.

This late afternoon I drove back through historic Bonavista with its narrow streets, old buildings, and crooked-pole, weathered fences holding in sheep and cows. Lilacs were out. Beyond the village, a huge iceberg floated off shore. I think I could have stayed there forever.

Bonavista was building a replica of the Matthew and an interpretation centre. John Cabot sailed into the harbour on the Matthew, discovering a "New World" that would now surely blow his mind. Although right there in Bonavista, it probably hadn't changed as much as in the rest of the world.

Near Goobies, I bought gas at a Big Irving Station and with paying over $138, they were delighted to let me spend the night. I stayed here a second night on my way back through.

During a conversation with two fellows waiting for the post office to open in a tiny village, one commented, "You're a long way from home. Are you traveling with a show?" I must have looked really puzzled. He pointed, "Your shirt." I was wearing a sweatshirt with "Shoji" on it that I had bought in Branson, Missouri, representing the Japanese violinist. That was funny.

Cupids is 400 years old, then we have Heart's Desire, Heart's Delight, and the one I was looking for, Heart's Content. In 1866, Heart's Content became the western terminus for the first successful transatlantic cable that stretched along the ocean bottom from Valentia, Ireland. Isn't it absolutely incredible that 132 years later I retrieved e-mail messages snatched from the air! I found only a tiny park with a glassed-in board telling what had happened there. The Cable Station was closed. And then there was Amelia Ear"hart."

I followed a narrow, horrendous gravel road toward the National Historic Site. The road was so bad, I thought I was lost again. I flagged down an older local couple who confirmed I was on the right track. We chatted a few minutes and he asked, "Are you alone?" I said yes. He said, "If you get into trouble, send for me, since you don't know anyone else here." We all laughed since I didn't know them either. They left without giving me their names. Good move.

That rough road finally ended where so many noted pilots had taken to the skies, including Wiley Post. In 1931, he flew around the world from this point. Amelia Earhart flew off this scenic point a year later. The historical marker reads, *"May 20, 1932...she took off from Harbor Grace, Newfoundland, in her red, high-wing Lockheed Vega monoplane...14 hours – 56 minutes later, after storms, wing icing and a fractured manifold ring, threatened destruction, she landed in a cow pasture outside Londonderry, Ireland, to become the first woman to solo fly across the Atlantic Ocean."*

The air field looked as rough as the road I had been driving on. It was a very short run downhill. Why here? I wondered what she was thinking when she took off, a true pioneer.

It was an interesting drive along the historical waterfront homes to The Custom's House, now the Conception Bay Museum. The curator gave me the scoop on Peter Easton, a legendary pirate of note in around 1600. She had researched him for 2½ years, finally losing his trail after, "He married a rich lady and moved to France at about the age of 40." She was so animated about this pirate, that I twitted her about a romantic infatuation. She didn't deny it.

Down the street the Cathedral of Immaculate Conception had flipped its lids. The two giant towers had been removed in a renovation process.

On to Witless Bay and the Atlantic shores where I drove under a fog bank and into the picturesque Petty Harbour and Maddox Cove villages. They were used as background for several movies. On Cape Spear, I was closer to Ireland than my daughter in Washington State. I wandered through the WWII bunkers and took pictures of the rugged rock shoreline below. I concluded that the only reason Cape Spear is North America's easternmost point, is that God couldn't see to go any farther; it was too foggy.

A short drive took me to Signal Hill above St. John's Harbour. Cabot Tower is a National Historic Site to commemorate John Cabot's voyage to Newfoundland and contains an exhibit on Guglielmo Marconi's receiving the first transatlantic wireless message in 1901. The tower also contained a very good second-year journalism student salesman. We talked writing while he sold me Newfoundland's unique bakeapple and partridgeberry sauce for my kids and T-shirts for the grandchildren.

With no time left to explore the considerable interests in St. John's and the rest of the island, I returned to Gander for two new front tires. I didn't know what I was getting into on the Trans-Labrador Highway but instinct prompted me to better front rubber and an oil change.

In the meantime, I did laundry. I shared the laundry with a non-committal young fellow, at least until I asked him a question. The floodgates opened. He had a wife and two kids in Virginia Beach, Virginia, where he was stationed. He was in Canada for "war games" and he sounded and looked homesick. At 27, he talked about retiring in another few years and I wondered where I had gone wrong. He was obviously homesick and once he started talking, I didn't think he was going to stop.

I headed north to see the Twillingate icebergs. I gnawed on chicken nuggets, drove through small villages, and admired the Long Point Lighthouse view over Notre Dame Bay (Notre Dame, a touch of home).

An unmarked gravel road led to that perfect two-berg picture. I went past a house and wound up in a boat yard. At that point, I wasn't sure the road was public. I had to back the Sprinter as far as the house, then turn around. The workers looked at me rather strangely.

At Lewisporte, the Sprinter and I boarded the ferry for the 35-hour trip to

Happy Valley/Goose Bay, Labrador.

I chose the top bunk because there was a reading light. Turning around in a cramped space, backing down a cold aluminum ladder that kills bare feet made me wonder if it was a mistake. It was gruesomely hot. I finally gave up and went on deck to watch the sunrise. Another early riser was there. This gentleman, probably in his mid-70s since he talked about being in WWII, retired after 37 years with the railroad. He was now traveling wherever possible by rail, probably for free.

It was more than a little mind-boggling to realize that those sun and water-sculpted ice mountains we were traveling through, might be 1,200 years old! They originate in the high Arctic and Greenland and may take two or three years to float the 1,800 nautical miles to Newfoundland.

It wasn't difficult believing this part of the ocean is called "Iceberg Alley." That's exactly what it was like, a corridor of icebergs. They were probably a ¼ or ½ mile away from each side of the ferry but they were huge even at that distance, when you consider what is visible is about 1/7th to 1/10th the size of the iceberg's total mass. The rest of it is under water. I thought a lot about the Titanic going down in the icy Atlantic off Newfoundland 86 years before on a night much like that one.

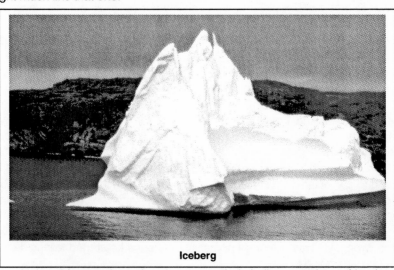
**Iceberg**

At breakfast and as the day unraveled, I discovered my friend was married and had been for many years but his wife has arthritis. She travels with him depending on the circumstances. He has an adventurous soul and has been everywhere. When a trip sounds like it is too much for her, she is content staying behind with the grandchildren and her crafts. They have found a happy meeting ground and I admired them for making it work.

Several of us shared my binoculars. My new grey-haired friend, slender, well dressed, and healthy and wealthy enough to do what he wanted to do, was really sweet. I juggled my glasses, sunglasses, binoculars, and camera.

He put my binoculars over his head when they weren't being used, and helped me keep track of everything else. Without being flirtatious on either side, I was comfortable with this well-trained husband who was so happily married.

We spent most of the time topside watching icebergs. They really were fascinating. He found figures in them and you really could. Several times between icebergs, we enjoyed drinks or dinner, joined by another single lady we had met. He was fun and had a nice sense of humor. Whenever he started to get into something funny, I gave him "The look" and that made him laugh. I got so I knew when he was going to pull my leg or hers.

We three shared a last cup of coffee as we pulled into Goose Bay. Margie was born in the part of Labrador I had just visited. She was staying a few days with her son who lived in Goose Bay. Our friend was staying the day and returning to Lewisporte that night. We said our goodbyes a couple of times, wishing each other well on our trips. and parted each to our own direction.

I never knew their last names and will never see either of them again but it was a nice acquaintanceship while it lasted. It is funny how warm and close you can become in a captive area, especially if you have a few things in common. I'm not into wanting somebody else's husband but he was so friendly, fun, and attentive, I remembered ten-fold what I am missing by not being part of a couple. I don't generally feel lonely but suddenly I was.

As I drove away from the ferry terminal, I saw the Goose Bay road crew. The crew was one person. He drove, stopped, got out and patched potholes, got back in and moved on to another pothole.

Knowing I would likely not return, I took a few hours and drove out to Sheshatshiu and North West River. Sheshatshiu appeared to be Native American housing only. I drove through North West River, central Labrador's oldest community. The Sprinter stood out like a sore thumb, as in many other places, but I enjoyed beautiful views of Lake Melville and Grand Lake.

Happy Valley/Goose Bay was a transatlantic aircraft ferry facility of the United States, Canada, and Great Britain during World War II. The base is still used as a tactical flight training facility by Canadian, British, German, and Dutch Air Forces.

Happy Valley/Goose Bay, the mainland portion of Newfoundland-Labrador, wasn't so different from any other North American community, with Burger King and Radio Shack. You can get most anything you need in this town of roughly 9,000. All of Labrador's 293,347 square kilometres has a population of only of 30,335 permanent residents. It is truly on the edge of the wilderness.

While the attendant pumped gas into the Sprinter, the guy across the aisle started talking and we were soon in a three-way conversation. They said the Trans-Labrador Highway wasn't bad but it was a "tote" road. He didn't discourage me from driving through that vast wilderness.

People "in the know," including those at the Visitor Center, did nothing to discourage me from driving this road with a RV. I can only think they really didn't know the true conditions, but then I've followed other people's ideas of "good" roads before.

The 180-miles to Churchill Falls was listed as "Pit run gravel - tote road only," but it was a fantastic gravel road. It was level, straight as an arrow, wide enough I wasn't intimidated by the sharp drop-off on either side, and scenic. I could travel their posted 70-km/hr-speed limit. I relaxed and admonished myself for being so suspicious. An American Airlines plane flew over. That was a good omen, right?

After approximately 60 miles of that mistaken confidence, I came to a screeching halt. The scene in front of me brought descriptive phrases to mind like, "Axle deep" and "Will I be here forever." It was then I remembered what should have been my first clue, "Car rental agencies will not rent vehicles for travelling on Route 500 (Trans-Labrador Highway)."

Suddenly gratefulness for the two new front tires, full tanks of propane and gasoline, at least a month's store of food, and the Sprinter's overall good condition, washed over me. The sharp rocks probably weren't good on the new tires, but it was better than having old ones punctured in that mess.

This wasn't the "tote" road at all. I had been traveling on the newly constructed section that *replaced* the tote road. An enormous loader pushed equally enormous boulders into ravines along with various grades of gravel and dirt over that. A roller packed it all down. They waved me across.

The next 60 miles were the rough, narrow, winding, one-lane tote road, which really wasn't a major problem. The problem was where the old road intersected with the new road and they built it while I waited! I could not believe the loose dirt and rocks I was driving through up to my axles. I think that is where I creamed my step into oblivion for the third time in four years. The good part was that they had the equipment to pull me out if I got stuck. I'm not sure the workers could believe a RV driving through there.

When I stopped for anything, the mosquitoes were bigger and more plentiful than I had seen anywhere else, including Alaska. I knew if I went outside, they would eat me for breakfast sans the eggs and hashbrowns. Most workers wore mosquito-netting hats.

The right-a-way was being surveyed and cleared. It finally dawned on me that the cute little red "cups" I saw packed into rocky areas, were dynamite set ups. No doubt about it, it was a dynamite experience, and I'm sure the end result will be just like the first 60 miles of great gravel road.

After surviving the worst part, a big converted bus passed me heading for Goose Bay. Behind it was the wife driving the tow car. I was certain the bus would get through but how on earth she made it with that low-clearance tow car, I can't imagine! A few cars went by that direction and I couldn't conceive how they made it when I doubted I would make it with my high clearance.

Only one semi came up behind me and I let him by. Later that one and one heading for Goose Bay were stopped talking to each other. A traffic jam, there in the middle of nowhere!

The last 60 miles into Churchill Falls were horrendous. It was washboardy and very bumpy with big rocks coming through very little gravel. The freezer door came off in my arms when I stopped for lunch. I was thrilled when the pavement near Churchill Falls came under my wheels.

It is saying something to say that was the worst 180 miles I have ever driven. I was a bit discouraged until the young man at the Churchill gas station said, " You've gone through the worst part of it. The 149 miles to Labrador City and the Québec border is 'pretty good.'" Fortunately, he was mostly right.

The modern town of Churchill Falls owes its existence to the Western Hemisphere's single largest hydroelectric generating station built in 1967. The huge underground turbines produce 5,225 megawatts of power from the 250' drop over the mighty Churchill River Falls.

I found a large empty gravel lot to park in for the night and slept sound. It had been an exciting day but exhausting. It had rained off and on all day and continued through the night. I took off again at 5:30 a.m.

Culvert ends are very black and resemble creatures. I've seen many a culvert bear in my time so when I saw a distant big black blob, I figured it was my eyesight playing tricks again. Someone had pointed out that with the entire wilderness to wander in, I was unlikely to see any creatures near the road, although Newfoundland/Labrador is supposed to have one of the continent's largest concentrations of black bears. At any rate this culvert sprouted ears and a nose and ambled across the road like he owned it...and indeed he did, a bushy black bear.

Other small animals, freshwater lakes, falls, spring flowers, ospreys, and eagles filled my day. I drove from low boggy land through boulder country into dryer, higher, wooded mountain country.

A small RV was camped on a riverbank. I thought it would make a nice cover shot. I took river pictures with this motorhome in the background. I went down the other bank and took Sprinter pictures. Realizing if I moved the Sprinter, I could get a couple spectacular pictures of it with the falls, trees, and mountains, I moved it down by the bank. I finished what I was doing and granted the falls was noisy, but I looked across the road and the mini-motorhome had stolen away. I didn't even hear it start up. A car had also been parked alongside the road. Hmmm.

It made me wonder if they were ready to leave when I came along (they were watching me take pictures)...or did they leave because I interrupted a clandestine liaison between a woman and a man for whom another belle toils. The fiction side of my brain went into overdrive.

As I got closer to Labrador City, I saw more cabins on the rivers and lakes. I crossed the Québec North Shore and Labrador Railroad tracks that run from Sept-Îles, Québec, on the St. Lawrence Seaway, north to Schefferville, Labrador. At the edge of town, I pulled off the road to check something, and realized a fellow in a pick-up truck had pulled in ahead of me. He walked back, "Are you all right?"

"I'm fine. I stopped to see what had crashed in the back of the motorhome."

"You're sure you're all right?"

I assured him I was. I didn't fit his image of what should be on that road and when I pulled off, he thought I had a problem. People are so much more concerned in wilderness areas like these.

The fellow at the gas station was chatty. "Are you from Wabush (a small nearby town)?

"No, I'm from Texas." His immediate response was, "Texas, oh my God!" I thought that was pretty funny.

Labrador City and Wabush have grown into modern towns with most facilities, due to North America's largest open-pit iron ore mining concentrate and pelletizing mineral operation. Amazingly to me, this area is also home to "Serious ski buffs, with unexcelled downhill and (world class) cross country skiing." I guess with the long winter season, it makes sense.

I crossed into Québec on Route #389. The rest of the 350 miles was varying stages from good to bad gravel, potholes, less harrowing construction, some good and some very good paved road. It was dryer country with higher mountains, lots of lakes and falls.

A big gravel pit cradled the Sprinter and I for the night but I didn't sleep well because all of the "little" noises. Either something was already inside the camper or fighting hard to get inside. Then, even though it was still dark, some big bird or something was on the roof. I finally gave up and drove. Finally stopped outside another big dam and slept until it was light, then got cleaned up and drove on into Baie Comeau.

Of special note in the Manicouagan Valley, were two of the largest hydroelectric power dams in the world. The Daniel-Johnson dam has a 490' waterfall and the largest arch and buttress dam at the Manic-5 generating station. The other was the Manic-2 generating station and dam with 230' waterfalls only a few miles before I reached the St. Lawrence Seaway (again) at Baie-Comeau.

Would I drive that 679 miles again. Probably not but then again, by this time the new gravel road has probably been completed. Am I glad I did it? Yes, Yes, Yes. I wouldn't have missed it for the world. My only regret is that I wasn't able to take more time. With a family reunion scheduled in Minnesota, I had to keep going. Actually, I always feel I haven't spent as much time as I should have.

I filled up with gas, delighted to be back on a main drag again, Route #138. Apparently I had forgotten the language barrier in Québec, with over 80% of its inhabitants speaking French. Perhaps it was because all other

Québec travels were near big cities and more people spoke English.

It was time to make a beeline for Minnesota. I had traveled the St. Lawrence Seaway, visited Québec and Montreal on another trip, and generally traveled across lower Québec and Ontario. I was also directly across the St. Lawrence from the Gaspé Peninsula, which was another beautiful part of Québec I had traveled. I turned on #172 to hit territory I hadn't been in before. I followed northernmost and paved routes across Québec, #172, #170, #169, #167, #113, eventually connecting with #117 that took me into Ontario. Québec is Canada's largest province and twice the size of Texas, so it seemed to take forever to cross it.

The roads were mostly two lane and in pretty good condition. Of course anything was beautiful and most tolerable after the Trans-Labrador and #389! The roads I loved, but after traveling through the wilderness I wasn't prepared for getting into this major tourist area and by June 26, they were coming out in full force. Although my time schedule didn't allow, this whole area from the St. Lawrence Seaway to Chicoutimi, basically the Saguenay-Lac-Saint-Jean area, is one that should be explored thoroughly.

I saw beautiful waterfalls, lakes, mountains, and followed rivers, and most importantly, bought some fresh strawberries to have over bread because I didn't want to take the office supplies out of the oven to bake.

At another Big Irving Station, the young man spoke very little English. Even at that, we managed to cover a lot of territory. He was curious about the motorhome and my travels after seeing the Sprinter's map. He reminded me of a young Tim Matheson. When I paid, I handed him a business card. He looked it all over, even though he had several customers waiting, and then said, "You are a person with many sympathies." I laughed and thanked him but have no idea what that meant. He said I could park for the night.

Along with the long, lonely trek northward through the Reserve Faunique Ashuapmushuan, it was also extremely hot by mid day and I don't do well with heat. It was pretty with many lakes and thankfully, lots of stops with picnic tables. At the first one I took a much-needed nap but then stepped out to get my hot water fired up and almost stepped on a snake that had probably been sleeping in the shade of the MH. That got my heart started I can tell you! I stopped often if no more than to take a break.

I drove on up to Chibougamau just to say I had driven to the end of the paved road but then turned onto #113 and the long downside trip to Senneterre and connection with Transcanada North, #117.

Late in the day I stopped to make a phone call. Two ladies sitting on a porch swing said hello to me and admired the motorhome. When I was through making my call, I talked with them. They were both widowed and lived there in the "Pension" house.

"Where will you be eating supper?"

"In the motorhome."

"Oh, you can cook in it too?"

I would have invited them inside but it was still messy from driving the Trans-Labrador. It was interesting that no one else had been able to speak English but these two charming ladies did quite well with it and they must have been in their early 70s.

By this time it was very hot, the air conditioning wasn't working all that well, and the alternator belt screeched when the engine was cold. I connected with #66 in Ontario and again chose the northernmost route #11 to Thunder Bay. I guess I was anxious to get "home." I crossed the border after dark. The border guard asked me routine questions plus.

"Do you like traveling alone?"

"It beats waiting on my front porch until someone asks me."

With "Good Luck" and a smile, I filled up with gas at $1.17 a gallon in Grand Portage, Minnesota. The attendant laughed when I asked if people coming across from Canada kissed the ground when they paid. Of course that was 1998, as I write this in 2001, we pray to ever see $1.17 again.

People often ask me where I will settle down when I "Hang up my wheels." The following is a partial hanging.

**Home Sweet Arizona Home**

# *Upsizing*

On September 4, 2001, I will celebrate my 15th year of full-timing. By October, the Sprinter will celebrate his 14th year with an odometer reading approximately 215,000 miles (after a fourth Alaska-Canada journey). In 1999, I received the deed for a 50' X 70' RV lot that I bought many years ago at the Escapees North Ranch Rainbow Park near Congress, Arizona. It is high desert country at 2,500' elevation with surrounding mountains occasionally covered with snow.

I parked on it off and on during winters when I wasn't in Mexico or other interesting warm-weather places. It was nice. I had electric, sewer, water, and a 10' X 12' shed with which the Sprinter and I could exchange "junque." Yup, a long-dormant "nesting" syndrome was reviving in a teeny tiny corner of my roaming heart.

In 2000, I revised a book, and landscaped the lot. This lot backs up against a large retention pond whose function is to prevent flooding. I was very excited about this. I pictured Noah-sized rainstorms. I would buy that long-desired kayak, build a pier, and spend my leisure days kayaking the pond and the drainage canal that runs through the park to another retention pond. I'm still waiting.

After making another giant loop around the lower 48, I returned to North Ranch. Friends dating back to high school also live in the park. One day Jan Carmichael took me cruising in her golf cart. Two fifth wheels sported "For sale" signs. We couldn't resist looking. My lot specifications were for either a RV or a park model but I hadn't planned on either one. Funny how things happen when you aren't looking.

The first one was nice but nice didn't do it. I'm not sure whether it was the condition of the next fifth wheel or the warmth of its owners, Sharon and Dick Docksteader, but with the scrawl of a pen, I started 2001 owning two RVs. The Royales International fifth wheel would be a winter base and the Sprinter for traveling. Life was changing again.

Upsizing from a 27' motorhome with roughly 22' of living space, into the 40' fifth wheel with a living room slide out, was almost as great a revelation as downsizing from ye olde Michigan homestead. The emptier the Sprinter became, the more his fenders grinned. On future trips to town, he fairly danced down the highway. Gas mileage improved radically.

I found things in the Sprinter I didn't remember I had. Underneath the clothesbasket, I found two new boxes of Crest Toothpaste. It must have been a three for one deal. My teeth were happy. Soup cans surfaced that predated the Civil War. As I carted "stuff" into the Royales, I wiped the Sprinter's upper cupboards clean. My dishcloth turned a puzzling brown. Then I remembered a bumpy Mexican journey and a coffee jar that rolled around sans its lid until the contents filtered into the lower cupboard. Always did like filtered coffee.

The dining table has leaves – just like real people. It's next to the kitchen where there are major drawers, shelves, cupboards, and a sliding pantry. I can start collecting again! This is a good thing? And whatever I put in the cupboards doesn't have to be glued down. It will only fall and break via earthquake, then it will be San Andreas' fault, not mine. The oven is empty. I can actually use it without emptying it of copy paper, manila envelopes, multi-talented labels, and spare printer refills.

The nooks and crannies fascinate me. I pulled up steps and found a potato nook. Lifting the foot of the queenside bed gave me not only a cranny, but almost another room. I could make a trap door under the bed that would let me out into the night, but then I haven't figured a scenario that would warrant it. Darn! But it does lend itself to a writer's fertile mind, don't you think? Remington Steele, where are you when I need you?

The bathroom provided a niche big enough to hold the giant-sized scales. I really don't need them. For my self-confidence, they are permanently welded at 120 pounds. The bathtub is about a foot bigger than the Sprinter's. I fit better. At least I can breathe while I'm wedged in this one. With the dressing room type bulbs around the bathroom mirror, I feel like a star. They are wrinkle-proof to go along with the permanent 120-pound scale.

The toilette top is made of leather. When they are made of leather, they are "toilettes." A little spray nozzle hangs behind the stool for spraying away extraneous material. This tells me a little about what the unit cost originally. The Sprinter toilets' only claim to fame is a cracked seat, the result of a 200,000-mile stretch of rough road.

I used to swing around the end of the Sprinter's bed and arrive in the bathroom without opening my eyes. Before I was accustomed to the tri-level Royales, I negotiated the first two hall steps, missed the bathroom completely, fell down the next two hall steps, completely negating my need to find it. The thigh-length bruise was a constant reminder to remember the steps and their order, succinctly.

One of my "stashed" mechanics came to see my new home. His comment on seeing the shower was, "At least it's high enough you won't hit your head when you shower." I looked up at his 6'1" frame from my 5' 2 ½" (providing I haven't shrunk) and said, "That was never a problem."

I brought spaghetti in from the Sprinter, no, not the kind that compliments garlic bread. Do you know how many cords run the surge protector, copier, mouse, CPU, monitor, keyboard, sound system, and telephone? As my oldest would say, "You've come a long way, Baby." What only a few short years ago would have driven me to that edge beyond which few return, I actually had no problem re-connecting. I am proof there is hope for those who are 60-something and reluctantly entering the 21st Century.

My kayaking buddy, Art, cut holes in a cabinet top. With the monitor and printer on top, the keyboard and mouse fit nicely on a sliding table beneath. A piano keyboard resided on it for the previous owners. The CPU, surge protector, and phone jack were installed behind cupboard doors below. Another revelation came with the office equipment. I didn't need to fasten it down because of its uncommon desire for flying lessons on abominably bad roads, or put inch-thick pads beneath it. I lovingly wiped at least three years of dust from it. The newly accumulated dust will never be as interesting as past dust gathered on North America's back roads.

The propane catalytic heater "whooshed" at me. Whoosh is synonymous with dangerous. I don't like things that whoosh at me. It did this several times until there was enough propane in the air to light up Cleveland. I have to get down on my knees to see the start button. Do you know how hard it is to get down on my knees at 4:30 in the morning? The Royales catalytic did a final "whoosh," and the pad glowed faintly. I turned it to high and prayed for the best. Several days later I read the directions. It still whooshes at me but there is a rhythm to it. We tolerate each other.

If anyone were even vaguely interested, they could follow my progress through the Royales by the lights. There are big flat switches. In the Sprinter I had to reach up and turn on a switch. Here I barely breath on them and behold, there is light. That's great except during a middle-of-the-night foray when I am feeling my way along the hall and blow any further sleep by accidentally brushing against a light switch. Lights, both AC and battery, are everywhere, big ones in the ceilings, tiny ones in the hall stairway and over the bed, four frilly lamps in the living room, another to light up a glass cabinet. Lights automatically come on in the closets.

Red lights prove the TV booster is on and that the refrigerator and water heater are working. They signal functioning clocks in the sound system and the microwave. Looking down the hallway, it resembles a red-light district! Hey, I was born in a log cabin; this is, well, Royales living.

In the living room is a complete sound system plus radio, TV, and places to hide all the CDs, tapes, and movies. It took me a few days to realize radio speakers live in the bathroom and bedroom.

The Sprinter is definitely not soundproof, but the night is more romantic considering I live alone. The Royale's bed can be made up as I walk around it. The Sprinter's bed is scrunched against the wall, but a push of the curtains, a slide of the window, and I am immediately transported to a world of magnificent stars or full moonlight at 3 a.m. I can hear the desert coyotes, a rushing mountain stream, the rustle of the cottonwoods, or soft rain sounds. The less luxurious side of life has its compensations.

While I love the new-to-me permanently skirted desert home, the Sprinter will always be my first love. The 40' Royales could never have fit into places I have parked or driven the Sprinter. Old Faithful has taken me to far away places with strange sounding names. He has patiently waited for me in airport parking lots while I flew to European adventures or to play with grizzlies or polar bears. He has lounged beside the still waters, or the not so still Yukon River, Schuswap Lakes, Yellowstone Lake, and the Sea of Cortez, while I kayaked or canoed. He has dawdled at the mountain's bottom while I hiked or paraglided off it.

How could I not love those Sealbeam eyes and the warmth I feel when I unlock the door and say, "Hi Honey, I'm home!"

It is nice to have a stationary place of my own to hang up the tires for a few weeks or a few months at a time but I do sort of wonder at the sundry tools that have taken up residence in the shed, wheelbarrow, shovels, rakes, and sprayers. For all these full-timing years I have moved by the time the grass needed mowing or gardens needed weeding or something required paint. But then again, there is joy in doing those jobs again and North Ranch is a perfect place to watch those incredible Arizona sunsets.

My friend, Steve, who has been full-timing for several years now, doesn't understand this "return to the soil" at all. He says, "I have waited for this full-time RVing freedom all my life and now that I am retired, I don't want to stop traveling until I can't do it anymore." I understand how he feels because until a couple of years ago I couldn't conceive of not traveling. I admit that being at North Ranch among friends, I feel content, but I also know that by spring and the completion of this book, I will have an impressive case of "itchy wheels," and be more than ready to fire up the rejuvenated Sprinter.

The Sprinter's winter months of quiet existence, except for a once-a-week church and shopping escape (until I get a car next winter), has provided him time for inside and outside scrubbing and repairing. The engine compartment "stuff," the underside, and tires have been checked and replaced where necessary. We'll shortly experience springtime in Canada and Alaska as we once again travel the gravel of questionable back roads. I'll watch rain clouds from mountaintops knowing they will only stick around long enough to say hello, sort of like a full-time RVer.

And speaking of living every minute (If you didn't notice, that was the whole point of the book!), I want to end *RVing Adventures with the Silver Gypsy* with a very special adventure.

# Bear with Me

A frigid November wind swirled around the solitary building, blowing snow between the steel bars. It clung tenaciously to the windowpanes, bringing the Arctic winter up close and personal. Shivering with the knowledge that I couldn't leave this building without armed guards, I quietly descended the ladder and snuck out of the crowded dormitory. I took a quick GI shower, dressed, and headed down the cold, bleak corridor. The dining area was cozy and fragrant at 6 a.m. Sizzling bacon and fresh coffee stirred my saliva. It was my third morning behind bars, waiting, waiting to see the Lords of the North, the polar bears of Churchill, Manitoba, Canada.

The room soon filled with 31 world-traveling Elderhostelers. Conversations ranged from kayaking to film festivals to the inevitable politics with Canadian and United States elections eminent. Limited exchange was given to aches and pains though we were all 50+.

A Cypress couple discovered I was a full-time RVer. She told me about, "This lady author traveled alone and...." The husband piped up with, "A guy wrote the technical stuff in the book and...." What fun to realize the book was *Freedom Unlimited, The Fun and Facts of Full-timing*, the book Bill Farlow and I co-authored many years before.

But let me back up a little. Except for a ticket screw up and my blouse buttons setting off the Houston Intercontinental Airport metal detector, the flights to Minneapolis and Winnipeg were uneventful. I boarded a small plane for the last leg, a 2½-hour flight. As we vibrated the 625 air miles to Churchill, I watched the frozen north disappear into the bad weather and the night. This was the real thing and I tingled with a new-adventure excitement by virtue of someone's last-minute cancellation.

The plane wasn't carrying enough meals and since I wasn't hungry, I declined the offer, not a hardship when you consider flight food. The lady ahead of me asked if I was going to see the polar bears. I soon discovered Jill Ferguson, a retired teacher from Sydenham, Ontario, was among several Elderhostelers whose earlier flight had been cancelled. Suddenly, I didn't mind the inconveniences...at least I was getting there.

We had our first taste of frigid air walking into the terminal. It felt good to feel the wind in my hair but not for long. That same howling wind and snow helped Melissa, the Assistant Director, and Dave, a Centre volunteer, scurry us aboard for a bumpy 15-mile ride along a reflector-lined road to the Churchill Northern Studies Centre.

Our first wild life viewing was a healthy-looking bushy-tailed red fox. Dave stopped. The fox trotted into the road, blinked into our headlights, and promptly dumped, perhaps a political comment on the audacity of the big yellow bus and its contents.

Our hectic late arrival at the former operations building of the Churchill Research Rocket Range, our home for the next five days, coincided with our first lecture. This began with Carley, the Program Coordinator, giving us the rules and responsibilities.

"We run a safe, comfortable facility. The iron-barred windows are due to the polar bear concentration here on the Hudson Bay Coast. This is one place people are not necessarily at the top of the food chain. Nobody goes out on his own. Guards with shotguns will accompany organized walks. Keep the doors closed at all times. Bears will come inside if given the opportunity.

"Be flexible. Things don't necessarily happen on time in Churchill. Being an old building, fire alarms go off occasionally. Don't run outside for a fire. Convene at the luggage area. If we have to move out, we'll go together."

The building housed a library, herbarium, reading room, lounge, gift shop, two classrooms, dormitories and laboratories. It is an active national and international research centre for northern plant and marine life research and polar bear behavioral work. Summer finds 30 to 40 researchers working there. On the off season, Elderhostel and other study programs utilize the Centre. The income supports the research.

Rupert Pilkington, a passionate young conservationist who came to North America nine years ago from Britain, taught four of our eight lectures, accompanied us on all activities, patiently answered questions, and doubled as a guard. His lecture painted a big picture of bears, other wildlife, humans, the ecosystem, how we all fit together, and what we should do to protect our interrelationship via public education and world-wide management sharing.

Then we met the roommates! Six women divided rough-cut bunk beds for a major pajama party, stuffing bare minimum but bulky cold-weather clothes and miscellaneous wherever we could stuff it. Since I had never gone to summer camp, it was new to me.

As one of the sturdier 60-something participants, my short legs manipulated the precipitous climb to postage stamp-sized quarters. At midnight, I encouraged a stiff, sitting-most-of-the-day body to disgorge its clothes and slide into sweats while maintaining a modicum of dignity and modesty. The modicum was soon ditched.

Five out of six of us were exhausted. One lady read her book by flashlight. Do you know how noisy page turning or how bright a tiny flashlight can be in the dead of night? This same dear soul who should never have been on a top bunk, was up and down that ladder at least three times until she gave up and slept on the floor (and later moved to another room and a bottom bunk).

The "snorer" was below me. By the third night, a sympathetic roomie offered me her extra set of earplugs. That solved my problem or at least toned it down. By then everyone else needed earplugs because my cough, though I didn't have a cold, was so bad it was keeping me awake too.

By 4 a.m., I was fully awake and feeling imprisoned. I grabbed my goody bag, stole down the ladder like an overgrown polar bear, stumbled across "the body" and out the door to freedom. Much to my surprise three other early-risers were up. We did amazingly well with limited bathroom facilities, one two-shower, two-lavatory bathroom each for women and men. As a full-time RVer, I could understand their conservation concerns. They haul all sewage and water.

I don't remember a flashlight being on our necessity list and it was a problem not having one. The third dark morning I swung my leg off the bunk, missed a rung, and my shin slid along a chairback that was next to my ladder, and all the way to the floor. Ouch! It's hard to whisper obscenities!

Our need for flexibility came when the weather wasn't conducive to helicopter flying. The alternative bus ride into Churchill gave us a daylight view of cold, rough Hudson Bay that chilled our bones. We visited Parks Canada Visitor Centre for locally made movies and interpretive historical displays. I suggested we get together and discuss the movies later. While very interesting, between a frigid morning walk and our lunch, it was a perfect nap setting. I think we each fell asleep during different segments.

The Eskimo Museum highlighted native carvings and artifacts dated from 1700 BC. My favorite was a painting of a

> With glaciers retreating, Hudson Bay ice forms later and breaks up earlier, a definite sign of global warming, and a significant dilemma for these creatures. When there is no longer ice, there will no longer be polar bears. The polar bear is a good way to study the healthiness of our own system. The early 1999-ice breakup and shorter feeding time revealed distinctly poorer polar bear condition.

sweet Eskimo baby reaching around from his back carrier to kiss his mommy. If there had been room in the Sprinter, it would have been mine.

The place to go in Churchill is the Gypsy Bakery, a restaurant, pastry, deli and coffee shop where we had snacks. As in visiting anywhere in Canada, every story had two sides, the English and the French.

On the return trip, a pale lemonade-colored polar bear padded across a lake. A lady squealed, "He's so cute. I'd love to hug him." Dave commented, "He'd appreciate it."

I did a double take every time I saw Michael Goodyear, Executive Director. He was the image of Anthony Edwards from the TV show, ER. On a later "city" trip, Mike pointed out a cavernous underground military storage depot with train tracks alongside, plus other abandoned military buildings.

Miss Piggy, a sight for sore eyes...or maybe a sore sight for any eyes, was a crashed C46. It took off from the nearby airport, couldn't make it, and sort of eased on to the snow with the tail dragging along the rocks. It has been used for graffiti-painting parties and who knows what else.

We passed the Bear Jail, the only one of its kind. It is home to as many as 23 "problem" bears that are taken out of circulation due to apparent "habituation" to town or the dump. This is especially necessary with a mother. Cubs are with the mother for two years. She teaches them how to live and if she teaches them that the dump or a town site is a good place to get goodies, her babies will become problem bears. This behavior is primarily discouraged by rubber bullets and pepper spray.

**How often do you hug a Polar Bear? Only once!**

Someone questioned why the dump wasn't fenced to keep the bears away. Obviously the speaker couldn't figure it out either. "We can't fence a dump? So basic. We put a man on the moon but we can't fence a dump and electrify the fence!"

Mobile traps are set up in a parameter around Churchill. Some are made of road-building culverts. When a bear pulls on the seal blubber-soaked burlap bag, a heavy steel door is released. Spring-loaded snares with 3/8" steel cables are used in permanent railroad-tie traps. The bears don't thrash or fight. When the snare catches a paw, the bear just lies down uninjured. The various traps are checked daily.

Sometimes a false camp is set up with someone inside shooting stinging rubber bullets. This plays on a bear's intelligence. It soon learns it doesn't want to go there. As a last resort, bears are darted with a safe commercial drug cocktail. When a female is darted and goes to sleep, her cubs climb on top of her. They are darted by hand and confined together.

The drug doesn't impair a bear's basic metabolic or physical function. While apparently there is no danger of overdosing, some feel this is not good for them in the same way that humans shouldn't have more anesthesias than absolutely necessary.

While these powerful animals are tranquilized, they are measured, marked with lip tattoos, ear tags, and given penicillin to avoid any infection from the handling procedure. It is questioned whether tattooing and taking a supposedly "unnecessary" tooth to determine the bear's age, is a good idea. The comment was "A non-essential tooth like a non-essential foot!"

Bears have minimal people contact and no contact with other bears during the 1 to 30 days until they are relocated. A bear (or mother and cubs) is loaded into a cargo net, placed in a sitting position to keep it off its airway passage (otherwise it might suffocate) and flown by helicopter to a safer zone or released on the ice.

> Extinction has always occurred, but the rate of extinction compared to the rate of human development and of pollution... is proceeding frighteningly fast. What happened previously over 10,000 years, is now materializing in mere decades! We are linked to these creatures but everything we do as a Society is running them into extinction.

We humans are so arrogant as to believe we are the only ones with thought processes. One bear was released in the wild after a Bear Jail stint. Handlers waited to see that he was o.k. After he recovered from the tranquilizer, he made his way back to the offending vehicle, took a distinctly "And don't fool with me again" hunk out of it and lumbered off.

The later the freeze, the more bears are trapped. Approximately 20 bears are picked up a season, but in the 1998 late freeze, 85 bears were trapped.

The male polar bear is the largest land carnivore in the world weighing in excess of 1,500 pounds, big enough I don't think I'd argue with one. Females weigh 330 to 550 pounds. Polar bears are black skinned for better heat absorption. Bear hair is hollow and contains insulating air. Well-fed bears also have an insulating fat layer. They are designed to live in exceedingly cold areas and overheat quickly.

The massive skull has a slightly shorter neck with a grizzly-like hump behind the neck. Their sight is comparable to our sight although even with water glare, they can detect fish in the water. Their noses are even better. Bears do not growl or roar. Vocal only in pain or fear, it is sort of a snorting cough.

They can run as fast as a horse at 30 miles an hour, but can't sustain the speed. The huge footprints are mainly toe pads and hair.

Heat expelled from their toe pads melts enough ice to give them a good ice-walking grip.

Bears are extremely curious. They stand on hind legs for a better view, possibly to a height of 9' to11'. If they don't perceive you as a threat, they will not attack you. That was good news. Some polar bears actually never go on land and can swim a hundred miles at a time. Because they are the biggest bears and usually have very little interaction with human beings, polar bears may live their life span of 25 to 30 years.

> With more recreational time, mobility, and disposable income, we are leaving heavy footprints on the land. We needn't necessarily give up our four-wheelers, motorcycles, and snowmobiles, but it is imperative that we ensure a balanced co-existence with other animals.

Polar bears do not usually go into hibernation. Lack of food rather than weather is what usually forces bears into hibernation. They breed on the ice in springtime. Delayed implantation develops in late September. Attempting to keep their babies away from males who prey on cubs and are often several times larger than they are, females utilize large inland peat banks for birthing dens. Hudson Bay Lowlands contains the largest peatland in North America.

These peat dens, possibly three meters thick and intertwined with growing tree roots, may have been used for over 300 years. A very stable inside temperature is maintained. Above and beyond that, the snow covereth.

Fine-haired, blind cubs, usually twins, are born in mid to late February and migrate toward the heat of the nipples. They weigh 1-1½ pounds, the smallest young in relation to adult animal size. They grow extremely fast on rich mother's milk. Eventually breaking through the snow, mother and cubs head for sea ice. Mama bear spends the entire pregnancy living on the fat she stored previously. The longest known fast is about eight months. In this harsh world, the mother is fierce, and must defend her babies when she is weakest.

Coinciding with the March ringed seal births, they sniff out the snow caves, hunting for the perfect polar bear snack. Polar bear diet consists of several hundred ringed seals per year. The polar bear is an extraordinarily clever animal. It stalks with nothing to hide behind so it covers its black nose, the only part a seal can see, with a paw. It creeps up to a seal breathing hole and waits in patient silence, eventually taking its primary food source out for dinner.

Ringed seals have a ringed-pattern pelt and are considered the "True Seal." They are earless and unlike the sea lion that walks on its flippers, true seals cannot bring their flippers up under them. They undulate. Breathing holes are kept open by continually clawing freezing ice that may eventually be eight feet thick, maintaining six or seven holes within a one to two kilometer range. Breathing holes are just large enough for the mother and her pups.

Mating takes place in May with a delayed implantation of 89 days. Mothers find breathing holes under snowdrifts and dig snow caves for hiding their pups when they are born. Usually only one pup, with a birth weight of 10 pounds, nurses for six weeks and gains weight unbelievably fast.

Polar bear cubs stay with their mother for two years, depending on

I'm watching you with my eyes closed.

whether she has more babies. Young cubs on their own are "subadults" who sometimes hang together, wandering up and down the coastline, tending to get into more trouble. They are not physically or sexually adult yet, and are not as skilled as adult bears.

Churchill, at the southern edge of polar bear range, is unique. Freezing ice catches on the Churchill promontory and the first solid ice forms there. Approximately 1,200 polar bears gather during November, waiting for Hudson Bay to freeze. This phenomenon doesn't happen anywhere else. They lie flat on land or early-forming ice, staying as cool as possible. Although summer berry hors d'oeuvres are occasionally eaten, polar bears often eat nothing until seal hunting begins. They rely very little on non-meat food. They have little energy and their fat is quickly depleting by the end of the long fast.

Our major Elderhostel activities were helicopter, dog sled, and tundra buggy rides, along with several walks accompanied by three armed guards, a point man, a middleman, and one in the back. We could count on cold, cold, and blowing cold. A playful black dog, "Bear," bounded along as our bear-warning device. He did an admirable job of startling winter-white ptarmigan into flight.

Considering my last-minute arrangements and lack of purchasing time for adequate gear, I put on everything I brought for walks. The drifted snow was a few inches to 12" deep and the way often icy.

Rupert took us to see the Centre's famous weather rock that hung from a tall tripod. "When it snows, it is covered with snow. When the wind blows, it moves back and forth. When it rains, it is wet." Truly scientific observations.

He showed us how a polar bear had accessed the Centre shed roof via a snowdrift. Footprints are often found around the building. One Elderhosteler and the kitchen crew sighted a bear one morning while we were there. Rupert explained the dangers were very real, "When walking around a building, corners are given wide berth because a bear could be and has been, right there." We hated going indoors again but with the chill factor, we didn't argue...especially with the guys with the guns!

One walk included a bus ride to Twin Lakes, the end of one of Churchill's few roads. There are no roads connecting with the rest of Manitoba. We crossed paths with a minx; otherwise, we saw only tracks. We drove from tundra to higher country supporting a boreal forest of Jack pine, white spruce, and tamarack. The difference was immediate, almost like drawing a line.

David scouted well ahead of our hiking column with his gun. Mike told us about the deeper glacial (kettle) lakes and the Laurentian Ice Sheet, "As the ice sheet receded, the land rebounded. The land is still rising up and the rivers are cutting down through it. You can tell the glacial movement by scratches on the rock tops."

I love any kind of flying but for my last group of the day, photographing polar bears or the sunset was a complete bust at 4:25. The helicopter was a beauty, maneuverable, comfortable, and a great ride. Through earphones we listened as the pilot pointed out bears and landmarks that we were mostly "almost" seeing. It was nearly dark by the time we landed, very disappointing and yet it had its good points.

His wry sense of humor and extensive experience made the lecture by musher and trainer, John Stetson, more interesting than the ride. "These dogs are valuable and meaningful to me. Dogs are just like people, except they are trustworthy and loyal. Dogs are dressed in jackets for extreme climates and always while racing. I wear a facemask for weather less than -40°F. I can't see much. I've traveled 70,000 miles but I've only seen 20,000 miles of them. When my fur changes direction, I know I'm off course."

> Ecotourism should be done in such a way that truly limits what we do to the land and our activities on the land where we are moving into creature habitats. It doesn't take much to impede large mammals in their travels. When a road, subdivision, or recreation site bisects their vitally large habitat, they won't cross it.

After showing his fascinating Antarctic expedition slides, he warned, "80% of those who watch these slides, get a team within two weeks." Hitching them to my Sprinter would definitely improve its gas mileage!

The sleds were not traditional dog sleds but big sleigh-looking affairs with wheels and room for several people. We were given lap robes and gloves but being jammed three to a seat kept us reasonably warm. It wasn't windy but it was clear and extremely cold. John said it was about 18°F per his mustache ice gauge but someone had seen a temperature gauge for 10°F.

The dogs were not traditional either. Rather than the Siberian Husky we usually associate with dog sledding, these dogs were slender with shorter coats and bred specifically for racing.

"They wear booties for foot protection and are harnessed tandem style, two by two. The bigger dogs protect the littler ones. Each dog has a unique appearance, personality, way of thinking, and a distinct voice. They form relationships with different levels of involvement."

We were urged to "Get on quickly. Sometimes the dogs leave without the people or me. We've taken them on wilderness trips where there are no trails. We choose the safest possible routes but still occasionally run into thin or bad ice or glacial crevasses. If the team ahead of you goes through, you know you should go around it.

"We raise all of our own dogs, socializing with them and teaching them about whatever they will run into in their lives. It takes nine months to get them used to the harnesses. They jump and bark, 'pick me, pick me.' They are absolutely nuts about pulling these sleds. We have Retirement Row for all sled dogs over 13 years. They jump four feet off ground when they are young. In Retirement Row they are still excited but they jump two inches." Someone in the back commented, "We can relate to that."

When asked where he lived, John said, "I have to paddle two lakes and do two portages to get to my house, four miles from the road."

> The "island" reserves we now have aren't big enough to be effective. We can lessen habitat loss and fragmentation by establishing "corridor" reserves with indistinct boundaries that lead from one protected area to another. This approach is now being adopted as a huge cooperative effort in the Rocky Mountains.

Somehow he fit that image. "The cardinal exploration rule is to get back," and we did, though our exploration lasted only long enough to experience some frigid northern exposure.

Our tundra buggy pulled itself slowly over orange lichen-covered rocks and boulders, through bogs and small lakes. For centuries the wind and snow have blown across the tundra…only padded polar bear prints and other animals broke the snow surface. Now it is criss-crossed with oversized balloon tire marks, the ultimate monster track.

With his heavy French accent, we were on our third rule before I understood our tundra buggy driver, JP. "Please be completely silent when bears are sighted." We were "reasonably" quiet when the first one came into view. What a thrill.

Two cubs nearly as big as their mother sparred and played until they were out of sight. Two subadults tested their way across the ice. One put his face and front quarters down, pushing himself along a snow patch, "Oh yeah, that feels soooo gooood."

The heated tundra buggy had seats, washroom, a railed outside observation deck, and windows we opened for that perfect shot.

Curiosity brought some bears upright and we were glad for the six-foot high, all-terrain tires. In between rushing from window to window, we ate lunches we prepared ourselves immediately after breakfast. The Centre provided coffee and lemonade.

Other tundra buggies were also vying for good viewing spots for their passengers. In the past (hopefully) people have put blubber on the wheels to attract bears but that is completely discouraged. With such a long fast, the bears are not all that active. The young ones have more energy. What's new?

One splayed out flat on the cold ground, napping and trying to stay cool in what was to him, hot weather. He watched our encroachment with an occasional, if only slightly concerned eye opening.

Out of 40 bears, the last was the biggest. He wallowed through a snowbank, shook snow from his plush coat, and gave us a show. He was magnificent. He pushed a little more snow, rolled in it, and stretched. We enjoyed his day almost as much as he did.

We bottomed out several times on the way back, hitting rocks really hard. JP said our brakes had gone out. We took it all in stride, feeling good about the beautiful day with the polar bears. We sang "*Row, Row, Row Your Boat,*" and other songs. My only fear was that since our experience was a great deal like a Girl Scout outing, someone would break out with, "*Ninety-nine bottles of beer on the Wall!*" That might have caused me to commit hari-kari right there on the frozen tundra.

Sitting on the Hudson Bay shoreline was the seasonal Tundra Buggy Lodge. It was the closest thing I saw to a RV in Churchill. It was a dozen tundra buggies hitched together to include photography platforms, plus sleeping, dining, and lounging buggies. As we scrambled in and out of our reasonably inexpensive Centre bunk beds, rumor had it that to stay in the Tundra Buggy Lodge was over $300/night. They couldn't possibly have had more fun than we did, even with the snoring and coughing.

> **Very seldom is deviant animal behavior evident in the wild. It is a learned pattern, usually a result of human contact. Feeding bears people food is incredibly stupid. We need to make them think we hate them.**

The cafeteria was a favorite gathering place, homey and comfortable. I loved watching Sarah make rolls early in the morning while I sipped coffee. We hoped our cold-weather activities neutralized the calories in the homemade rolls and desserts, not to mention the mouth-watering stews, ribs and other goodies. Paul and Sarah made all-you-can-eat creations from scratch and butter into pure deliciousness. Food and drink was always available for between meals or midnight snacks. Sarah's husband, Rob, was the Centre Jester, Jack-of-all-trades and doubled as a guard on our outings.

We were divided into groups for clearing tables and washing dishes. Carley said she had never seen anyone change the dishwater before. I changed it several times. The Health Department discipline I learned back at the Bar-M Dude Ranch wasn't lost on me! Everything was pre-washed, washed, then put into a sterilizing machine that was really slick. Wish I had had that back at the ranch.

Scuttlebutt was that a weasel lived in the kitchen but few people saw him. He worked full time keeping the rodent population in check. Someone suggested his other function was running a wheel that powered the Centre.

Marvelous polar bear posters and photographs lined the walls everywhere including the bathrooms. Where else could you find an advertisement for, "Fifty pounds of ground whale meat." It took two full days to learn the way from the dorm area to the dining room without entering strange rooms. Jill admitted, "I congratulated myself thinking I had finally found my way, and then opened a door into the machine shed."

On our fifth and last night, Rupert ended his class with a reading that was quite emotional for him, nice to see in a man. The staff gave a farewell wine and cheese party where we mingled for parting conversations. Our completion certificates and Elderhostel books were duly signed and stamped to prove our participation. This was the 42$^{nd}$ Elderhostel for one lady, and the 30$^{th}$ for another. All of the first-timers vowed it wouldn't be their last. The "Roomies" gathered for pictures.

> Rupert left us with this thought: "The eloquent spiritual arguments supporting conservation are often unconvincing to those who promote development. Scientific facts, based on conservation biology, which illustrate the need and 'benefits' of conservation management to both the general environment and its human population, however, are harder for non conservation-minded individuals to refute."

Afterward, a few diehards remained. Rupert explained his dream of building a Centre for Environmental Education. When he isn't lecturing at the Centre, he lives sans electric and other amenities in British Columbia's Rocky Mountains.

Our last evening ended on a high note but we were disappointed not to have gotten a glimpse of the Aurora Borealis. Rupert promised to knock on our doors if the sky cleared.

The last morning, groups departed for the two-day train trip to Winnipeg or the airport to wherever home existed. The five days were so packed, you wished for a few relaxing minutes but when it was over, it was strange to have nothing to do.

I was dropped off at the Tundra Inn for my remaining three solo days to wander historic Churchill, Canada's only Arctic seaport. Jill and her husband were about to become grandparents so she shopped while waiting for her evening train. Later in the afternoon we shared Chinese cuisine and became better acquainted. I walked her to the train station where we met others from the group who were also leaving.

It was a hazardous icy walk back to the Tundra Inn. The snow was blowing hard and even with streetlights, it was difficult to see. Over the next three days I did a lot of crunching through the cold and snow. I found the hospital and considered recruiting a doctor for what felt like walking pneumonia by that time, but I toughed it out. I revisited the Visitor Centre and Museum for gifts, souvenirs and information.

Returning for coffee, I could easily spot the difference between the locals and visitors mingling at Gypsy's. Locals wore one or two layers of clothes. Visitors stripped for 10 minutes! Observing from my warm corner, I watched people struggle against the wind and listened to giant snow removers. Snowmobiles buzzed down the streets, along with truckloads of snow, and van buses with "Tundra Buggy Tours" or North Star Tours" printed on the side. Train or ship transported all vehicles to Churchill.

Gift shops decorated with white and colored lights, beckoned from early morning to nine at night, their income dependent on summer Beluga whale watching and November polar bear sightings.

Occasionally I wondered what a full-time RVer who follows the sun was doing plowing through two-foot snowdrifts to get into stores. In my frozen heart I knew. No road led to it, but it was another adventure.

Shopkeepers were very friendly. At the Northern, a huge warehouse-type grocery store, the fellow who waited on me was talkative and interested in my Churchill stay, as was the lady at the museum. In a gift shop, I lamented I didn't have anyone to take my picture. The clerk pleasantly offered to do just that and did, coatless in the freezing cold.

Beyond my winter reach were historical places attained by boat or helicopter. I left such trips to the summer Beluga visitors. The English and French had battled for fur-trade control. Begun in 1717, the Hudson's Bay Company started a trading post at the mouth of the Churchill River and in 1771 completed the Prince of Wales Fort, a stone fortress used to defend the bay. For all their thinking that the fort was invincible, in 1782 the French took over without a shot.

Across the river from the fort, a stone battery was built at Cape Merry for additional protection. Two miles upriver, Sloop Cove is named after the small vessels repaired there. The "sloops" were used in whaling expeditions and trading. These three, plus York Factory and Norway House, were a network of Hudson's Bay fur trading posts, now National Historic Sites.

Well before the Europeans arrived, the area was settled in 900 BC by the Cree, Dene, and Inuit. Well after, in 1929, The Hudson Bay Railway was constructed from Winnipeg to Port Churchill.

Pat, the lady who owned the Tundra Inn with her husband, had lived in Churchill for 38 years, having come with the military. They liked living in Churchill but she said they would probably retire somewhere with less extreme weather.

With winds blowing 50-70 KPH, I limited my walks to twice a day. In the comfort of my room, I took hot baths, slept, watched TV, and re-arranged notes I had taken on my NEC laptop computer. Churchill is well off the beaten track but not so far that it can't keep up with the rest of the world. I thought about the fellow Elderhosteler whose luggage may still be wandering the world. Little did I know mine would be lost between Churchill and Winnipeg on the way back. I filled out all kinds of forms because it wasn't going across the border with me. Fortunately, they found it before the next leg of my journey.

On my last day the wind wasn't as bad, and breakfast at the Churchill Motel and Restaurant was pleasant. On the way to the airport, the taxi driver told me that two weeks previously a child walked through town oblivious to being in a polar bear path. Someone drove into the bear to scare it off. He said there are usually one or two incidents a year involving bears in town.

We were soon up, up, and away. Just 500 miles south of the Arctic Circle, Churchill's winter days would soon be mostly dark. I knew that below me ghostly white tundra buggies stole silently across Hudson Bay's grey horizon in the blowing snow. Black Taiga, the land of little sticks, outlined frozen lakes and bogs. I had found beauty in its starkness. It was desolate, yet wonderful and beautiful and exciting, another dimension of God's creation.

And while we are still riding high...

# 'Til We Meet Again

It is time to say, "So long until we meet again." I don't expect you to follow in my treadmarks, but I hope and pray you will reach out for some adventure in your own life.

God willing, and my excellent health continues, I am not through traveling. If anything happens to my travel-mate, the Sprinter, I may not replace him, but I might turn a different direction. Elderhostel programs, Habitat for Humanity, working in a historical village, sea kayaking and a llama trek trip all appeal to me. Alaska's Inside Passage and Tasmania are on the "to do" list, and maybe a summer on Prince Edward Island. Publishing the Great American Novel with a recommendation from Oprah wouldn't be bad either. *The list goes on...*

My dreams change from time to time but as I have written on my book covers, *the dream continues...* I can't say I have done it all or seen it all but I'm still giving it a good honest try! In whatever **you** choose to do, don't put off living your dreams. Life is going on whether you notice or not. Don't waste a minute of it.

I hope you've had as much fun reading *RVing Adventures with the Silver Gypsy*, as I did living it and sharing it with you. May God bless you richly in whatever you do with your life.

The Sprinter is packed. We're ready to go. It is very early as I type this last message. The stars are going home for the day. The coyotes are snuggling down for a nap as the birds awaken. The sun is rising over the Bradshaw Mountains and all is well in my world. I left home 250,000 miles ago to follow my dream. I wish you the very best in following yours.

God Bless

"Charlie"

*I know how it feels to have wings on my wheels,*
*and my wheels are so ready to fly...*

# All Non-Fiction Titles
## Sharlene "Charlie" Minshall

### RVing Alaska! (and Canada)

A **"How-to"** and **"Why-not"** book that gives vehicle and mental preparation, map information, where-to-stay, when-to-go, what to take, and road conditions, plus practical suggestions and strong comments regarding safety, vehicle breakdowns and boondocking. Add to the misadventures of playing with the grizzlies in Katmai National Park and canoeing the Mighty Yukon River, and you have information plus entertainment.

**Excerpt:** Please remember, speed is directly relational to anguished springs, broken axles, chipped windshields, and creative alignment.

**Excerpt:** ...at the Yukon Territory and Northwest Territories border, I drove into a totally different world. It was dark, snowy, and windy. It was more ominous looking than I wanted to admit because I didn't want to turn back. I thought hard for milliseconds, then put the Sprinter in gear, and inched toward Inuvik, 205 miles north of the Arctic Circle.

### Full-Time RVing: How to Make it Happen (Completely Revised 2000)

A "How-to" book that lets you in on the mobile lifestyle that millions are enjoying! How do I get started? What should I keep? What should I take? How do I keep relationships with family and friends intact? How do I cross borders into Canada or Mexico? What happens if I break down? How can I prevent breaking down? What is the daily life of a full-time RVer really like? It has two full-time budget comparisons, ways to cut costs, info on personal safety, getting mail, establishing residency, and the nitty-gritty details you need to know to become full-time or extended-time RVers.

### In Pursuit of a Dream

"Charlie," widowed at 45, inspires you with a positive and personal story of "How and Why" she quit her 9 – 5 job to become a full-time RVer, writer-photographer, and public speaker. Laugh and shake your head as you read her tales of Alaska, new romance, and living on a beach in Baja, Mexico.

### Freedom Unlimited: The Fun and Facts of Fulltime RVing
(Co-author Tech Writer Bill Farlow)

A view from all sides of the full-time spectrum by two long-time, full-timing RV columnists. Learn the "Nuts and bolts" of full-time RVing from such chapters as "Is the Impossible Dream Possible?" (Finances and Costs), and "Cutting Your Apron Strings" (Roots to Enroute) about maintaining contact with your family, friends, mail, phone and church. From the technical to the "fluff stuff," the authors cover questions about the full-time or extended-time RV lifestyle in a personal and humorous style.

### RVing North America, Silver, Single, and Solo    OUT OF PRINT
Follow the Silver Gypsy in her adventures into Mexico, Alaska, Canada, and all around the "lower 48." These are tales of the traveling life of a full-time RVer. The stories are previous to *RVing Adventures with the Silver Gypsy*. Please let Gypsy Press know of your interest in this book. This may be reprinted in the near future.

# ORDER FORM

**For AUTOGRAPHED copies, complete form and send a check or money order (US Funds) to:**

**Sharlene Minshall
% Gypsy Press
150 Rainbow Drive PMB #5024
Livingston, TX 77399-1050**

*RVING ADVENTURES with the SILVER GYPSY (**SPRING 2001**)*.........................$14.95

*RVING ALASKA! (and Canada)*..........................................................................$14.95

*FULL-TIME RVING How to Make it Happen* -- **Completely Revised 2000**...........$14.95

*IN PURSUIT OF A DREAM* .............................................................................$ 8.00

*FREEDOM UNLIMITED The Fun and Facts of Fulltime RVing*
*(Co-authored by Bill Farlow)* ...........................................................................$ 8.00

*RVING NORTH AMERICA Silver, Single & Solo* **OUT OF PRINT**.......................$12.95

Name _____

Address _____

City, State, Zip _____

|  | Price | Qty | Total |
|---|---|---|---|
| RVING ADVENTURES with the SILVER GYPSY | $14.95 | _____ | _____ |
| RVING ALASKA! (AND CANADA) | $14.95 | _____ | _____ |
| FULL-TIME RVING: HOW TO MAKE IT HAPPEN | $14.95 | _____ | _____ |
| IN PURSUIT OF A DREAM | $ 8.00 | _____ | _____ |
| FREEDOM UNLIMITED | $ 8.00 | _____ | _____ |
| $2 **DISCOUNT** on combo of three books | **Subtotal** | _____ | |
| $3 **DISCOUNT** on combo of five books | **Discount** | | -_____ |
| **Postage & Handling** | Subtotal | | _____ |
| **$3.50 for one book** | **P&H** | | +_____ |
| **$1.00 for each additional book** | **Total** | | _____ |

**Canadian orders: Add $1.50 to above shipping costs for each book.**

**NOTE:** Please let me know of your interest in RVing North America, Gypsy Press may print it via Book on Demand.

Please allow six weeks for delivery.

Printed in the United States
25305LVS00002B/511-606